T0321065

A Theory of Insurance and Gambling

A Theory of Insurance and Gambling

Replacing Risk Preferences with Quid pro Quo

JOHN A. NYMAN

OXFORD
UNIVERSITY PRESS

OXFORD
UNIVERSITY PRESS

Oxford University Press is a department of the University of Oxford. It furthers
the University's objective of excellence in research, scholarship, and education
by publishing worldwide. Oxford is a registered trade mark of Oxford University
Press in the UK and certain other countries.

Published in the United States of America by Oxford University Press
198 Madison Avenue, New York, NY 10016, United States of America.

Library of Congress Cataloging-in-Publication Data
Names: Nyman, John A., author.
Title: A theory of insurance and gambling : replacing risk preferences with
quid pro quo / John A. Nyman.
Description: New York, NY : Oxford University Press, [2024] |
Includes bibliographical references and index. |
Identifiers: LCCN 2023045395 (print) | LCCN 2023045396 (ebook) |
ISBN 9780197687925 (hardback) | ISBN 9780197687949 (epub) |
ISBN 9780197687956 (online)
Subjects: LCSH: Insurance. | Risk.
Classification: LCC HG8051.N96 2024 (print) | LCC HG8051 (ebook) |
DDC 368—dc23/eng/20231004
LC record available at https://lccn.loc.gov/2023045395
LC ebook record available at https://lccn.loc.gov/2023045396

DOI: 10.1093/oso/9780197687925.001.0001

Printed by Integrated Books International, United States of America

Over the years I have been lucky enough to know a disproportionate number of very smart and accomplished people. Many have been an inspiration to me, but none more so than Charles Breunig, my history professor at Lawrence University, and Dorothea Tanning, my artist and poet aunt. I dedicate this book to their memory.

Contents

Contents

Preface

I began thinking about why people buy health insurance about 25 years ago. I had always been troubled by the notion that all the additional healthcare consumed when insured—moral hazard—was inefficient (Pauly 1968). It seemed to me that a lot of people purchased and benefitted from health insurance because they were able to gain access to care that they could not otherwise afford to purchase if uninsured. In 1999, I published two theoretical papers on health insurance (Nyman 1999b; 1999a). The first identified access as an important motive of the demand for health insurance. The second showed that even for insurance that paid off by reducing the price of a covered commodity (like health insurance), a portion of the additional healthcare purchased was due to an income transfer and was therefore efficient.

This thinking led me to the theory that the demand for health insurance was essentially a demand for an income transfer (from those who bought insurance and remained healthy, to those who bought insurance and become ill,) rather than a demand for certainty. A paper (Nyman 2001c) describing this theory soon became a full-length book (Nyman 2003). During the same period, I also recognized that the conversion of the Friedman and Savage (1948) analysis to a gain perspective could be applied to insurance in general, not just health insurance (Nyman 2001a).

Thinking about insurance led to my thinking about gambling. To me, economists had overlooked what seemed like the basic gambling motive by not recognizing that the dollars that made up the wagers were not the same dollars as those that made up the winnings: the former typically required labor to obtain, but the latter did not. An early version of a theory of the demand for gambling was written up (Nyman 2004) and later published in two papers where the theory was laid out as an introduction to the empirical analysis (Nyman, Welte, and Dowd, 2008; Nyman et al., 2013). The theory in this book builds on that early analysis.

The next step was the realization that the theories of insurance and gambling were very similar. Uncertainty in insurance and gambling was important not because risk preferences were motivating demand, but simply because the uncertainty was a vehicle for augmenting the payoffs, compared to the premiums and wagers. That is, both insurance and gambling are transactions that generate augmented amounts of income that are received by consumers in states of the world that are different from the states where the premium or wager is paid, and these different states affect the utility or value that the consumer derives from the income transfers. An early version of the quid pro quo theory of insurance and gambling was written up (Nyman 2020), but was really too large to be contained in a single journal article. Therefore, it was revised and expanded into the present book.

I would like to thank David de Meza at the London School of Economics, Jeremiah Hurley at McMaster University, and a third reviewer for thoughtful comments on how an earlier version of the book could be improved. I would also like to thank my editors at Oxford University Press for all their work on my behalf: James Cook, Alexcee Bechthold, Niccola Perez, Anne Sanow, and Barami Selvan. It has been a pleasure to work with such a skilled and competent group of professionals. Finally, I would like to thank my wife, Patricia, for her support in writing this book and for her excellent editing and other advice when issues came up along the way.

1

Introduction

Conventional Theory

What is insurance and how does it differ from recreational gambling, the type done typically at a casino, racetrack, or a betting website? For economists, a behavioral definition of insurance has been widely accepted from the time that it was formally proposed by Friedman and Savage in 1948: insurance is purchased by consumers because they are averse to the risk of a loss, and insurance converts an uncertain loss into a certain one of the same expected magnitude (Friedman and Savage 1948). This behavioral definition is derived from the assumption that for most consumers, utility increases with income or wealth at a decreasing rate.

This risk aversion definition of insurance demand is widely held by economists. This definition, and its corollary that consumers seek insurance to smooth and eliminate variation in consumption across states of the world, represent the cornerstones on which virtually every economic model of insurance is built. The centrality of uncertainty and the consumer's aversion to it in motivating the demand for insurance was established early on and is illustrated by the many terms that have been used by economic theorists to describe the core beneficial effect of insurance: consumers purchase insurance so as to "avoid," "eliminate," "hedge against," "kill," "manage," "shed," "protect against," "bear," or "shift" uncertainty (e.g., Mossin 1968; Schlesinger and Doherty 1985; Mayers and Smith 1983; Cook and Graham 1977; Arrow 1963b; Feldstein 1973; Feldstein and Friedman 1977; Feldman and Dowd 1991; Manning and Marquis 1996; Johnson et al. 1993). And, although one can point to no surveys of economists that query their views on why consumers purchase insurance, if such a poll existed, "because consumers are risk-averse," would surely gather the most endorsements. As Fels observes, "there is hardly a question in [e]conomics to which members of the discipline—proverbial in their inclination to disagree—seem more unified in their answer" (Fels 2019, 2). The same author goes on to observe that this

A Theory of Insurance and Gambling. John A. Nyman, Oxford University Press. © Oxford University Press 2024.
DOI: 10.1093/oso/9780197687925.003.0001

definition is so embedded that economists often switch the behavior with the explanation and hold the connection tautologically: consumers are risk-averse because they purchase insurance.

In their seminal paper, Friedman and Savage (1948) also provide a formal behavioral definition of the demand for gambles: consumers gamble because their utility functions are increasing at an increasing rate and so they prefer the chance of either receiving a payoff or losing a fair wager to the certainty of the status quo. These authors further observe that many people who purchase insurance also gamble, more or less simultaneously. The question then arises: If consumers are generally averse to risk because they exhibit diminishing marginal utility of income (or wealth), how can they also gamble at the same time, since the desire to gamble requires that the marginal utility of income be increasing in income or wealth? Rather than viewing this fact as a contradiction of the underlying theory and a reason to question it, economists generally have accepted it as a theoretical puzzle and have sought to find an accommodation for the insurance-purchasing gambler that fits within the Friedman–Savage framework.

Quid Pro Quo Theory

In this book, an alternative behavioral definition of the demand for insurance is suggested that does not pose a similar internal contradiction, nor does it conflict with empirical findings. Instead of a desire for certainty in the face of an uncertain loss and the elimination of variation in consumption across states of the world, the theory in this book holds that consumers demand insurance because they seek to transfer income to, and to augment consumption in, a state of the world where the income and consumption are more valuable. Insurance is therefore a quid pro quo exchange: purchasers of insurance seek additional income in a state where it is more valuable, and are willing to pay for it with income in a state where it is less valuable. Converting the demand for insurance from the conventional risk aversion model into a quid pro quo exchange is, on the one hand, a simple change in the specification of the insurance decision. On the other hand, it changes the purview of insurance, and does it so extensively, that it changes the welfare implications of insurance (Nyman 2003). Specifically, it implies that insurance is far more valuable, and that the welfare costs of insurance are far smaller, than they were thought to be under the conventional model.

Also in this book, an alternative behavioral definition of the demand for gambling is proposed. Instead of a desire for uncertainty, this book holds that consumers gamble because they desire additional income in a state of the world where the labor cost of acquiring it is smaller. Gambling is therefore a quid pro quo exchange: gamblers desire additional labor-free income and are willing to pay a wager of earned income in order to acquire it. This approach removes the motivation to gamble from the shape of the utility function and focuses it instead on the utility of labor and the costs of acquiring additional income. As a result, the quid pro quo approach to gambling does not contradict the theory of the demand for insurance and can accommodate the insurance-purchasing gambler.

Uncertainty is important in the theory of both insurance and gambling, but it does not represent the consumer's motivation. Rather, its role is mainly to facilitate the supply of insurance and gambling contracts. With regard to insurance, its primary role is that it allows for the payout, and thus the income transfer, to be a multiple of the insurance premium. That is, the insurer would not be able to charge premiums that were a fraction of the payout if everyone who paid the premium received the augmented payout. By limiting the number of beneficiaries who receive a payout to a fraction of them, uncertainty is the factor that makes such an augmentation of the payout possible. Similarly, uncertainty is important in gambling because it allows for the winnings, and thus the income transfer, of a roulette game or horse race to be a multiple of the wager. This would also not be possible if every wager resulted in the augmented payoff. So uncertainty is the facilitator of the insurance contract and of the gambling transaction, rather than the consumer's motivation.

To show the similarities between these behaviors, this book now begins by proposing parallel definitions for insurance and gambling, and the quid pro quo motivations for each. Both the demand and supply sides of the exchange are considered.

Insurance is a contract between an insurer and a consumer that exploits the uncertainty of some future triggering event to augment the insurance payout compared to the premium. Consumers who purchase insurance do not desire certainty of income in the face of a potential loss, but instead they desire the acquisition of additional income or consumption in a future uncertain state of the world—determined, for example, by becoming ill or having an auto accident—where the income and consumption are comparatively more valuable to the consumers. In exchange, consumers are willing to forego a smaller payment, the premium, in a state where the income is comparably less valuable.

The insurer is willing to agree to transfer a larger payout to the insured consumers for a smaller premium because the payout is uncertain and because the insurer writes a large number of similar uncertain contracts more or less simultaneously, thus reducing the uncertainty it faces by shrinking the variance of the payout. Because of the welfare gain from the additional income to consumers, the insurer is able to charge premiums that in the aggregate, exceed the expected payouts of these contracts and thereby is able to cover the firm's administration and profits (the load).

Gambling, as exemplified by casino or racetrack gambling, represents an implicit contract between the gambling house and a consumer that exploits the uncertainty of some future triggering event to augment the payout of winnings compared to the wager. Gamblers do not desire uncertainty, but instead desire an amount of additional income and consumption in a future state of the world—determined, for example, by a lucky roll of the dice or a lucky spin of the roulette wheel—where the income is comparatively less costly to obtain. In exchange, gamblers are willing to forego a smaller payment, the wager, which is paid for with income that was obtained largely through work.

The gambling house is willing to take on these implicit contracts to pay a larger amount of winnings for a smaller wager because of the uncertainty of the payout and because it makes a large number of similar uncertain contracts more or less simultaneously, thus reducing the uncertainty it faces by shrinking the variance of the income payout. Because of the utility savings to the consumer from not having to work for additional income, the gambling house is able to charge and receive wagers that in the aggregate, exceed the expected payouts of all contracts and thereby cover the firm's administrative costs and profits (the house take).

The intent of this book is to further develop this quid pro quo theory of insurance and gambling. Before beginning, however, a number of preliminary decisions should be explained.

Income Versus Wealth

One decision is whether to base the analysis on the utility of income or on the utility of wealth. Friedman and Savage (1948) used income as the argument for their utility function, but by the 1970s, wealth had become more widely used in theoretical studies of the demand for insurance. Although some may regard the choice between these two concepts as arbitrary, there are some important differences worth mentioning.

Perhaps most important is the difference with regard to meaning. Income is a flow concept. It is an amount of money that has a time dimension: US$1,000 per week in pay, for example. Wealth is a stock concept that captures an amount of money in an instant of time: US$1,000 in a bank account. This difference began to matter more with the promulgation of Kahneman and Tversky's prospect theory in 1979. This is because the point representing the origin in Kahneman and Tversky's prospect theory diagram also represented a reference point that could vary with the money remaining after the loss of an asset (Kahneman and Tversky 1979). As a result, wealth seemed more appropriate than income as the argument of the value function because it could better accommodate a reduction in money due to a loss. Moreover, because the positive portion of the value function was assumed to be increasing at a diminishing rate and to represent a portion of an underlying function that covered all wealth levels, the wealth level at which this reference point occurred on the value function could affect the curvature of this portion of the function, and thus the demand for insurance. This became especially important for those studies, like Kőszegi and Rabin (2006), which based their explanation of the variation in the demand for insurance on the variation in the reference points for the value function.

In the analysis that follows, however, this book retains the original income as the argument of the utility functions, rather than wealth, and uses income as the argument for the prospect theory value functions as well. There are a number of reasons for this stance.

First, analysis of the utility of income is sometimes more appropriate because the type of insurance in question pays off with periodic payments of income rather than a single payment. For example, periodic income payments are made directly by worker's compensation, unemployment insurance, annuities, disability insurance, and others. Other forms of insurance, like long-term care insurance or prescription drug insurance, may also cover expenditures that occur periodically and so also have a time dimension. Although using utility of income to analyze insurance coverage of a single large expense is a departure from reality in some cases, it would be a similar departure to use utility of wealth to analyze insurance coverage of periodic payments that occur with annuities or unemployment insurance. This book intends to provide a generalized theory of all insurance, and so a single approach is desirable as being representative of the general theory.

Second, regardless of whether the insurance payoff is a single payment or an amount that is paid periodically, the premium payment is almost always periodic and paid out of income. Therefore, for the quid half of all quid pro quo insurance transactions, income is almost always the more appropriate argument of the utility or value function than wealth.

Third, even though some types of insurance pay off with a single large payment, such coverage often obviates the need for periodic payments out of income from the perspective of being uninsured. For example, the healthcare that is covered by health insurance, especially if expensive, may have required taking out a loan if uninsured. Therefore, the repayment of the loan would come out of income and those periodic payments would represent the opportunity cost of the absence of such insurance coverage. Liability insurance would represent a similar case. Moreover, for assets that would be lost, even though insurance would pay off a contract with a single payment, that payment would often cover costs with a time dimension if uninsured. For example, a house fire would often mean new monthly rental payments or mortgage payments if the house were uninsured, and possibly double mortgage payments if the house destroyed by fire had not been completely paid off and a new house were purchased. The same would be true of automobile insurance. Thus, a number of different types of insurance would produce settlements that would cover payments of a periodic nature, and so are replacements for income, from the perspective of being uninsured.

Fourth, the theoretical analysis of insurance that pays off by reducing price of a covered commodity decomposes the additional spending due to insurance (that is, the moral hazard) into portions that are (1) due to using price to transfer the income and (2) due to the income transfer itself. In previous work, these effects have been referred to as (1) price effects and (2) income-transfer effects, or simply, income effects (Nyman 1999a; 1999b; 1999c; 2003).[1] These effects are similar to the substitution and income effects from the welfare analysis of an exogenous price change (Hicks 1946). They are different because they do not emanate from an analysis of an exogenous

---

[1] Actually, there are two important income effects that matter in insurance that pays off by reducing the price of a covered commodity. One is the effect of the income transfer in generating additional purchases of the commodity covered by insurance, and the other is the effect of paying a larger premium to obtain a smaller coinsurance rate, and the effect that this reduction of income has on the quantity demanded of the commodity covered by insurance in the *ex post* period. These are discussed in chapters 2 and 8.

change in the market price, but instead from a price reduction that must be purchased with a premium in order to exist (Nyman 2003). In previous work on unemployment insurance, the wealth equivalent of the income-transfer effect has been called a "liquidity" effect (Chetty 2008). This is because, for these types of insurance—for example, unemployment insurance or worker's compensation insurance—even though the insurance payment to the beneficiary occurs periodically and is a payment of income, such a payment would substitute for the unemployed household's liquidization of assets if uninsured. In other words, Chetty's use of the concept of a liquidity effect to convert periodic insurance income payments into their wealth equivalent is analogous to using an income-transfer effect to convert a single insurance payment into its income equivalent.

Thus, the analysis of insurance in this book relies primarily on income in order to keep the story consistent throughout and to emphasize the idea that the welfare gain from insurance is derived from the transfer of income from those who purchase insurance and do not experience a triggering event, to those who purchase insurance and experience a triggering event. This income transfer is more directly apparent if the argument of the utility or value functions is modeled as income. Nevertheless, the insurance coverage of some assets still raises the issue of whether to convert wealth losses into their income equivalent, or whether to analyze insurance coverage of an asset loss as a loss and a transfer of wealth. This issue is taken up again in chapters 2 and 5, where readers can determine better for themselves whether this represents an exception to the general theory.

For gambling, the utility of wagers and winnings are constrained by the theory to be amounts that are consistent with income. This is because the gains from gambling are derived from the disutility saved from not having to work for the additional income represented in the winnings. Therefore, the analysis of the demand for gambles uses income as the argument for the utility or value functions. The exception is lotteries where the winnings may far exceed any level of income that a consumer could possibly hope to earn. For this and other reasons, lotteries are gambles that are analyzed separately.

Income Versus Consumption

Another issue, closely related to the previous one, is whether to focus on the additional income as the reason for the demand for insurance and gambling, or to focus on what that income would purchase—the consumption. This is an issue for insurance because some insurance contracts pay off with consumption rather than income. Health insurance, fire insurance that covers the replacement of a home, consumer product warranties, and automobile collision insurance are all examples of insurance contracts that pay off with consumption rather than income. Some gambling games, too, pay off with direct consumption rather than income. For example, new cars are jackpot prizes for some slot machines (also known as "fruit machines") at casinos and a quantity of meat is the prize in some raffles at taverns. For insurance that pays off with consumption, however, it is not clear whether consumers think through the provenance of this consumption and recognize that it relies on a transfer of income from the pool of premiums. That consumers may generally lack sufficient sophistication to understand this mechanism is suggested by the studies that document the lack of numeracy and understanding exhibited by most buyers of flood and health insurance (discussed in chapter 5). Therefore, the use of income transfer to model and describe the reason for the demand for either insurance is a useful generalization, intended to describe the demand for insurance for the analyst, and not necessarily to describe the thought process of the consumer.

This difference between income and consumption generally has little effect on the analysis of the welfare, except in two instances related to the demand for insurance. The first is the case of consumption insurance that pays off by reducing the price of a covered commodity, for example, health insurance or automobile collision insurance. The reduction of price might cause the purchase of more healthcare or more extensive repairs than would be the case if uninsured. This has traditionally been regarded as moral hazard, a welfare-decreasing inefficiency. The fact that there is an income transfer behind the additional consumption changes the welfare implications dramatically. This issue is addressed in chapter 2.

The second is the case of consumption insurance that pays off with actual consumption, as is the case with consumer warranties. Because the consumer at one time had been willing to purchase the insured commodities reveals that there might be an additional value to these commodities over and above the income that would be required to replace them—a consumer surplus. This consumer surplus might increase the demand for insurance that replaces a covered commodity with a new one, compared to the demand for insurance that pays an amount of income equal to the cost of replacing the same commodity. This consideration is discussed in chapter 8 in more detail.

The difference between income and consumption is not an issue with all insurance. Clearly, this is not an issue with insurance that pays off income losses directly with income, such as is the case with unemployment insurance or workers' compensation. In this book, the discussion of the demands for insurance will retain the term "income transfer" as the basis for the demand, but the reader should recognize that because of this simplification in the quid pro quo model, the *quo* might have a consumption meaning to consumers instead of an income-transfer meaning.

With regard to gambling, additional income obtained through gambling may imply a different mental accounting than income obtained through working, for many consumers. Specifically, an additional dollar of gambling income may generate more consumption than an additional dollar of income obtained through working. This increase in consumption may then represent an additional incentive to gamble—the splurge in consumption that is associated with gambling winnings. This demand factor is discussed further in chapter 3.

Gambling and Insurance Defined

Another issue is whether to use the quid pro quo gambling model to explain the demand for all gambling, or to limit its application to the types of gambling that are typically supplied by gambling firms. Such firms would include bingo parlors, racetracks, internet gambling sites, organizations that provide pull tabs at bars, and casinos. In casinos, it would include the portion of casino games—blackjack, roulette, craps, and slot machine games—that are generally played for modest stakes, but would exclude games like kino that are often played for very large stakes. If this distinction were followed, it would also exclude gambling such as neighborhood poker games, office pools, sports betting, risky investments, and lotteries.

The intended distinction between these two groups is the directness with which the quid pro quo model can be applied. That is, the quid pro quo demand model is more apparent for gambling done at casinos and commercial gambling houses, because fewer alternative motivations are involved. With the exception of gambling by a professional gambler, all forms of gambling have the fundamental demand characteristic that the winnings are work-free and so differ from the wagers, which are typically obtained through working. However, this motivation is sometimes hidden deeper within the gambling experience and may even be superseded by other motives. For the neighborhood poker game, these other motives might include the social aspects of the game and challenge of competition in the more strategic aspects of the game. For the large stakes lottery and kino games, the dramatic change in lifestyle implied by such a large increase in wealth might be salient. For office pools and sports gambling, loyalty to a school or hometown sports team may be the main motivating factor. For risky investments, the strategic aspects of the portfolio decisions and the challenge of competition with other investors may take precedence. And for the professional gambler, demand motives may include the psychological aspects of the game, plus the fame and acclamation from success. However, since gambling represents work for the professional gambler, work is not being avoided by the gambling winnings and so professional gambling must be excluded from the analysis.

In almost all cases, too, there is an important entertainment aspect of gambling. Entertainment was suggested early on in the literature as an alternative demand motive for gambling and as an explanation for the insurance-purchasing gambler (see chapters 3 and 9). While it cannot be denied that entertainment and social interactions contribute to the motivation for many types of gambling, the type that best exemplifies the quid pro quo theory is gambling that would be done in the absence of the entertainment and social motivations. And, while casino gambling is far from this ideal, it is perhaps closer to this concept than the other forms of gambling mentioned above.

Perhaps one way to distinguish those forms of gambling where the entertainment motive dominates is to determine the portion of gamblers who would continue to play the game if the betting were for meaningless tokens. That is, those forms of gambling that would likely *not* persist if played with meaningless tokens are the types of gambling for which the quid pro quo theory best applies. For example, the number of slot machine customers at a casino would likely drop dramatically if consumers were constrained to betting tokens that had no value, in hopes of gaining other tokens that similarly had no value. Therefore, the demand for slot machine games at casinos represent a form of gambling that might be considered exemplary of the quid pro quo theory.

Although playing for real money is requirement of the quid pro quo theory, the more important requirement is playing for real money for which the consumer does not need to work. This means that except for the case of the professional gambler, the quid pro quo theory is a general theory that applies to all gambling. Nevertheless, this book acknowledges that the demand for additional "free money" is more important in some types of gambling than others. For this reason, the book focuses on the modest-stakes casino games as representing, perhaps, the clearest and least-contaminated example of the type of gambling explained by the quid pro quo theory.

With regard to insurance, there are many aspects of life that represent a form of insurance: the pooling of resources within a family, the mutual defense contracts implicit in clans and villages, national income redistribution through taxing and spending programs, the hedging of some risky investments with alternative investments, and so on. In this book, insurance is limited to formal contracts that are sold by a firm and that take advantage of uncertainty to pay out income transfers that are a multiple of the premiums. They include insurance contracts for fire and casualty, automobile accidents, healthcare, long-term care, pharmaceuticals, annuities, injury compensation (workers' compensation), income lost from unemployment, liability judgments, loss of art and jewelry, and so on.

State-Dependent Utility Functions

The decision to use state-dependent utility was another important step in the development of the quid pro quo models of the demand for insurance and for gambling. The historical impetus for making utility dependent on the state of the world was apparently the realization that death, which would imply a drop in income (perhaps to 0), would also have the unreasonable effect of increasing the marginal utility of income of the dead person, if a state-independent single argument utility function were assumed. To my knowledge, this issue was first recognized by Eisner and Stortz (1961) in their analysis of the demand for flight insurance, where arguments in addition to income were included in the utility function. In some early analyses of health insurance, health status itself was included as an argument of the utility function along with income or wealth (for example, Phelps 1973; Arrow 1974b), but more often, health status was used to distinguish between utility of different states in the analysis of health insurance, with income or wealth as the argument (for example, Hirshleifer 1966; Zeckhauser 1970).

In their analysis of utility functions that depend on health status, Viscusi and Evans (1990) write that if $U(Y)$ represents utility, U, of income, Y, when healthy, and $V(Y)$ represents utility, V, of income, Y, when ill, "for any given level of income, one's overall level of utility is greater when in good health than in ill health, or $U(Y) > V(Y)$. This assumption is not controversial" (Viscusi and Evans 1990, 354).

But in reality, what this inequality actually means is that the utility derived from a certain level of income if healthy is greater than the utility derived from that level of income if ill. Thus, Viscusi and Evans's statement *is* controversial because it is entirely possible that, if focusing on the functional relationship between income and utility alone, the utility of income per se could be greater in the state of ill health than in the state of good health. That is, although utility overall may be greater if healthy than if ill when every determinant of utility is considered, if income is the only determinant of utility considered, the effect of income alone in determining utility might result in greater utility for a given level of income when ill than when healthy. In addition, the marginal utility of income if ill may exceed the marginal utility of income if healthy.

This aspect of state-dependent utility represents one of the central propositions of the quid pro quo theory described by this book: income is often more valuable—that is, it generates greater utility—when ill than when healthy. Or more generally, income is often more valuable in the *ex post* state of the world after the insurance payoff-triggering event has occurred, than in the *ex ante* state of the world before the insurance payoff-triggering event. And, because the intent of insurance in this quid pro quo model is to transfer income to the triggering state in the *ex post* period, the effect of income on utility in that state is central to understanding the demand for insurance.

For health insurance as the example, the triggering event is becoming ill. Becoming ill increases the value of income because with illness, a new commodity—healthcare—is added to the list of commodities that would be purchased with a given household budget, a budget that is assumed to be fixed were it not for the income transfer of insurance. Thus, becoming ill makes income more valuable in general, and therefore shifts the utility function upward, compared with the utility function if the consumer remains healthy. To the extent that this shift also increases the marginal utility of the insurance income transfer, this shift would increase the demand for insurance. This same shift occurs with the triggering events of other types of insurance. For example, with fire insurance, a fire that destroys a house would create additional rent or mortgage payments necessary if uninsured. These additional expenses would also mean that the income in a household budget is more valuable, again shifting upward the utility function. This state-dependent quid pro quo theory is further developed with additional examples in chapter 2.

Previous economic theory of the demand for insurance focused exclusively on the shape of the utility or value function and changes in income or wealth that cause movements along that function. The possibility that a shift of the utility function could increase demand for insurance—a shift caused by a change in health status, a house fire, a car crash, or any other change in state represented by an insurance-payout triggering event—has been overlooked generally by economists. There are, nevertheless, a few antecedents for this theory in the literature.

The antecedents include work by the present author who has suggested that the demand for health insurance represents a desire for a transfer of income from the healthy state of the world to the ill state (Nyman 2001c; 2003) and that the demand for all insurance represents a similar income transfer to a "bad" state (Nyman 2001a).[2] These papers emphasize the effect of insurance in transferring income, and thereby gaining access to consumption, in states where access to such consumption would not otherwise be possible. The antecedents of this theory with regard to gambling also derive from the suggestion that the utility of the gambling winnings and the utility from earning the same additional income by working are a form of state dependence where the state is determined by being dealt a winning black-jack hand or picking the winning horse at the racetrack (Nyman 2004; Nyman, Welte, and Dowd 2008; Nyman et al. 2013).

The antecedents also include Fels's suggestion that all insurance represents a shifting of income to a state where it was more "needed" (Fels 2019). In a revision of his earlier paper, Fels (2021) goes on to focus on how this shifting of income might work with regard to annuities, showing diagrammatically a gain from utility due to changing from utility in a dead state to utility in the state of being alive, and how an annuity can improve expected utility by shifting income to the living state where it there is more "need" for it. Thus, Fels (2021) shows the demand for annuity insurance is due to a shifting of the

---

[2] The quid pro quo theory described in this book was originally described in a discussion paper and its revision (Nyman 2020; 2021). These papers described the quid pro quo theory of the demand for insurance as a desire for an income transfer because of the shifting of the utility function in response to a change in the state of the world. They also described the corresponding quid pro quo theory of gambling. Although these papers postulate a shift in the utility functions for both insurance and gambling, the analysis presented in this book is substantively different from the analysis suggested in these papers.

utility function across states, but does not go on to attribute the demand for any of the other types of insurance to this shifting. Instead, Fels writes,

> In other situations, there is a variation in financial needs across states. In these cases, insurance redistributes wealth into states with larger financial needs, thereby aligning the variation in financial resources to the variation in financial needs. In health insurance, for example, the primary purpose of the wealth transfer is not the compensation of a loss, but the financing of (medical) expenses satisfying the needs that are exclusive to the state (of sickness). (Fels 2021, 16)

In addition, Fels holds that "exclusive consumption opportunities" and "expenses that only have value in certain states" are sources of the demand for other (unspecified) types of insurance. Thus, Fels's definition of insurance focuses on changes in the financial needs—a difficult concept for economists to operationalize—and, with the exception of an annuity, does not make the important transition to a theory that focuses generally on how the triggering state shifts the utility function and the valuation of the insurance payoff. Nevertheless, Fels's model of insurance is closest to the one described in this book (Fels 2021).[3]

The empirical work that estimates state-dependent utilities for health states has been reviewed by Finkelstein, Luttmer, and Notowidigo. These authors "define health state dependence as the effect of health on the marginal utility of a constant amount of nonmedical consumption" (Finkelstein, Luttmer, and Notowidigdo 2009, 116). This definition is important because it expressly excludes healthcare consumption. It is, however, the introduction of healthcare consumption into the budget that is exactly the type of new consumption that, under the quid pro quo theory, is held to shift the utility of income upward in response to becoming ill. This excluded consumption is the source of the additional value of income in health insurance. Thus, the definition of consumption that these authors use does not capture the effect of insurance in generating transfers of income that can be spent on any consumption, including healthcare. None of the studies reviewed by these

---

[3] Fels also suggests that insurance and gambling both derive from the same motivation, namely, to concentrate resources in a subset of states of the world in order to overcome affordability constraints (Fels 2017).

authors captures the effect on utility of additional income that is used to provide healthcare. This issue is again discussed in chapter 10.

It should be recognized, however, that the change in health status may impinge on the utility of income in ways other than through an increased desire to purchase healthcare. For example, even though a change in health status may increase the demand for the healthcare (where such a demand did not exist before the change in health status), it might also reduce that utility that the ill consumer derives from income that would otherwise be spent on commodities like travel or restaurant meals. Thus, the increase in utility of income may be different than it would be if focusing on the demand for the new covered commodity alone. With health insurance, the effect of health on the utility from other forms of consumption could result a decrease of utility that would lessen the net increase or cause a net decrease, or it could reinforce the increase of the value from the new commodity generating an even larger increase in utility. Of the six studies reviewed, Finkelstein, Luttmer, and Notowidigdo (2009) find that the additional income spent on nonmedical consumption increased utility with a change of health status in two studies, decreased utility in three, and was ineffective in one. Thus, to find the total effect of insurance on welfare, the effect of income spent on both the commodity covered by insurance and of income spent on other commodities would need to be evaluated.

In summary, although much of the intuitive appeal of the quid pro quo theory is the presumption that the recognition of a potential change in state would increase in the demand for insurance, a change in state may have negative effects on the demand for insurance as well. Thus, differences in this factor across types of insurance and across consumers may generate both positive and negative variation in the demand for insurance. This issue is addressed further in chapter 2.

Risk Versus Uncertainty

One relatively minor decision was whether to use the term "risk" or the term "uncertainty" in the analysis. Knight (1921) distinguishes risk from uncertainty by defining risk as a stochastic event where the probability is known and uncertainty as one where the probability is unknown. In this book, there does not seem to be any need to distinguish between these terms on this basis, so the terms will be used interchangeably.

Overview of Chapters

The remainder of the book consists of nine chapters. Chapter 2 presents the Friedman and Savage (1948) model of insurance, and shows how the quid pro quo approach is a simple respecification of that model, if the same assumptions were to prevail. It then shows how the conventional approach has led to at least five erroneous conclusions regarding the welfare consequences of insurance, and how the quid pro quo approach captures a number of welfare gains from insurance that have previously been ignored, or worse, that were thought to represent welfare losses, because of the widespread acceptance of the conventional model.

Chapter 3 presents the corresponding conventional model of the demand for gambling and an alternative model derived from the demand for entertainment. The quid pro quo model for the demand for gambling is then described.

Chapter 4 addresses the supply side of insurance and gambling. It focuses on the development of insurance underwriters of shipping cargos and of gambling casinos during the early and late renaissance period in Italy. This history is revealing because it shows the reasons why these firms took the forms that they did. Moreover, it shows that the understanding of the concepts of probability and the law of large numbers in these firms probably far predated the formal description of these concepts by academic thinkers.

Chapter 5 expands and updates the conventional theory of the demand for insurance to account for the empirical studies that have informed prospect theory. It suggests that theories based on the use of many varied reference points are perhaps the most recent incarnation of the conventional theory, but that these theories are unlikely to represent the thought processes that ordinary consumers use when purchasing insurance. Far more likely is the application of a quid pro quo approach, because that approach is the one that consumers use when purchasing almost all other commodities. This chapter concludes by showing the quid pro quo decision to purchase insurance in the context of prospect theory.

Chapter 6 continues to model the quid pro quo theory from the basis of prospect theory, but concentrates on the importance of loss aversion in understanding the demand for insurance.

Chapter 7 returns to the theory of demand for gambling and the application of prospect theory to the quid pro quo approach to gambling. This chapter reviews the empirical studies on the motives to gamble and shows how these studies find that the desire for additional income is a far more common motive for gambling than is the desire for uncertainty, entertainment, or social interaction. Moreover, some of these studies show that if the motivation to obtain additional income were not present, the other seeming motivations to gamble would no longer exist.

Chapter 8 addresses the empirical estimates of the income-transfer effects, compared to the price effects, across a number of different types of insurance that pay off by reducing the price of the covered commodity. These studies show that income transfers generate most of moral hazard in a number of instances. These studies also show that the models that recognized the access value of health insurance increase welfare by an order of magnitude compared to conventional models, and that optimal coinsurance rate for health insurance approaches zero when the access value of insurance is included in the analysis.

Chapter 9 reviews some of the approaches that have attempted to explain the insurance-purchasing gambler in light of conventional theory. Economists have generally regarded the insurance-purchasing gambler as a puzzle to be explained, rather than a reason to question the underlying theory. The insurance-purchasing gambler, however, is neither a puzzle under the quid pro quo theory nor a reason to question that theory.

Chapter 10 addresses the question of why the findings that consumers prefer uncertain losses to certain ones is not more widely recognized in insurance theory. It also addresses the question of why income transfers have not been more widely accepted by economists as an explanation for moral hazard, especially by economists who write about health insurance. The chapter and book conclude by reiterating of the thesis of the book as found in the book's abstract.

2

Demand for Insurance

Preference for Certainty or Desire for Additional Income

Utility

The concepts of utility and diminishing marginal utility of income can be
traced to the work of Daniel Bernoulli, a Swiss mathematician who came
from a celebrated family of scientists and thinkers. In 1738, Bernoulli
proposed a solution to the St. Petersburg paradox, a puzzle that had perplexed
many members of the early learned societies of Europe at the time (Bernoulli
[1738] 1954). His solution applied a concept that had been alluded to in *La
logique, ou l'art du penser* (*Logic, or the Art of Thinking*), a tract published
anonymously by the Port-Royal Monastery near Paris in 1662 (Muir [1961]
1996). *La logique* suggested that people determine their fear of a harm by
both the gravity of the harm and the probability of the harm occurring.
While the latter concept—the probability of the harm—was also relatively
new at the time, the former—the gravity of the harm—was perhaps first formally acknowledged as a separate factor in this tract (Hacking [1975] 2006).
"Gravity" implied that individuals needed to give a personal evaluation to
whatever harm would happen. This subjective appraisal was a precursor to
Bernoulli's concept of utility (Bernstein 1996). Indeed, because of its popularity among the learned during this period, it was likely that Bernoulli had
read *La logique* before his paper on utility was published (Bernstein 1996).

Bernoulli's concept of utility differed from the accepted thinking of the
day that the value of an uncertain commodity to a consumer was simply its
expected monetary value. For example, if a fair coin toss determines whether
one receives US$1,000 or US$0, the value of that coin toss game to anyone
who would want to purchase it was exactly [0.5(US$1,000) + 0.5(US$0) =]
US$500, the expected value. Bernoulli held, however, that the value of the
US$1,000 was not fixed, but depended on how much income or wealth a
person already had, implying that an individual's subjective appraisal of

A Theory of Insurance and Gambling. John A. Nyman, Oxford University Press. © Oxford University Press 2024.
DOI: 10.1093/oso/9780197687925.003.0002

the value of money varied systematically with existing income or wealth. Specifically, he wrote that "utility resulting in a small increase in wealth will be inversely proportionate to the quantity of goods previously possessed" (Bernoulli, quoted in Bernstein 1996, 105). Thus, utility is increasing with wealth, but at a decreasing rate. Bernoulli used this concept of diminishing marginal utility to explain the St. Petersburg paradox.

The St. Petersburg paradox is based on an individual's willingness to pay to play a coin toss game where the winnings from the game increase with the number of successive heads that appear when a coin is tossed a series of times. The individual who purchases this game would win US\$1 if the first toss is heads, US\$2 if the second is also heads, US\$4 if the third toss in a row is heads, and a doubling of the winnings for every successive heads after that, until the first tails is tossed, ending the game. Because a heads on a coin toss has a probability of $1/2$, the expected winnings for the first throw are US\$1*$(1/2)$ = US\$0.50. The probability of winning on the second throw is $[(1/2) * (1/2) =] 1/4$, so the expected winnings for that toss are US\$2*$(1/4)$ = US\$0.50. A win on the third has a probability of $1/8$, so winnings are US\$4*$(1/8)$ = US\$0.50, and so on indefinitely. The expected value of the game is, therefore, the infinite sum of these expected values or an infinite amount of money. The paradox is that, even though the expected value is infinite, no one would pay more than a few dollars to play such a game.

Bernoulli's explanation for the paradox was that the value of ever greater winnings is diminishing to the individual consumer. So even though the amount of the winnings on, say, the 51st heads in succession is astronomical, it would have had a negligible effect on what a consumer would pay for the game because of all the money the consumer would have won on the preceding 50 heads. That is, these previous winnings would have so reduced the marginal utility of income that the additional winnings from the 51st heads are virtually valueless.

Interestingly, the solution to the St. Petersburg game does not rely on diminishing marginal utility. A computer program simulated the same St. Petersburg game described above and found that, after 1 million such games, the average winnings are only US\$9.82 per game (Nyman 2007b). Thus, the paradox—an expected value of the game that is infinite, but a subjective willingness to pay for it that is small, perhaps less than US\$10—is not explained by the diminishing utility of the winnings, since each US\$1 of winnings was valued at exactly US$1 in the computer program. The reason for the small experimental value of the game is that a streak of many heads in a row is simply unlikely in a single game, and potential purchasers recognize that fact either intuitively or perhaps after briefly experimenting with a fair coin (Nyman 2007b).

Specifically, focusing on the distribution of streaks of heads in the computer simulation study of 1 million games, about ½ of those 1 million games would result in no winnings at all because a tails would appear on the first throw, implying a streak of 0 heads and US$0 in winnings. Another ¼ of the games would end in US$1 winnings because of a tails thrown on the second throw (a "streak" of 1 heads), another 1/8 of the games would end in (US$1 + US$2 =) US$3 of total winnings because of a tails on the third throw (a streak of 2 heads in a row), and another 1/16 of the games would end in (US$1 + US$2 + US$4 =) US$7 of winnings because of a tails on the fourth throw (a streak of 3 heads). So about (50 + 25 + 12.5 + 6.25 =) 93.75 percent of the 1 million St. Petersburg games would result in streaks generating winnings of US$7 or less. Thus, the individual considering the purchase of one game would be unlikely to experience, and so never need to contemplate, winnings even approaching an amount of money where diminishing marginal utility would be a factor in evaluating the game.[1]

Nevertheless, the concept of diminishing marginal utility of income is so intuitively reasonable that it is accepted by most economists today and represents a basic assumption in much of economic theory. The concept implies that an additional US$1,000 is more valuable to a poor person than it would be to the same person if they were rich. Or equivalently, if it were possible to hold all else constant, a poor person tends to derive more utility from a marginal increase in income than a rich person. Diminishing marginal utility of income or wealth is the basis for the conventional theory of demand for insurance that was proposed by Friedman and Savage (1948).

---

[1] This analysis may be affected by streak selection bias that finds that the probability of tossing a T following any H in a finite series of fair coin tosses is slightly greater than the iid estimate of the probability of tossing a T on a random toss (Miller and Sanjurjo 2018). If so, it would bias the expected value of the St. Petersburg paradox game downward. The St. Petersburg paradox, however, does not apply to streaks after Hs in an ongoing series of coin tosses, but to streaks beginning with the first toss of the coin. Thus, how this bias affects these results is not clear.

Risk Aversion Versus Quid Pro Quo

The Friedman–Savage insurance demand model assumes that a potential loss exists, which is uncertain but exogenously determined (Friedman and Savage 1948). For example, a consumer with y_1 in income incurs a loss of $(y_1 - y_0)$ of that income because of incurring the cost of repairs from an automobile collision, leaving only y_0 in income. Or, a consumer with y_1 in income incurs a loss of $(y_1 - y_0)$ of that income because of medical expenditures, again leaving only y_0 to spend on other goods and services. The consumer is assumed to exhibit a utility function that increases with this income at a decreasing rate—what has become known as a "risk-averse" utility function among economists.

In the conventional Friedman–Savage model, the consumer is assumed to be presented with the choice: either purchase insurance or remain uninsured. The consumer's decision depends on the expected utility with or without this insurance. The lump-sum insurance payoff is $(y_1 - y_0)$ and it is assumed to be equal to, and thus cover completely, the exogenously determined loss. The probability of the loss, π, is exogenously determined, and the insurer charges an actuarially fair premium of $\pi(y_1 - y_0) = (y_1 - y^*)$, thus the model assumes that the insurer has no administrative costs or profits. The expected utility without insurance is:

$$EU_u = \pi U[y_1 - (y_1 - y_0)] + (1 - \pi)U(y_1) = \pi U(y_0) + (1 - \pi)U(y_1) \qquad (2.1)$$

and expected utility with insurance is:

$$EU_i = \pi U[y_1 - (y_1 - y_0) + (y_1 - y_0) - (y_1 - y^*)] + (1 - \pi)U[y_1 - (y_1 - y^*)]$$
$$= \pi U(y^*) + (1 - \pi)U(y^*) \qquad (2.2)$$

$$= U(y^*) \qquad (2.3)$$

The gain from becoming insured is therefore

$$EU_i - EU_u = U(y^*) - [\pi U(y_0) + (1 - \pi)U(y_1)] \qquad (2.4)$$

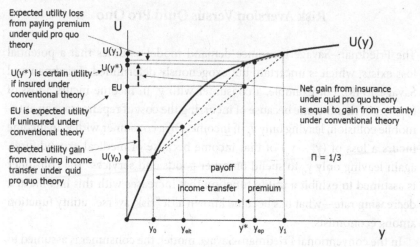

Figure 2.1 Conventional v. *quid pro quo* theory

With Friedman and Savage's model, the consumer appears to be presented with a choice between equation (2.1), being uninsured and having an uncertain outcome with an expected utility, or equation (2.3), being insured and having a certain utility. If the consumer chooses to become insured, the consumer appears to be opting for certain utility over uncertain utility. The authors write,

> An individual who buys fire insurance on a house he owns is accepting the certain loss of a small sum (the insurance premium) in preference to the combination of a small chance of a much larger loss (the value of the house) and a large chance of no loss. That is, he is choosing certainty in preference to uncertainty. (Friedman and Savage 1948, 279)

Thus, the demand for insurance has conventionally been interpreted as a demand for certainty or, equivalently, for avoiding risk.[2]

Figure 2.1 illustrates this choice. In this diagram, the probability of loss, π, is shown as 1/3. Endowed income is y_1, and y_0 is income after the loss $(y_1 - y_0)$. Expected utility without insurance is represented by EU and expected utility with insurance by $U(y^*)$, so the gain in utility is the upward-pointing dashed

---

[2] The demand for insurance is sometimes referred to as the demand to smooth consumption over states of the world. Even though Friedman and Savage do not use this language, this is equivalent to their concept of a demand for certainty.

arrow representing $U(y^*) - EU$. This gain represents the theory behind the conventional demand for insurance.

Rather than a choice between uncertainty and certainty, the same insurance problem can be presented as a quid pro quo exchange, the type of transaction that dominates the day-to-day commercial activity of consumers and firms, and that is ubiquitous in a market economy (Nyman 1999a; 1999b; 1999c; 2001c; 2001a; 2003). With a quid pro quo exchange, the demand for insurance becomes a demand for additional income—and, implicitly, additional consumption—in a state where it is more valuable to the consumer. In this specification, a premium is paid in exchange for additional income if the insured event occurs. Substituting equation (2.2) for equation (2.3) in equation (2.4), and collecting terms according to the state of the world in which the utility is experienced, results in equation (2.5):

$$EU_i - EU_u = \pi U(y^*) + (1-\pi)U(y^*) - [\pi U(y_0) + (1-\pi)U(y_1)]$$
$$= \pi[U(y^*) - U(y_0)] + (1-\pi)[U(y^*) - U(y_1)] \qquad (2.5)$$

If the event occurs, a premium payment would have been made, but the consumer receives the premium payment back as a portion of the total payout from the insurer, resulting in a net gain to the consumer equal to the income transfer, $(y_1 - y_0) - (y_1 - y^*) = (y^* - y_0)$. The expected gain from purchasing insurance can, therefore, be interpreted as receiving additional income equal to $(y^* - y_0)$ if the event occurs, so the expected gain in utility is represented by $[U(y_{eit}) - U(y_0)]$ in Figure 2.1, or the portion, π, of the gain in utility from $U(y_0)$ to $U(y^*)$. The premium payment is also uncertain because the payment only occurs if the event does not occur. The expected loss of utility from paying the premium if the event does not occur is $[U(y_{ep}) - U(y_1)]$ in Figure 2.1, or the portion, $(1 - \pi)$, of the loss of utility from $U(y_1)$ to $U(y^*)$.

In Figure 2.1, the size of the expected gain in utility from the income transfer if the triggering event occurs (an illness, an automobile collision, and so on) is represented by the upward pointing solid arrow from $U(y_0)$. The size of the expected loss of utility from paying the actuarially fair premium if the triggering event does not occur is the downward pointing arrow from $U(y_1)$. The net gain from this quid pro quo interpretation is the difference and, for utility functions that are continuous and twice differentiable like the one depicted in Figure 2.1, this difference is equal to the welfare gain from the conventional interpretation of the insurance problem (see Nyman 2003 for examples of the net welfare gain from specific utility functions).

Because the utility gains are the same, the difference between the conventional theory and the quid pro quo theory lies in the different interpretations of the motives for the demand for insurance. The conventional theory suggests that it is the consumer's preferences regarding the risk of a loss that lead to the demand for insurance: a certain loss is preferred to an uncertain one of the same expected magnitude. The quid pro quo theory suggests that it is the desire for an expected utility gain from receiving an income transfer that is greater than the expected utility loss from paying the premium that motivates the purchase of insurance.

Uninsured Loss and Income Assumptions

These welfare gains are the same only because the quid pro quo approach adopted the same assumptions as the Friedman–Savage model. Perhaps the most important of these assumptions is that the payout with insurance is equal to the loss without insurance, thus enabling the consumer to compare the expected uninsured loss to a certain one—the insurance premium—of the same expected magnitude, and so choose certainty over uncertainty by purchasing insurance. With a quid pro quo approach, however, there is no such constraint: the insurance payout can be determined by the consumer's preferences for additional income after the triggering event has occurred, and thereby create a mismatch between the actuarially fair insurance premium and the expected uninsured loss. If so, insurance would no longer generate certainty against the uninsured loss. Such contracts, of course, would still be actuarially fair as long as the premium equals the expected insured payout.[3]

Moreover, the conventional interpretation of utility in the Friedman and Savage (1948) model measures the utility derived only from y, income spent on other goods and services. For example, a "loss" due to spending on

---

[3] In contrast to the assumption of conventional theory that insurance is demanded to achieve certainty of the uninsured loss, there is empirical evidence that suggests that consumers do not actually regard the loss as part of the insurance decision in the way that it is conventionally described: a choice between a certain loss and an uncertain loss of the same expected magnitude. Instead, the loss is separate from the insurance decision: it is part of the context in which a quid pro quo contract for a gain is purchased, but not part of the calculation itself (see Connor 1996; Nyman 2003, 56–58). This issue is further discussed in chapter 5.

medical care reduces the income available to spend on other goods and services alone, not on all goods and services, including medical care. This focus on the effect of insurance on only the uninsured commodities, however, does not allow for additional purchases of the insured commodity with the income that is transferred through insurance. A more general model would show the effect of insurance on Y, income that can be spent on *all goods or services*, including those, like healthcare or automobile repair, covered by the insurance contract. If Y_1 is original income, Y^* is income after the premium is paid, and Y_0 is income after a loss of $(Y_1 - Y_0)$ amount of income, then the quid pro quo welfare gain would be written:

$$EU_i - EU_u = (1 - \pi)[U(Y^*) - U(Y_1)] + \pi[U(Y^*) - U(Y_0)]. \qquad (2.6)$$

Equation (2.6) represents the difference between the expected utility lost from paying the premium if the triggering event does not occur and the expected utility gained from receiving the income transfer if the triggering event occurs, income that can be spent on anything. This specification implies that all of the utility gain from the income transfer in insurance is captured by the utility function, including the utility from consumption of the commodity covered by insurance.

Because the quid pro quo approach makes the payoff independent of the uninsured loss (since the achieving certainty of the uninsured loss is no longer the insurance demand motive) and because it takes into account that the income transfer can be spent on any commodity including the commodity covered by the insurance contract (since the payoff is modeled in terms of Y instead of y), insurance is more valuable under this approach than under the conventional risk aversion approach. Indeed, the conventional model has misled economists from appreciating the full welfare gain from insurance in at least five ways. The following represent five welfare gains not acknowledged by conventional theory.

Welfare Gain 1: Direct Income Effect

First, Friedman and Savage's (1948) model of insurance generates certainty because it assumes that the consumer will spend exactly as much on the insured commodity with insurance as without. This is the case even though insured consumers in the Friedman and Savage model have received a lump sum income transfer from the insurer that could be spent on anything of their choosing. However, as de Meza (1983) has suggested, if the insured commodity is a normal good, this income transfer would be expected to generate an increase in spending on both the other goods and services and the insured commodity. And such a freeing up of the consumer to spend according to his or her preferences, rather than forcing the insured to spend the same as without insurance in order to achieve certainty, would likely increase welfare.

Table 2.1 illustrates this issue for the case of health insurance by comparing the Friedman–Savage assumption that the insurance income transfer generates no additional medical spending with the quid pro quo alternative where the same income transfer generates an increase in medical care spending. Row 1 shows that without insurance, the consumer with US$100,000 would purchase US$60,000 of medical care if he or she became ill. Row 2 shows the conventional Friedman–Savage interpretation of insurance, where the insured consumer purchases US$60,000 of medical care if ill, but achieves certainty across the health states by spending only US$80,000 on other goods and services, regardless of being healthy or ill, and US$20,000 on an insurance premium. The difference between the US$20,000 premium and the US$60,000 of medical care spending represents a US$40,000 transfer of income from the insurer to the ill consumer. However, if the ill consumer has US$40,000 in additional income that could be spent on medical care or other goods and services, and both were normal goods, we would expect that some of the US$40,000 would be spent on additional medical care.

Row 3 of Table 2.1 shows the effect of being insured that is consistent with the quid pro quo approach: US$70,000 is spent on medical care (an increase of US$10,000 from the US$60,000 of spending without insurance) and US$70,000 would be spent on other goods and services (an increase of US$30,000 from the US$40,000 in spending without insurance) for a total of US$140,000 in spending, the same total amount of spending as with the conventional approach. That is, it would only be by chance that consumers would find it optimal to spend the same amount on medical care with insurance as without, given they have an additional US$40,000 to spend on anything of their choosing from insurance. Because insurance costs the same under this quid pro quo approach as under the Friedman–Savage approach in Row 2, permitting consumers to rearrange their spending to better maximize utility

Table 2.1 Insurance without the Certainty Constraint

Insurance approach	Health status	Original income (y_0)	Prob of illness	Insurance premium (y_0-y^*)	Insurance payoff as a lump sum payment upon diagnosis	Income transfer	Total income after transfer	Medical spending	Additional medical spending generated by the income transfer	Spending on other goods and services
1. No insurance	healthy	$100,000	1/3	$0	$0	$0	$100,000	$0	—	$100,000
	ill	$100,000	1/3	$0	$0	$0	$100,000	$60,000	—	$40,000
2. Conventional Friedman–Savage	healthy	$100,000	1/3	$20,000	$0	$0	$80,000	$0	$0	$80,000
	ill	$100,000	1/3	$20,000	$60,000	$40,000	$140,000	$60,000	$0	$80,000
3. Quid pro quo	healthy	$100,000	1/3	$20,000	$0	$0	$80,000	$0	$0	$80,000
	ill	$100,000	1/3	$20,000	$60,000	$40,000	$140,000	$70,000	$10,000	$70,000

with the additional US$40,000 (compared to their uninsured choice) would result in a welfare gain.

Welfare Gain 2: Income-Transfer Effect

Second, rather than paying off with a lump sum income transfer if an injury or other triggering event occurs, many insurance contracts pay off by paying for the expenses of the insured, essentially reducing the price that the insured consumer pays for purchasing or repairing the commodity covered by insurance. For example, pharmaceutical insurance reduces the price of drug purchases and automobile collision insurance reduces the price of a car repair. Because of the emphasis in conventional insurance model on only covering the uninsured loss in order to achieve certainty, economists have focused attention on evaluating the additional "loss" that is caused by insurance, that is, the spending over and above the spending that would have occurred without insurance: the moral hazard.[4]

---

[4] Moral hazard is a term that was originally used to describe the additional costs that insurers of merchant ships experienced when they insured the cargo of a ship on a commercial voyage, compared to when the cargo was not insured (Dembe and Boden 2000). It became clear to perceptive insurers that insured ships had a greater chance of loss than those that were not insured. The insurers attributed this to a moral failing of the merchants and ship captains who were less cautious when insured than when uninsured or who fraudulently disposed of their cargo on the voyage before returning to port and claimed otherwise. Hence, the "moral" part of the hazard in "moral hazard." Arrow (1963b) was perhaps first to identify the concept of moral hazard as an important issue in economic theory and Pauly (1968) provided an analysis of the welfare loss from *ex post* moral hazard that was consistent with the Friedman and Savage (1948) theory. As is mentioned in chapter 10, this analysis was probably appealing to economists in part because it was consistent with the notion that anything provided free of charge in an economy where resources are scarce would be overconsumed.

There are two types of moral hazard: *ex ante* moral hazard, where the probability of loss increases if insured (Erlich and Becker 1972), and *ex post* moral hazard, where the size of the loss increases if insured (Pauly 1968). With insurance, both types of moral hazards are concerns but most of the analysis for insurance has been devoted to the study of *ex post* moral hazard. Nyman (1999a) presented a model where *ex post* moral hazard was decomposed into an efficient income-generated portion and an inefficient price-generated portion. Cutler and Zeckhauser (2000) suggested shortly thereafter that that moral hazard should only be defined as the inefficient portion of the *ex post* moral hazard. They write,

> In the terminology of demand theory, moral hazard is the substitution effect of people spending more on medical care when its price is low, not the income effect of people spending more on medical care because of insurance, by efficiently transferring resources from the healthy state to the sick state, makes them richer when sicker [De Meza (1983)]. (Cutler and Zeckhauser 2000, 577)

To my knowledge, the issue of what is meant by "moral hazard" has not been resolved within the economics profession and the term is often used to refer to both efficient and inefficient types, combined. Indeed, some economists do not recognize income effects and the efficient portion of moral hazard at all. In this book, moral hazard refers to both the efficient and inefficient portions combined, and when the portions are separated, they are identified as such.

Pauly (1968) was first to analyze the welfare effect of moral hazard, as applied to health insurance. Pauly interpreted becoming insured as causing a movement along a Marshallian demand curve for medical care. This is because insurance reduces the price of medical care from the market price to a fraction of the market price as represented by the coinsurance rate, and therefore causes an increase in quantity demanded. He calculated the welfare loss from moral hazard as the difference between (1) the cost of producing the additional medical care, where the market price was assumed to represent the marginal cost, and (2) the value the consumer derived from that care, as measured by the consumer's willingness to pay for the additional care, the area under the Marshallian demand curve. Because the conventional model based its welfare gain from insurance on covering only the uninsured loss in order to achieve certainty, it would stand to reason that covering the cost of any additional care represented a welfare loss. Pauly thought that this welfare loss from moral hazard was substantial and could even be so large as to exceed the welfare gain (described in Figure 2.1) from achieving certainty for the risk-averse insurance purchaser, thus making the purchase of insurance welfare-decreasing (Pauly 1968). Because of this, the existence of moral hazard would require major cost-sharing provisions to reduce this additional spending and, thus, the moral hazard welfare loss.

Pauly's argument is represented by his famous diagram, as shown in Figure 2.2. Demand for the commodity in question is the Marshallian

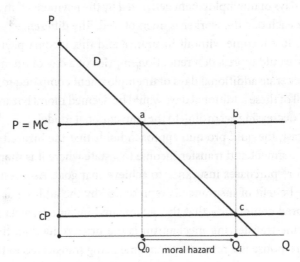

Figure 2.2 Conventional moral hazard welfare loss

demand, D, and is downward sloping. Given the market price, P, the amount of the covered commodity that would be consumed without insurance is Q_0. The purchase of insurance changes the effective price that the insured consumer faces from P to cP, where c is the coinsurance rate, such that $0 \leq c < 1$. The consumer responds to the lower price by purchasing Q_i of the commodity when insured, with $(Q_i - Q_0)$ therefore representing moral hazard. If it is assumed that the market price, P, also represents the marginal cost (MC) of producing each unit of the insured commodity, then the production cost of moral hazard is area Q_0abQ_i in Figure 2.2. The value of the moral hazard is the area, Q_0acQ_i, under the demand curve, representing the most the consumer would be willing to pay for these additional units of Q. The difference, area abc, is the welfare that is lost from becoming insured and purchasing more of the insured commodity, that is, the moral hazard welfare loss.

This diagram was originally applied to health insurance and has represented the dominant theoretical approach that economists have used to analyze many of the most important health policy issues over the years. It can also be applied to other forms of insurance where the payoff is made by reducing the price of the insured commodity, and where any spending on the insured commodity over and above the amount of the uninsured "loss" is interpreted as an inefficiency. Examples of this moral hazard are increased spending on car repair with automobile collision insurance and increased spending on drugs with insurance coverage of pharmaceuticals. Another example is unemployment insurance where moral hazard is represented by the additional days of unemployment generated by the payment of an amount of income for each day the worker is unemployed. The difference between the consumer's lost income without insurance and this income payment from the insurer would represent a reduction in price of a day of unemployment and may generate additional days of unemployment compared to being uninsured. All of these additional days would be deemed moral hazard and thus be welfare-decreasing according to the conventional model.

In contrast, the quid pro quo approach holds that the insured consumer intends to augment and transfer income to a state where it is more valuable and therefore purchases insurance to achieve that goal. As a result, a large part of the benefit of insurance is represented by the additional purchases of the insured commodity that this augmented income transfer generates. If the income-transferring mechanism is the price reduction, then within that price response is a response to income being transferred to the injured consumer. This transfer, for example, might be from those consumers who have purchased homeowners insurance and who do not incur storm damage on their house, to those who purchased homeowners insurance and who do incur storm damage. The latter consumers then draw upon the pool of insurance premiums to make home repairs, some of which (claims adjusters permitting) the storm-damaged homeowners might not otherwise have made if uninsured and relying solely on their own resources.

To determine the size of that income response, it would be necessary to pay to the storm-damaged consumers a lump-sum amount (that is, an indemnity payment) equal to the amount that the insurer would have paid out for storm-damage repairs under the homeowner's original insurance. This amount would be income that the homeowner could spend on anything of their choosing. Thus, any purchases of storm-damage repairs out of this income payment would be efficient because the consumer's willingness to pay implicitly exceeds the price of the repairs, which is assumed to remain constant. These purchases would represent the income-transfer effect of insurance that pays off by reducing price. The difference between the cost of the repairs made under the original insurance and the cost of the repairs made if the insurer is paid off with this indemnity payment is the inefficient portion of moral hazard.

A more specific illustration can be derived from the decomposition of moral hazard from health insurance (Nyman 2003). In that illustration, Elizabeth contracts breast cancer. Without insurance, it is assumed that she would purchase a mastectomy for US$20,000. With insurance that pays for all her care (coinsurance rate = 0), she would purchase a mastectomy for US$20,000, plus a breast reconstruction for US$20,000 and two extra days in the hospital to recover for US$4,000. Moral hazard is therefore represented by the expenditures for the breast reconstruction and extra hospital days. To determine whether this moral hazard is efficient or inefficient, it would be necessary to present Elizabeth upon her cancer diagnosis with a cashier's check for an amount equal to the cost that the insurer incurred to pay for her care (US$20,000 + US$20,000 + US$4,000 = US$44,000) and see what medical care she would purchase. Assume that with her original income (minus the premium paid) plus US$44,000, she would purchase the US$20,000 mastectomy that she would have purchased without insurance plus the US$20,000 breast reconstruction, but not the two extra days in the hospital for US$4,000. Because she could have purchased anything of her choosing with the additional US$44,000 and chose to purchase the US$20,000 breast reconstruction, we know that this portion of moral hazard is worth at least the US$20,000 that she spent on it and is efficient. Because she did not purchase the two extra days in the hospital for US$4,000, we know that this portion of moral hazard is inefficient and was purchased only because it was free and her insurer was paying for it.

Figure 2.3 illustrates the quid pro quo theory's evaluation of moral hazard. Marshallian demand, representing the consumer's response in quantity demanded to an exogenous change in price, for the commodity in question if uninsured is represented by D_u and is downward sloping. Without insurance, the consumer purchases Q_0 but with insurance that pays off by lowering the price to the coinsurance rate, c, the consumer purchases Q_p, the difference $(Q_p - Q_0)$ representing moral hazard. The welfare implications of becoming insured, however, must recognize that a portion of the moral hazard represents an amount that the consumers would have purchased if they had been paid off by the insurer with a lump sum income transfer equal to the same spending as the insurer would have done under the coinsurance rate, c. This amount would represent an increase in consumption of the insured commodity that was intended when purchasing insurance and whose expected costs were included in the insurance premium. That is, it might reflect a consumer's intended desire to purchase more complete car repair after a

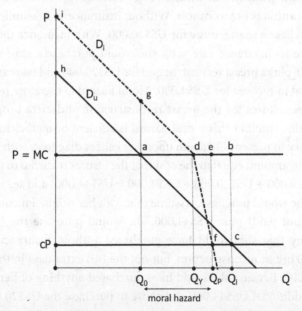

Figure 2.3 *Quid pro quo* model of the welfare effects of moral hazard

car crash (automobile collision insurance), a costly medical procedure that the consumer would not otherwise be able to afford (health insurance), or a few extra days searching for just the right job (unemployment insurance), if insured. Thus, a portion of the moral hazard represents a shifting out of the insurance demand curve that would be generated by the income transfer. The degree to which the insurance demand shifts out from Marshallian demand would depend in part on the coinsurance rate: lower coinsurance rates would imply a greater income transfer and a greater shift in demand.

In Figure 2.3, this income transfer would shift demand out to the insurance demand, D_I, the dashed demand curve. Of the total moral hazard, $(Q_P - Q_0)$, the portion of total moral hazard that is generated by the income transfer is $(Q_Y - Q_0)$. The welfare gain from moral hazard would recognize that consumers with more income have an increased willingness to pay for the covered commodities. Thus, the value of this portion of moral hazard is area $Q_0 gdQ_Y$ and the cost of producing it is area $Q_0 adQ_Y$, so the welfare gain from this portion of moral hazard is area agd.

This income transfer was achieved by reducing the price of the insured commodity from P to cP. Therefore, a second portion of moral hazard might be the consumer's opportunistic response to the insurer's using a price reduction to transfer income. This portion is illustrated in Figure 2.3 by $(Q_P - Q_Y)$ and represents a movement along a portion of the insured demand curve, but one that is steeper than the Marshallian demand. The increased steepness of this portion of the insurance demand curve is due to a second income effect that accounts for the fact that, as the coinsurance parameter, c, falls from 1 to 0, insurer would need to charge an ever-larger premium *ex ante*, and that larger premium would reduce the income available to purchase the insured commodity in the *ex post* period. For example, with health insurance, a common coinsurance rate might be 0.2, but a family insurance policy with that coinsurance rate might cost US$22,000 a year, if purchased privately with no subsidy around the year 2021 in the US. For those families with incomes of US$80,000 a year (about the median household income in 2021 in the US), spending such a large amount of a budget on a premium up front would reduce demand for healthcare, even if insured and paying only 20 percent of the medical bill (US Department of Housing and Urban Development 2022). Of course, for those families making less than the median income, this income effect might be more pronounced. In any case, the moral hazard welfare loss from using a price reduction to pay off the insurance contract is the difference between area $Q_Y deQ_P$, representing the cost of the additional consumption of Q, and area $Q_Y dfQ_P$ representing its value. This amount, area def, is smaller than area, abc, in Figure 2.3, the welfare loss from all of moral hazard according to the conventional model. The net welfare effect of the moral hazard under the quid pro quo model of insurance is the difference between the welfare gain from moral hazard, area agd, and the welfare loss from moral hazard, area def.

It needs to be emphasized that this second indirect income effect represents yet another important difference between the quid pro quo approach and the conventional approach. The quid pro quo approach recognizes that any price reduction *ex post* must be purchased *ex ante* in order to exist and this has implications for *ex post* behavior. This is different from using the Marshallian demand curve to determine the welfare loss from moral hazard. The use of the Marshallian demand in the conventional model assumes that consumers respond to insurance in the same way that they would respond to an exogenous change in the market price and that the insurance premium has no effect on demand for the insured commodity.[5]

Much has been made of the conventional moral hazard welfare loss in the analyses of health insurance policy since the publication of Pauly's model in 1968. Influential studies have estimated the welfare gain from risk avoidance (represented by the dashed upward-pointing arrow in Figure 2.1) net of the welfare loss from moral hazard (represented by area abc in Figure 2.2) to determine the net welfare effect from health insurance, and then have used those estimates to develop policy recommendations for the coinsurance rates that would choke off the optimal amount of moral hazard. As Pauly predicted might be the case, the existing welfare costs of moral hazard in some of the most famous analyses of health insurance were found to exceed the welfare gains, making it necessary to raise the coinsurance rate considerably in order for health insurance to generate a net welfare gain. For example, Feldstein (1973) found that existing moral hazard generated such a large welfare loss that the coinsurance rate in health insurance should be raised to 66 percent (or higher) in order to improve welfare. Similarly, Manning and Marquis

---

[5] Note that the text quoted in footnote 3 from Cutler and Zeckhauser (2000) assumes that the decomposition of the moral hazard is one that would be appropriate for an exogenous decrease in price, not a price decrease that must be purchased in order to exist. In Nyman (1999a), the decomposition depicted is a Hicksian decomposition that would have been appropriate for an exogenous change in price, but not a change in price from insurance. This error was required by the paper's editor at the *Journal of Health Economics,* who would not have permitted the publication of the paper if the decomposition depicted had been one consistent with a change in price purchased by an insurance premium. This error was later corrected in the analysis in Nyman (2003).

(1996) used data from the RAND Health Insurance Experiment to conclude that raising the coinsurance rate to 45 percent for all medical care, across the board with no maximum on coinsurance spending (that is, no "stop loss"), would be optimal.

It is, perhaps, surprising that income effects in the analysis of the price reduction in insurance were ignored in these studies. After all, the original Friedman–Savage model assumed insurance paid off with a lump sum income payment and by 1983 de Meza had shown that such a direct income payment could generate additional spending (de Meza 1983). Moreover, most economists understood that the welfare consequences of an exogenous price reduction must recognize both income and price (substitution) effects to be accurate (Slutsky 1915; Hicks 1946; Friedman 1962). Why these early studies postulated price changes from insurance that were the same as exogenous price changes along a Marshallian demand curve, but ignored any welfare-increasing income effects in the corresponding welfare analysis, is a puzzle. On the other hand, if the intent of insurance under the conventional theory was to achieve certainty of the uninsured loss, any additional spending on the insured commodity when insured compared to spending when uninsured had to be inefficient and welfare-decreasing. This is because any additional spending on the insured commodity if insured would mean that the expected "loss" was no longer the same without insurance as it was with insurance, and so insurance would not achieve certainty. Thus, any recognition of efficient income effects would mean that insurance no longer achieved certainty. If this consideration dominated the thinking of the early theorists, it would be understandable why income effects were ignored.

Interestingly, income effects are still being ignored. For example, Finkelstein's 2012 Kenneth J. Arrow Lecture on what economists have learned about moral hazard in health insurance since the publication in 1963 of Arrow's famous paper on the welfare derived from health insurance does not mention income effects at all (Finkelstein 2014).[6] Similarly, Einav and Finkelstein (2018) summarize what we know and what we do not know

---

[6] Rather than referring to work by economists in peer-reviewed economics journals, Finkelstein (2014) takes issue with a quote by the popular science writer and noneconomist Malcolm Gladwell (2005): "the moral hazard argument makes sense . . . only if we consume health care in the same way that we consume other consumer goods, and to economists like [John] Nyman this assumption is plainly absurd. We go do the doctor grudgingly, only because we are sick" (Gladwell, 2005, 47). Finkelstein does not cite or further explain the position taken by Nyman (1999b; 2003; 1999a), namely, that moral hazard exists, but that the issue is whether it is all welfare-decreasing as Finkelstein and others hold that it is, or whether some of it is welfare-increasing because a portion of it represents an income effect.

about moral hazard in health insurance, but again parrot the conventional theory, failing to acknowledge the importance, or even the possibility, of income effects in generating additional care, implicitly holding that they are either not relevant theoretically or that they do not exist empirically. Thus, the conventional model of insurance has been remarkably durable.

Because the conventional insurance model derived a welfare gain from covering only the loss if uninsured, Pauly (1968), Zeckhauser (1970), Feldstein (1973), Manning and Marquis (1996), Finkelstein (2014), Einav and Finkelstein (2018), and others assumed that all of the additional spending generated the price reduction represents a welfare loss.[7] However, with the quid pro quo model, much of moral hazard is welfare-increasing. That is, what was thought to be a welfare loss is actually a welfare gain when income effects are recognized. A decomposition of moral hazard that takes account of income effects would be necessary to determine the true welfare implications for health insurance, automobile collision insurance, unemployment insurance, homeowner's insurance, pharmaceutical insurance, some forms of long-term care insurance, or any other insurance that pays off by reducing price. This decomposition and the nature of the welfare loss when using a price reduction to transfer income are further explored and refined in chapter 8.

Welfare Gain 3: Access

Third, under the conventional model, the welfare gain from certainty is determined by an insurance payoff that covers the uninsured loss. However, many types of insurance cover spending that would not have occurred if uninsured, because that level of spending would be unaffordable. The prime example is health insurance and the coverage of healthcare procedures that would otherwise be too expensive to purchase privately. The demand for insurance coverage of such care is not a source of certainty because there would be no financial "loss" to the ill consumer without insurance, since the procedure could not be purchased if uninsured. Moreover, such expensive care is

---

[7] Interestingly, Manning and Marquis (1996) claim to use a compensated demand curve to determine the welfare loss, but do not recognize that the income effect of insurance would generate an insurance-demand-increasing income effect. Moreover, their estimate of Marshallian welfare loss is smaller than their estimate using the compensated Hicksian demand, which clearly does not make sense and calls into question what they were using as a compensated demand curve.

sometimes life-saving and therefore very valuable. Such coverage represents the access function of insurance and is another motivation for the demand for insurance (Nyman 1999b).

The access function of insurance can be represented by the expensive drugs—for example, the "specialty," "biologics," or "orphan" drugs—that pharmaceutical insurance coverage allows, or the higher-quality nursing home care that a private patient receives because of the payoff from long-term care insurance.[8] Access demand could also be used to describe the demand for expenditures—such as the costs of college educations for children—that would have been unaffordable without life insurance, if the coverage were limited to the uninsured loss as represented by the expected earnings lost at death. Annuities allow the insured to gain access to consumer goods and services in added years of life beyond those that could have been purchased from savings. Similarly, unemployment insurance allows a worker to access extra days of job search that would otherwise be beyond the capacity of the worker's savings or other assets to finance.

Gaining access to this income or these commodities would not be possible without the uncertainty of insurance. For example, consider access to an expensive medical procedure like a liver transplant operation. If a liver transplant procedure costs US$300,000, few Americans would be able to purchase it privately, because even if a consumer were able to liquidate all their assets, the median net worth of American households in 2019 was less than US$125,000 (US Census Bureau 2021). However, if an individual has an uncertain 1/75,000 chance of needing a life-saving liver transplant procedure in a year, health insurance coverage of that procedure could be purchased for an actuarially fair price of (US$300,000/75,000 =) US$4 annually, the expected cost. Thus, the unaffordable procedure is affordable with insurance because of the uncertainty of the change in a consumer's health condition that would require a liver transplant.

Moreover, even though such additional expenditures are a form of moral hazard, the access spending could also be demonstrated to be welfare-increasing. In the above example, if the insurer paid off with a US$300,000 cashiers' check upon diagnosis and the insured consumer voluntarily

---

[8] Private and Medicaid nursing home patients generally receive the same quality of care within a given nursing home. Because private per diem rates are set at a higher level than Medicaid rates, private pay patients are better able to choose among nursing homes, especially in markets where a shortage exists, and thus are able to obtain care in a facility with higher quality care overall (Nyman 1988a).

purchases the US$300,000 procedure that he or she otherwise could not afford, the procedure would have been shown to be welfare-increasing. This is because the consumer has demonstrated that his or her willingness to pay is at least as great as the price by purchasing the procedure. For the same reasons, otherwise unaffordable spending in long-term care insurance, life insurance, unemployment insurance, annuities, and other forms of insurance could also be shown to be welfare-increasing.

One issue, however, is that in some instances, savings or borrowing can allow for the same sort of access and so it might be the case that these other vehicles for gaining access to expensive spending are substitutes for insurance. De Meza (1983) addresses this issue with regard to health insurance and shows that obtaining otherwise unaffordable care through insurance is more efficient than either saving or borrowing. This is because insurance takes advantage of the fact that the payoff is uncertain and so requires a premium payment that represents only a fraction of the consumption costs that savings or borrowing would have required in order to gain access to the healthcare. For example, in order to have sufficient savings to cover a US$300,000 liver transplant procedure, a household would need to save about US$30,000 a year for the 10 years preceding the need for care (ignoring interest payments and compounding). For most Americans, such savings would represent a huge and, in many cases, impossible cost in terms of present consumption foregone. Borrowing would have a similar consumption cost, only with the payback consumption costs occurring in the years subsequent to the loan. In comparison, through insurance, annual coverage would cost only US$4 because of the mere 1/75,000 chance of needing a procedure, so over 10 years the consumption cost of that coverage is only about US$40 (ignoring discounting). Because of the large difference between the present consumption cost of saving or borrowing, on the one hand, and the present consumption cost of a fair insurance premium, on the other, de Meza's model shows that insurance is generally efficient.

There are, however, additional differences among saving, borrowing, and insurance that make the actual welfare comparison more complex than de Meza's model suggests (de Meza 1983). With regard to savings, the savings amassed to cover a liver procedure could also be used to cover other healthcare expenditures, or even expenditures that would be covered under other types of insurance, like unemployment insurance or annuities. Savings are more flexible than insurance payoffs because they could also be used in purchasing any consumption, if no triggering event ever occurs, or they could be bequeathed. Borrowing would not need to be done ahead of time, and so it could be related to the occurrence of a single specific event (such as an unemployment spell) that would have already occurred. However, a loan might be difficult or costly to obtain if it is for a medical procedure, for an unemployment spell, or for any other spending where the risk of failing to pay off the loan is greater because of the nature of the triggering event (such as becoming ill or unemployed). Borrowing could result in an immediate influx of income, but savings would require time, so sufficient savings might not have accumulated before the triggering event occurred. Insurance coverage would be immediate because it would only require a premium payment for the period in which the triggering event occurs, but once the premium is paid, even though small, it would represent an unrecoverable loss to consumption if the triggering event does not occur. Moreover, for types of insurance like health or automobile insurance, coverage of a single medical procedure, a single type of car crash, or another specific triggering event is usually impossible. These considerations make the comparison between insurance, on the one hand, and savings or borrowing, on the other, more complex than de Meza's model suggests. Nevertheless, even though there are cases where saving or borrowing might still be preferred, in most of the cases, insurance generates a greater welfare gain than savings or borrowing, because of insurance's exploitation of the uncertainty of the payoff.

The quid pro quo approach recognizes that much of the additional consumption spending with insurance (including the additional spending that would otherwise be unaffordable) is the intended result of transferring income to a specific state of the world and is (largely) welfare-increasing. As will be discussed in chapter 8, surveys show that having access to otherwise unaffordable medical care is a principle motivation behind the demand for health insurance. This spending is not recognized as beneficial by conventional theory because it holds that only a preference for certainty of the expected uninsured loss motivates the demand for insurance. In the quid pro quo approach, welfare is increased when access to otherwise unaffordable healthcare is achieved through the transfer of income. This access motivation would also apply to spending on other valuable but expensive commodities covered by other types of insurance.

Welfare Gain 4: Shift of Utility

Fourth, the conventional model of the demand for insurance explains how certainty is achieved when a single risk-averse utility function (Figure 2.1) is used to represent the utility consequences of changes of income in both states of the world: the state of the world where the event that triggers the insurance payout occurs and the state where the event does not occur. Under a quid pro quo approach, however, there is no reason that the utility functions in these two states of the world would need to be the same. That is, the utility of income in the state where the triggering event occurs, *event utility*, could be different than the utility of income in the state where the triggering event does not occur, *no event utility*. The following is therefore the expression for the net quid pro quo gain in expected utility from insurance with state dependent utility:

$$(EU_i - EU_u)_{QpQ}$$
$$= (1 - \pi)[U_{no\,event}(Y^*) - U_{no\,event}(Y_0)] + \pi[U_{event}(Y_1) - U_{event}(Y_0)] \quad (2.7)$$

where Y_0 represents original income, $(Y^* - Y_0)$ is the payment of the actuarially fair premium, and $(Y_1 - Y_0)$ is the income transfer. Again, the quid pro quo approach omits the effect of paying the premium in the no event state because it is paid back as part of the insurance payout in the event state. However, because these states now have different implications for utility, omitting these factors may have an effect on expected utility of insurance, as will be shown in the next section. Thus, because of the assumption of state dependent utility, equation (2.7) now is only a partial accounting for the welfare implications of insurance.

Recognition of state dependent utility may increase utility in the event state compared to the no event state. Such a shift in utility would occur because the change in state increases the value of all income in the triggering event state. For example, with health insurance, becoming ill triggers a demand for medical care in addition to the demand for all the other goods and services commonly consumed by a household. This demand for a medical procedure is new and so adds another draw on the consumer's budget, increasing the utility of income. That is, in addition to all the consumer's regular expenses— food, shelter, clothing, transportation, and so on—the ill consumer now has another item that must be paid for out of his or her income: medical care. As a result, after illness and the addition of medical care to the budget, income would become dearer and utility of income would increase.

This shift in utility might also increase the marginal utility of the income transfer. For example, with health insurance, illness may create an urgency in the need for medical care. As a result, the income transfer, if spent on medical care, might have an unusually high marginal utility compared to the same increase in income if healthy. Or, the consumer when ill might rearrange spending to cut back on regularly purchased commodities and spend more on medical care. If so, the higher willingness to pay for the more essential commodities remaining in the consumer's nonhealthcare budget would have increased the marginal utility of the income, compared to when the consumer was healthy. Or, the disruption to normal life caused by becoming ill may increase the ill consumer's appreciation for many of the commodities—shelter, food, transportation—consumed as part of the uninsured budget, and so generate an increase in the marginal utility of all income including the marginal utility of the income transfer. There are no doubt other mechanisms that could cause an increase in the marginal utility of the income transfer.

On the other hand, a change in state may have a mixed effect on utility and the marginal utility of income. Perhaps the best example of this is long-term care insurance, where the triggering change in state is represented by the consumer's becoming dependent in performing the activities of daily living. This change in state may increase the utility and marginal utility of income used to purchase the nursing home care, but may decrease the utility and marginal utility of income that is used to purchase some of other commodities, such as recreational travel or restaurant meals, that had been purchased when healthy. The net effect may be a utility increase from the income transfer when dependent that is not sufficient to overcome the utility loss from paying the premium in the no event state, when the consumer is independent and can better enjoy this other consumption. For some consumers, the utility of additional income when dependent may even be reduced overall. Either or both of these factors may explain the limited demand for private long-term care insurance that is observed in the US.

Thus, the quid pro quo theory not only identifies another source of utility, but it also provides a potential explanation for the variation in demand for insurance across types of insurance, and perhaps across consumers, too. This effect is not captured by conventional theory because only income intended for the purchase of other goods and services is considered, and because the function describing the utility of this income is assumed to be fixed and not dependent on the state of the world that triggers the insurance payoff. While acknowledging state dependent utility functions is hardly a new theoretical concept (see, for example, Eisner and Strotz's model from 1961), to my knowledge no studies have used different utility functions and this definition of income to evaluate the welfare gain from insurance, either theoretically or empirically. This specification implies that the entire utility gain from the income transfer in insurance can be captured by the positioning of the utility function and its shape, because the function now includes the change in utility from income intended for both the consumption of the commodity covered by insurance and the consumption of other commodities.

In the following analysis of the demand for insurance, three cases are considered: (1) insurance against a triggering event where there is no uninsured loss of income or assets, like health insurance, only a change in state; (2) insurance against an uninsured loss of income, like unemployment insurance; and (3) insurance against an uninsured loss of an asset, like fire insurance of a home. For all three cases, with the quid pro quo approach, the effect of paying the premium is evaluated along the no event utility alone because the premium is paid in the *ex ante* period when the event has not yet occurred. The effect of receiving the income transfer in the *ex post* period is evaluated by a movement along the no event utility function, if the triggering event does not elicit a shift in the function, or by a movement along the event utility, if it does.

As for the first case, Figure 2.4 illustrates the net utility gain from insurance under a quid pro quo approach, where there is no loss of income or assets, but where the consumer is transferring income to a state of the world where it is more valuable. Again, Y_0 is original income, Y^* is income after the premium is paid, and Y_1 is income after the income transfer from insurance. The expected loss of income from paying the premium is $(Y_{ep} - Y_0)$ and the expected income gain from receiving the income transfer is $(Y_{eit} - Y_0)$. The expected utility loss from paying the premium if the payoff-triggering condition does not occur is represented by the length of the downward pointing arrow and the expected utility gain from the income transfer if the triggering condition occurs by the length of the upward pointing arrow. Because the latter is greater than the former, receiving the income-transfer portion of the insurance payout would contribute to the demand for this insurance.

Figure 2.4 shows the utility gain from the income transfer as originating from the income level, Y_0, which is the level of income after accounting for

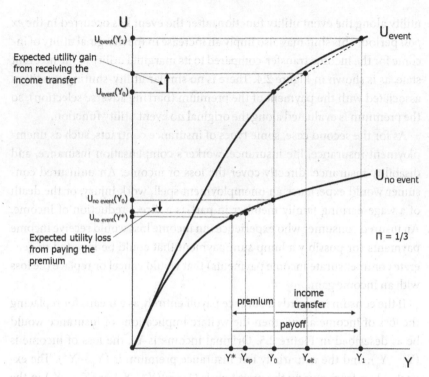

Figure 2.4 *Quid pro quo* net welfare gain from insurance with no loss

the repayment of the insurance premium. Evaluating the income transfer from Y_0 also assumes that there is no loss of income derived from the triggering event. This assumption is appropriate for the demand for types of insurance—such as health insurance, pharmaceutical insurance, long-term care insurance, annuities—where the triggering event does not involve an actual loss of income, only a change in state. For example, unless there were health consequences from an illness that reduces work, becoming ill does not generate a loss of income in itself. The issue for the uninsured ill is how to spend the consumer's original income budget to best maximize utility once the consumer has become ill. As described above, becoming ill shifts the utility of income upward because with illness an additional type of commodity is now demanded—medical care—which would not have been included in the consumer's budget if the insured consumer had remained healthy. This additional demand means that all income is dearer, and to reflect this, utility as a function of income shifts upward. The income transfer with these types of insurance is therefore evaluated by expected change in utility along the event utility function, after the event has occurred in the *ex post* period. This shift may also imply an increase in the marginal utility of income for the income transfer, compared to its marginal utility in the no event state, as is shown in Figure 2.4. There is no similar utility-shifting condition associated with the payment of the premium (barring adverse selection), so the premium is evaluated along the original no event utility function.

As for the second case, some types of insurance contracts, such as unemployment insurance, life insurance, worker's compensation insurance, and disability insurance, directly cover the loss of income. An uninsured consumer would experience an unemployment spell, work injury, or the death of a wage-earning family member in part as a direct reduction of income. An insured consumer who experiences an income loss would receive income payments (or possibly a lump sum payment that could be invested to generate commensurate income payments) that would cancel or replace the loss with an income gain.

If the consumer regards insurance payoff entirely as a means for replacing the loss of income alone, then the welfare implications of insurance would be as described in Figure 2.5. Original income is Y_1, the loss of income is $(Y_0 - Y_1)$, and the actuarially fair insurance premium is $(Y_1 - Y^*)$. The expected loss from paying the premium is $(1 - \pi)(Y^* - Y_1)$ or $(Y_{ep} - Y_1)$ in the diagram. The payoff here is assumed to be equal to the loss of income (for ease of exposition), so the income transfer with insurance is $(Y^* - Y_0)$. The expected income transfer is $\pi(Y^* - Y_0)$ or $(Y_{eit} - Y_0)$ in the diagram. The

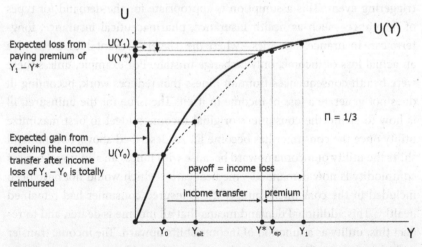

Figure 2.5 *Quid pro quo* net welfare gain with income loss and no shift in utility

expected gain in utility from the income transfer is represented by the upward pointing arrow and the expected loss in utility from paying the premium is represented by the downward pointing arrow. The net difference is positive so this net gain would contribute to the demand for insurance.

The analysis of this case is the same as the analysis of all insurance under the conventional model and is shown here to emphasize the fact that, while the quid pro quo model may reject the notion that insurance is demanded to achieve certainty of the uninsured loss, it does not reject the possibility of diminishing marginal utility of income. Nor does it reject the idea that expected utility is the basis for explaining decisions under uncertainty. In the foregoing analysis, the gain from insurance is derived solely from the assumed shape of the utility function: diminishing marginal utility of income. The loss of income triggered by, say, unemployment would mean that an actuarially fair income transfer from insurance would generate a larger gain in expected utility than paying the premium because of the shape of the utility function. Thus, in the case of insurance that is perceived to simply cover income losses and not to shift utility, the shape of the utility function alone and gain in expected utility would generate the demand for insurance.

However, with this type of insurance, there may be reasons that the triggering event would also make income dearer to the consumer in the *ex post* state after the event has occurred. If so, the analysis may also need to recognize a shift in the utility function. The reasons why this shift could occur would vary with the type of insurance. With unemployment insurance, the loss of a job means there are new drawdowns on income to cover the additional cost of a job search. There might also be added expenses due to disruption of household activities during an unemployment period that did not exist when working. Thus, the income transfer from unemployment insurance would be evaluated after the shift to a utility function where income is dearer than it was in the no event *ex ante* period. For life insurance that replaces the income of a worker in the household, additional funeral, moving, and other adjustment costs may be generated by death of a family breadwinner. With worker's compensation and disability insurances, a new work injury or disablement would likely mean new medical costs, and new nonmedical costs—making home entrances accessible or remodeling bathrooms—that are associated with coping with the injury. Moreover, the increased pain and discomfort when working would increase the value of income provided by the insurer (compared to earning it) and so that too would shift the utility function upward. As a result, the income transfer from insurance would thus represent a gain in utility that is derived from both (1) the shape of the event utility function and the income after the income loss, and (2) the shift from the no event utility function to the event utility function. Both would contribute to the demand for insurance.

Using the same variable labels as were used in Figure 2.5, Figure 2.6 shows how an income transfer would generate the expected utility gain if both the shape of the utility function and the shift in utility were taken into account. Notice that in this diagram, the income transfer is evaluated on the event utility function before the portion of the insurance payout representing the repayment of the insurance premium is accounted for. This treatment of the income transfer is consistent with the way it was evaluated in Figure 2.5, but opposite to the way it was evaluated in Figure 2.4. Whether to evaluate the income transfer before or after the repayment of the premium in the insurance payout is accounted for is arbitrary, so both ways are shown in these two diagrams. However, if combined with the net effect of paying the premium in the no event state and recovering the premium as part of the insurance payoff in the event state as described in the next section, the arbitrariness of the welfare conclusions would go away.

It should be noted, however, that Figures 2.5 and 2.6 could have instead depicted insurance for actuarially fair payoffs that exceed the loss of income if uninsured. Again, in some instances, these additional payoffs may not have

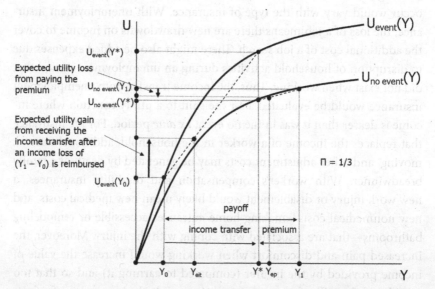

Figure 2.6 *Quid pro quo* net welfare gain with income loss and shift in utility

generated shift in utility. For example, it is typical for liability settlements against insured consumers to exceed, and sometimes far exceed, the income payments that such consumers would have been required to make if uninsured. There would be no corresponding shift in utility because it is assumed that the consumer derives no additional welfare from the additional payments to an injured third party, other than the avoidance of the loss of income represented by the uninsured liability payments. In other instances, payoffs in excess of the uninsured loss of income might need to be evaluated using a utility function that has shifted upward reflecting the additional utility from some added expenditure. For example, for disability insurance that pays off with an amount that covers lost earnings plus the additional costs of remodeling the disabled consumer's home to make it accessible and for the additional equipment necessary to cope with some disabilities, the utility gain from the payoff would need to be evaluated on a shifted utility function.

As for the third case, some types of insurance contracts cover a loss of assets, such as fire or theft (homeowner's) insurance, automobile insurance, and the like. The triggering event might also cause there to be additional expenditures that, if uninsured, would largely be paid for out of income for most Americans. For example, a fire that destroys an uninsured home would require either new monthly rental payments or a new course of mortgage payments to buy a new house. These payments would be in addition to any existing payments to the bank to cover the remaining equity debt on an uninsured house that burned down. Because the median level of home equity in 2019 in the US was about US$130,000 but the median amount of housing debt was about US$140,000, a typical uninsured house fire would likely require a substantial number of additional housing payments out of income (US Census Bureau 2021). A similar situation would obtain for an uninsured automobile. A car crash would mean additional costs for transportation, and often represent costs over and above the monthly payments on the uninsured car, since the median amount of US$15,000 household vehicle debt in 2019 in the US (US Census Bureau 2021)—all of which would represent additional expenses in a household budget that would make each dollar income more valuable to the consumer or household if the event happens than it was in the no event *ex ante* period. These events would shift up utility as a function of income in uninsured because income is dearer with these additional claims on the budget and they might also increase the marginal utility of income.

The effect on utility of insurance that covers these types of asset losses might also depend on the consumer's perspective. If the consumer adopts the perspective that insurance simply cancels the asset losses as if they never existed, then the gain from the income transfer would be as described in Figure 2.5. Assuming again full insurance that would cover the entire asset loss, this perspective would mean an income transfer that would result in an expected income gain of $\pi(Y^* - Y_0)$ and expected utility gain of $\pi[U(Y^*) - U(Y_0)]$ in Figure 2.5. However, if the consumer adopts the perspective of having experienced a house fire or car crash and being uninsured, the insurance income transfer would mean a savings of the additional uninsured spending required for the additional housing or transportation payment services that the triggering event engendered. From this interpretation, the income transfer from insurance would generate an increase in utility as described by Figure 2.6.

In this third case, the loss of an asset would need to be translated into its income equivalent to be represented in Figures 2.5 and 2.6. This is reasonable because without insurance, the housing or car payments would likely be paid out of income. Thus, a lump-sum payment from the insurer for, say, a home that was destroyed in a fire would likely translate into its equivalent in mortgage payments, and also be similarly treated with a lump-sum car settlement. As mentioned in chapter 1, this is consistent with, but just the opposite of, Chetty's treatment of income (unemployment) insurance using a wealth model (Chetty 2008). Even though unemployment insurance pays off in the *ex post* period with income payments, Chetty modeled the income payments as having had an effect on wealth by reducing the need for uninsured consumers to convert assets (wealth) into liquidity in the *ex post* period. In the present income model approach, the effect of the lump-sum payment for coverage of an asset (wealth) loss is modeled as reducing the need for the uninsured to make additional income payments in the *ex post* period.

In addition to the shifting of the utility function upward because of the additional expenses that arise due to the triggering event, the quid pro quo theory later in chapter 6 suggests that consumers are so averse to losses that an income transfer that cancels a loss could generate an additional shift in the event utility function in the *ex post* period. Loss aversion would, therefore, represent another reason for evaluating the income transfer according to a utility function that had been shifted upward as in Figure 2.6. This shifting up of the utility function is due to the prospect theory finding that the value lost from monetary losses exceeds the value gained from similar sized monetary gains (Kahneman and Tversky 1979; 1984; Tversky and Kahneman 1981). Thus, when purchasing insurance, consumers would evaluate the income transfer vis-à-vis this loss, and the willingness to pay for insurance would increase by an amount that reflected the loss aversion. Loss aversion is discussed in detail in chapter 6 when the demand for insurance is considered from the context of prospect theory.

Some asset losses, however, simply do not fit the present analysis because they are pure losses of wealth that do not have any implications for added consumption expenditures out of a fixed income budget. For example, insurance coverage of art, coin, stamp, or similar collections, or of jewelry would represent a loss of wealth that would generate little, if any, additional consumption demand and so would have little effect on shifting utility as a function of income. For insurance that covers these types of assets, it may be more appropriate simply to model utility as a function of wealth and to focus on loss aversion as the reason that the utility of wealth function would shift upward and generate a demand for insurance. As mentioned, the effect of loss aversion on the demand for these assets will also be addressed in chapter 6.

Finally, the event utility function in this analysis is intended to capture the gain in consumer surplus from the additional consumption of the covered commodity that is purchased because of the income transfer in insurance. The event utility for otherwise unaffordable medical care might represent the case where this gain is most apparent. Conventional theory would evaluate health insurance based only on a welfare gain from nonmedical spending and would regard medical spending in excess of the uninsured amount as generating a welfare loss. In contrast, the quid pro quo theory would postulate an event utility function that includes the utility from medical care. As a result, it includes the additional willingness to pay for any medical care consumption purchased because of the income transfer. Thus, any increase in the consumer surplus from insurance-produced consumption would be registered in the event utility function. Because of the inclusion of this consumer surplus, the event utility function might also exceed the no event utility function, which would represent the value of the income in the no event state that does not include the purchase of this medical care. This issue is addressed in chapter 8 when the welfare gains from an increase in the consumer surplus are further discussed.

Returning to the theme of this chapter, the shifting of the utility function (to capture the effect of the additional consumption that is often required after a triggering event occurs) represents an increase in the utility from insurance that is not recognized by the conventional theory. This increase in utility may also generate an increase in the marginal utility of income that increases the demand for insurance. This increase does not occur consistently across all types of insurance, but may be of primary importance in some types, like health insurance and annuities, where the triggering event is not a loss of income or assets but instead a change in state alone. This welfare effect cannot be recognized if the gain from insurance is evaluated only on the basis of a static utility function.

Welfare Gain 5: Recovery of the Premium Payment

Fifth, one seeming advantage of the quid pro quo approach is that the welfare evaluation of insurance is simpler because the premium payment is cancelled by an equivalent portion of the payout if the triggering event occurs. In this way, the analysis focuses on difference between the expected premium loss and the expected income-transfer gain. Under the assumption of state dependent utility, however, this advantage is reduced because the payment of the premium is evaluated on a different utility function than is the recovery of that payment in the insurance payoff, if the triggering event occurs. Thus, this canceling of the premium payment with a portion of the payoff may also contribute to the demand for insurance. In order for the welfare calculations to be complete, the welfare effect from this difference would also need to be accounted for.

If these factors were added back into the analysis, the expression for the net gain from insurance would become:

$$(EU_i - EU_u)_{complete}$$
$$= [U_{no\ event}(Y^*) - U_{no event}(Y_0)] + \pi[U_{event}(Y_1) - U_{event}(Y^*)] \quad (2.8)$$

That is, the gain from insurance would be represented by the reduction of utility from paying the premium with certainty in the *ex ante* period evaluated by no event utility, in exchange for the expected insurance payoff (that includes both the recovery of the premium and the income transfer) in the *ex post* period evaluated by event utility. This expression would represent

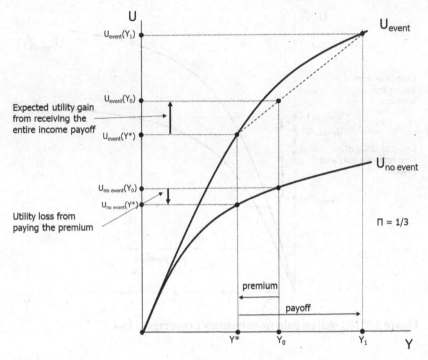

Figure 2.7 Net welfare gain from insurance with no loss

the *complete* accounting for the expected gain from insurance, and so is indicated as such.

Figure 2.7 shows the corresponding net gain from insurance when there is no income loss, but instead an increase in the utility of income and the marginal utility of income, accounting for both the gain from the income transfer and from recovering the premium payment in the insurance payoff.

Comparison of Figure 2.4 with Figure 2.7 shows that the addition of the recovery of the premium in the *ex post* period would generate a larger expected increase in utility than the expected increase in utility derived from the income transfer alone. This conclusion would, of course, depend on the shapes and positioning of the utility functions.

With regard to the expansion of the case shown in Figure 2.6 to account for both the payment of the income transfer and the recovery of the premium in the insurance payout, the effect on utility would depend again on how the event and no event utility functions manifested themselves. Figure 2.8 shows

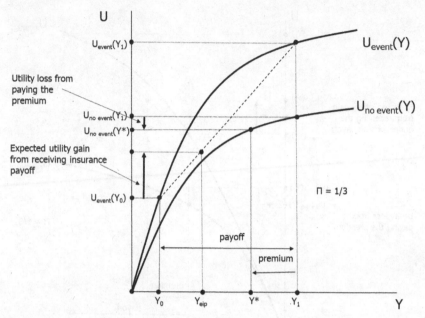

Figure 2.8 Net welfare gain from insurance coverage of loss

the corresponding diagram for the case where the recovery of the premium is taken into account in the *ex post* period.

The upward-pointing arrow, representing the expected increase in event utility from the expected insurance payout, $(Y_{eip} - Y_0)$, exceeds the downward-pointing arrow, representing the decrease in no event utility from paying the premium, and implies the purchase of this insurance.

This treatment of the premium payment might strike some readers as being more natural than the original treatment because in this version, the premium is being paid with certainty, in exchange for an expected insurance income payoff in the event state. Moreover, when the triggering event causes a change in utility, this analysis more completely captures the expected utility gain from becoming insured. The advantage of the original approach, however, is that it focuses attention on the income transfer as the basic motivation for the purchase of insurance. This approach is important because income transfers have largely been ignored in past analyses, thus creating errors and biases in the analysis of the welfare implications of insurance, especially with regard to the analysis of health insurance and of health insurance policy. The recognition that an additional factor—state dependent utility—may potentially increase the welfare derived from income transfers would add another reason to keep the quid pro quo approach prominent. However, regardless of which approach deserves prominence, the bottom line is that neither income transfers nor state dependent utility have been recognized sufficiently in past work and so their recognition in the present model represents an important advance in the theoretical understanding of the demand for insurance.

Digression on Price Effects and Welfare

As mentioned above, the insurance price reduction is not exogenous, but one that must be purchased by the consumer with a premium in order to exist. More importantly, under the quid pro quo approach, the intent of insurance is to transfer income and so the insurance price reduction is the vehicle used to accomplish that. Thus, the decomposition of moral hazard caused by an insurance price decrease focuses on the income transfer— the motive for demand for insurance under the quid pro quo model—and differs from the decomposition of the increase in quantity demanded caused by an exogenous price decrease. Specifically, the insurance price decomposition results in a smaller price effect, and therefore a smaller welfare loss, than the corresponding Hicksian or Slutsky–Friedman price effects from the decompositions of an exogenous change in price (Hicks 1946; Slutsky 1915; Friedman 1962; Nyman 1999c; 2003; Nyman and Maude-Griffin 2001).

Figure 2.9 illustrates the differences between the Hicks and Slutsky–Friedman decompositions, and the decomposition that is appropriate when the intent of insurance is to transfer income. In that diagram, Q is the commodity covered by insurance and for which the coinsurance rate, c, applies. Spending on other goods and services is y. Without insurance the consumer spends at point O. With insurance that reduces the price of Q from P_Q to cP_Q, the consumer spends at point I. All three income effects are determined by the same income expansion path (labeled as such in Figure 2.9) using the new prices. To facilitate the comparability among the three decompositions, the effect of paying a premium is not shown in Figure 2.9. Since the level of Q remaining after the income effect has been accounted for is not affected by omitting the premium payments that are all the same, this would not affect the relative amounts of moral hazard that would be generated by the price effects alone.

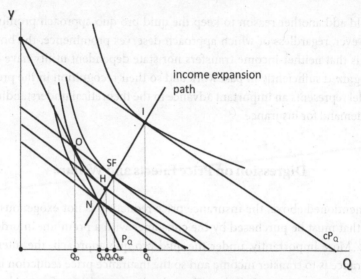

Figure 2.9 Hicks, Slutsky/Friedman, and new insurance decompositions

The various decompositions result in different sized price effects after the income effects have been acknowledged. The Slutsky–Friedman decomposition of an exogenous price decrease subtracts sufficient income to purchase optimally a bundle, SF, on a budget constraint that would allow for the purchase of the original bundle of goods. The Hicks decomposition of an exogenous price decrease subtracts sufficient income to purchase optimally a bundle, H, on the original indifference curve. The appropriate decomposition for the insurance purchase of a lower price subtracts the entire income transfer, that is, sufficient income to purchase optimally a new bundle, N, which lies on the original budget constraint. The welfare-decreasing quantity of moral hazard represented by optimal bundle N, namely $(Q_N - Q_O)$, is smaller than the quantities of inefficient moral hazard that would be represented by either of the other two optimal bundles—SF, with inefficient moral hazard purchases equal to $(Q_{SF} - Q_O)$, or H, with inefficient moral hazard purchases equal to $(Q_H - Q_O)$.

None of the empirical welfare analyses of health insurance recognizes a decomposition of moral hazard, much less one that is appropriate for insurance (e.g., Pauly 1968; Zeckhauser 1970; Feldstein 1973; Manning and Marquis 1996; Finkelstein 2012; Einav and Finkelstein 2018). These studies apparently do not recognize income effects because the motivation for purchasing insurance is to establish certainty. To establish certainty, the desired spending if insured must be the same as the loss if uninsured, and any additional spending on the insured commodity if insured is deemed to be inefficient. Since additional consumption due to increased income is clearly efficient, its recognition would raise fundamental questions about the validity of the conventional theory of demand for insurance, and so this income effect is ignored.

Moreover, whether the price effect from the insurance decomposition is actually a welfare loss is debatable. Insurers use a price reduction to pay off an insurance contract because, with some types of insurance, doing so is less costly administratively than paying off with a lump sum income transfer as an indemnity payment. For example, a health insurer could establish an indemnity payoff schedule for the various disease diagnoses, but doing so would require additional costly legal and health services research input to determine the amounts of the payouts. Even with contingency payments, such a system would probably still not be able to adjust completely for the idiosyncratic nature of diseases, comorbidities, and the varying effectiveness of disease treatments. Moreover, paying off with a lump sum income payment would require additional expensive monitoring for fraud by health professionals. Paying off the insurance contract by reducing the price of a procedure ensures that the insured person would have received the procedure before the payment is made. Thus, the pain, discomfort, and danger associated with many medical procedures serves as a natural check on fraud when a price reduction is used. Therefore, to the extent that the inefficient portion of moral hazard is merely a transactions cost, it may be ignored in the welfare calculations, because any other way of transferring income to the insured consumer would be more costly.

The reluctance of consumers to receive healthcare unnecessarily is an intuitively understandable explanation for using a price reduction to pay off a health insurance contract. A number of other types of insurance, however, use a price reduction to transfer income, and have triggering conditions and treatments for "injury" (in the legal sense) that many would find too costly to assume fraudulently. For example, the fraudulent triggering of automobile collision insurance would require a possibly injurious car crash and need to secure an alternative source of transportation over the period of time required for car repair. Likewise, an unnecessary accessing of worker's compensation insurance payments would require an often painful physical injury, and the fraudulent triggering of homeowner insurance might entail the loss of irreplaceable heirlooms and photographs in a fire. All these represent ways in which administrative costs are reduced by using a price reduction to transfer income.

Summary

This chapter began by considering the origins of the concepts of utility and diminishing marginal utility of income, and showed how conventional theory used the latter concept to conclude that the demand for insurance is a demand for certainty. The conventional theory, however, requires that the spending if insured be equal to the loss if uninsured in order to achieve certainty. This assumption represented an unnecessary constraint that has reduced the welfare gain from insurance in at least five ways. The alternative quid pro quo approach holds that insurance is purchased in order to obtain additional income in a state where income is more valuable. Because of the changes in the approach to the insurance demand problem, the quid pro quo model is able to identify new welfare gains or reduce the size some of the welfare losses under conventional theory. Indeed, some of the welfare losses under conventional theory are either eliminated altogether by adopting a quid pro quo approach or, even more dramatically, become welfare gains. In chapter 5, we return to the demand for insurance to reconsider it from the perspective of prospect theory. In chapter 6, the impact of loss aversion on the demand for insurance is also considered. In chapter 8, the empirical work around the issue of moral hazard and access is considered, and how the consumer surplus from the goods being insured may also increase the demand for insurance.

3

Demand for Gambling

Preference for Risk or Desire for Work-Free Income

Quid Pro Quo Model

The quid pro quo model of the demand for gambling is similar to the quid. pro quo model of the demand for insurance: the demand for gambles is due primarily to a desire for an income transfer gained in a state of the world where, instead of the income being more valuable to spend, income is less costly to obtain. The income transfer is the difference between the wager and the winnings and represents the source of the potential utility gain from gambling, compared to the consumer's situation without gambling. The change in the state of the world is a lucky roll of the dice or spin of the roulette wheel. This event is important because it means that, in contrast to the wager, the additional income that is obtained from gambling does not require work. This event shifts the utility function of income upward. The increase in utility is due in part to the income being unearned, but as is explained herein, it may also be due to its source as an unexpected windfall. The latter may increase utility because of the consumption implications that such windfall income generates. Nevertheless, the bottom-line motivation to gamble is the desire for a transfer of additional income in the state of the world where the utility function shifts upward by eliminating the disutility of labor.

In this model, *no event* utility is a function of income. In this case, however, income determines utility through both the value to the consumer in the goods and services that can be acquired with it and the impact on the consumer of the labor required to obtain it. The former increases utility, but the latter may increase or decrease it. *Event* utility is also a function of income, but income here determines utility only through the value of the commodities that can be obtained with it. It is not determined by the cost of the labor since no labor, or only trivial labor, is required to obtain it. It is assumed that both functions are concave, but that event function lies somewhere above the no event utility function over the range of income

A Theory of Insurance and Gambling. John A. Nyman, Oxford University Press. © Oxford University Press 2024.
DOI: 10.1093/oso/9780197687925.003.0003

represented by the income transfer. That is, because the disutility saved from not having to work for income only exists for the gambling income transfer, the shift of the utility function only occurs over that portion of the utility function representing the income transfer from the winnings. Unlike becoming ill, which generates new demands for goods and services at every level of income, a winning roulette number saves the disutility of labor only for the income transfer represented in the winnings, not any previously earned income. According to the theory, it is primarily the characteristics of the job and the worker that determine the level of disutility from labor and therefore the distance in utility between the no event utility function from earned income and the event utility function from unearned income.

Specifically, assume that the probability of winning is π, original income is Y_0, Y^* is income after the wager $(Y^* - Y_0)$ is paid, and Y_1 is the income after the winnings $(Y_1 - Y^*)$ are received. The wager is assumed to be actuarially fair so that $\pi(Y_1 - Y^*) = (Y_0 - Y^*)$. The income transfer is that portion of the winnings in excess of the wager, $(Y_1 - Y_0)$. If $U_{\text{no event}}$ is the utility function of income for earned income, and U_{event} the utility function for unearned income, the gain in utility from gambling, ΔEU_g, is represented by equation (3.1):

$$\Delta EU_g = (1 - \pi)[U_{\text{no event}}(Y^*) - U_{\text{no event}}(Y_0)] + \pi[U_{\text{event}}(Y_1) - U_{\text{event}}(Y_0)] \quad (3.1)$$

This is the gambling equivalent of the insurance equation (2.7). Gambling implies that the expected gain in utility from receiving the income transfer, evaluated by the event utility function, is greater than the expected utility loss from making the wager, evaluated along the no event utility function.

Note that again the wager is recovered in the winnings, if the event occurs. Moreover, the wager is paid with income that theoretically would be evaluated by the no event utility function and is recovered with winnings that would be evaluated by the event utility function. Whether this aspect of state dependency affects the demand for gambling is not clear because it is not apparent that the gambler views the recovery of the premium in the gambling winnings as being work-free and different from the payment of the wager. Moreover, in many gambling games—such as slot machines, blackjack, and roulette—the payment of the wager and the receipt of winnings occur both simultaneously and instantaneously. Because of these considerations, the wager if the gamble is won is excluded from the analysis in this chapter, but in chapter 7 the assumption will be changed to show the net gain when both the wager and its recovery are included in the analysis.

Utility and Disutility of Labor

The difference between the two functions requires further explanation. In general, for the additional income represented by the income transfer, this difference can best be described as a disutility of labor. Therefore, gambling is valuable because it represents the prospect of gaining a transfer of additional income which does not require such labor. As a result, the motive to gamble can be described as the reduction in the utility cost of obtaining additional income or the avoidance of the disutility of labor.

Because the disutility of labor is so central to understanding the motivation for gambling, it is important to review the history of the ways economists have viewed this concept. After the revolution in economic thinking that replaced the labor theory of value with marginal utility theory, economists adopted three different ways of thinking about the utility of labor (Spencer 2003). Initially, economists like Jevons ([1871] 1970) and Marshall ([1890] 1910) thought about what it was like to work and recognized that although some work is tedious, burdensome, or worse, other work may actually be pleasurable. For many workers there might be an optimal amount of labor supplied, which is determined both by gain in utility from the earnings and from having a job, and an eventual net disutility from working too much. That is, even if initially work were more pleasurable than being unemployed, few would be able to work to the limits of their physical or mental capacities without experiencing a reduction in that pleasure, if not a transformation to work becoming burdensome, fatiguing, or painful. Moreover, the number of hours worked is rarely at the discretion of the worker because of widespread acceptance of the standard (now eight-hour) workday and (now 40-hour) workweek. Thus, even if workers could specify an optimal amount of working hours, they would typically not have discretion to work only that long. So at the end of the workday or workweek, some workers might experience various levels of disutility from labor, depending on how the characteristics of the job interacted with their personal characteristics and work preferences.

By the early part of the twentieth century, however, influential economists like Knight (1921) and Robbins (1930) adopted the view that the characteristics of the job were beside the point. What mattered in evaluating labor was the value of the leisure time that was forgone when working, the opportunity cost of labor. Since it was difficult to measure the *value* of leisure time, the *amount* of leisure time foregone in order to work was used to evaluate labor without further refinement. If only leisure mattered but it could not be further evaluated, then there was a fixed opportunity cost of an hour of work, as represented by an hour of leisure forgone. Later, however, Becker (1971) and others recognized that some occupations were more desirable than others. Because of that, the minimum wage required for an individual to forego leisure and to work in an occupation would reflect the desirability of each job, and so this "reservation wage" could be used to refine and so evaluate the leisure forgone.

In the most recent wave associated with work by Alchian and Demsetz (1972), Shapiro and Stiglitz (1984), and Williamson (1985), the disutility of labor was captured by workers shirking their job responsibilities in order to reduce their effort and so obtain leisure when on the job. This "on-the-job-leisure" implies that there is something about the work effort that is generally to be resisted. Although evidence of shirking exists (e.g., Bradley, Green, and Leeves 2007), economists have not reached a consensus on exactly what aspect of the job is being resisted by shirking.

All three of these approaches suggest that for most consumers, there is a difference between the utility of winning an income transfer of, say, US$1,000 in a gamble and the utility of having to work longer hours in a workday or more days in a workweek at their current job in order to obtain an additional US$1,000 of income. This disutility of labor may derive from undesirable characteristics of the job or working longer than desired due to the lumpiness of the workday or workweek. Alternatively, this disutility might be related to recognizing that desirable leisure is forgone when working or by the evidence that some workers seek to reduce the effort they supply while on the job by shirking. While there may be sufficient reason to distinguish the two utility functions of income on the basis of any one of the three different theories, the one that seems to fit best the theory of gambling presented here is the first. This is because the nature of the job (the amount of effort required, the working conditions, the management, the coworkers, the stress and expectations, and so on) interacts with the nature of the worker (physical and mental ability, stamina and resilience, age, gender, race, family characteristics, place of residence, and so on), and both together determine how much an individual would value not having to work in order to obtain additional income.

Exactly how the introduction of labor would transform the utility function of earned income into the utility of unearned income, however, is not clear. One possibility is that the absence of labor could represent an additive utility "premium" for every dollar of income that is unearned. Thus, unearned event utility could be represented by a curve that traces out the familiar diminishing marginal functional form, but at a higher utility level. This view, however, does not account for the fact that having a job is typically better than being unemployed and so work can increase utility of earned income, at least initially.

An alternative transformation of the entire function is that the utility of earned income exceeds the utility of unearned income over some initial range of income, because having a job and doing some work is better than being unemployed, then drops below unearned income after some exhaustion level has been reached, as was suggested originally by Jevons ([1871] 1970). It is assumed that gambling winnings would occur after the workday or workweek has occurred, thus an income transfer from gambling would be evaluated over the range of income where the disutility of labor exists. Over this range of additional income, the utility from unearned income exceeds the utility from earned income.

Empirical evidence in support of this latter transformation comes from Rätzel (2012). Rätzel used the German Socio-Economic Panel to estimate the effect of different amounts of working hours in a day on life satisfaction. A life satisfaction variable was based on a 10-level scale of responses to the question, "How satisfied are you with your life, all things considered?" The author interpreted this variable as measuring "happiness" or "utility." The German panel captured about 120,000 person-years of observations, over the 23 years from 1984 to 2006. The life satisfaction variable was regressed on the number of hours worked in a day and hours squared, holding constant monthly income and a number of other variables in a fixed-effect regression analysis to address endogeneity. The analysis showed that utility is significantly higher if working, up to a maximum of 7.7 hours worked in a day for men and 4.2 hours for women, then it becomes lower if working. Thus, for the average German man (woman) working 8.8 (6.7) hours in a day, he (she) experienced positive utility from working for most of the workday, but disutility from working at the end of the workday, holding the amount of income and other things constant.

This analysis, however, did not account for the fact that some, who get more satisfaction from work, might opt to work longer hours. To address this form of selection bias, Rätzel (2012) constructed a variable representing the difference between a variable capturing the respondent's desired working time and how much the respondent actually worked. The difference reflected the lumpiness and assumed exogeneity of work hours in the implicit labor contract for the worker. Rätzel found that working more than desired significantly lowers life satisfaction, but more for men than women.

This analysis suggests that for most people who are employed, working initially adds to utility of income because having a job is better than being unemployed. The work that is done toward the end of the workday or working longer hours than the job calls for in a workday to obtain additional income, however, would be associated with a disutility of labor. It stands to reason that a similar relationship would prevail between the number of days in a workweek and utility, or the number of workdays in a year and utility, but to my knowledge, no studies have investigated these relationships. Nevertheless, it is reasonable to postulate that for most workers, obtaining additional income from a gambling income transfer would increase utility more than working additional hours to obtain the same increase in income.

This empirical study suggests another gain from the income transfer. The disutility of labor might cause the utility function of earned income to turn downward after some level of earnings. Moreover, this would raise the possibility that a forward-looking consumer might view the gain from gambling by adding the expected utility gain from the income transfer ($Y_1 - Y_0$) when unearned, to the expected utility loss avoided if that same increase in income had to be earned (Nyman 2004; Nyman, Welte, and Dowd, 2008). For example, a worker might desire additional consumption for some specific reason and gamble because, when considering the standard ways of obtaining additional income to finance that consumption such as taking another job or working longer hours, a gamble would appear to be the least costly option.[1] If so, the gain from gambling would be evaluated according to equation 3.2.

---

[1] The ability of some workers to work overtime for a higher wage might reduce the demand for gambling and if so, might lend empirical support to the theory described in equation 3.2. To my knowledge, no existing study has investigated the relationship between (1) having the option to work for overtime pay and (2) the amount of gambling. In addition, the fact that firms must pay increased wages to entice workers to work overtime voluntarily is consistent with Rätzel's (2012) finding that utility of labor declines for work performed at the end of the normal workday, and the assumption that this decline would extend to hours worked beyond the normal workday.

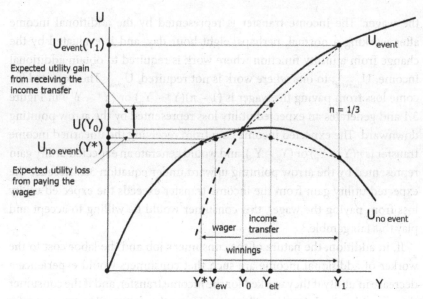

Figure 3.1 *Quid pro quo* theory of the demand for gambles

$$\Delta EU_{g2} = (1-\pi)[U_{\text{no event}}(Y^*) - U_{\text{no event}}(Y_0)]$$
$$+ \pi\{[U_{\text{event}}(Y_1) - U_{\text{no event}}(Y_0)] + [U_{\text{no event}}(Y_0) - U_{\text{no event}}(Y_1)]\} \quad (3.2)$$

If the disutility of working is great enough to make $U_{\text{no event}}$ turn downward and the income transfer is large enough, the comparison represented by equation 3.2 might generate a greater motivation to gamble than the comparison represented by equation 3.1. Future empirical analysis might be able to shed light on this issue.[2]

Figure 3.1 illustrates the gain from gambling according to a quid pro quo approach. The wager is evaluated along the utility function where work is required, $U_{\text{no event}}$. According to the Jevons's ([1871] 1970) theory and Rätzel's (2012) empirical study, initial work is utility increasing, so no event utility lies above the event utility over the range of income that is used to obtain

---

[2] In the original quid pro quo theoretical model, the consumer was assumed to choose optimal income and leisure, and then gamble from that optimal level of income and leisure (Nyman 2004). The gain in utility was evaluated by the difference between the utility from unearned income and utility from the earned income. The present model is perhaps more realistic in that it does not assume consumers are already working optimally.

the wager. The income transfer is represented by the additional income after working a normal, perhaps, eight-hour day, and is evaluated by the change from a utility function where work is required to obtain additional income, $U_{no\ event}$, to one where work is not required, U_{event}. The expected income loss from paying the wager is $(1 - \pi)(Y^* - Y_0)$ or $(Y^* - Y_{ew})$ in Figure 3.1 and generates an expected utility loss represented by the arrow pointing downward. The expected income gain from receiving the unearned income transfer is $\pi(Y_1 - Y_0)$ or $(Y_{eit} - Y_0)$, and would generate an expected utility gain represented by the arrow pointing upward under equation 3.1. Because the expected utility gain from the income transfer exceeds the expected utility loss from paying the wager, this consumer would be willing to accept and play this fair gamble.[3]

If, in addition, the nature of the consumer's job and the labor cost to the worker of additional income are such that consumers would experience a decrease in utility if they worked for the income transfer, and if the consumer then considers both (1) the utility gained from the unearned income transfer and (2) the disutility saved by not having to work for the income transfer as reflected in equation 3.2, then the demand for gambling would be greater. This would increase the size of the upward pointing arrow, but is not shown on Figure 3.1.

Variation in Gambling

Variation occurs across consumers with regard to how much they gamble, or whether they gamble at all. Variation may derive from (1) differences in how consumers view the wager, (2) differences in how much consumers desire the consumption splurge from the gambling winnings, and (3) differences in whether consumers also consider in their gambling decision the cost savings from not having to earn the income transfer.

First, regarding the wager, the quid pro quo theory suggests that those who evaluate the wager along the no event earned income utility function in Figure 3.1 would be likely to gamble. In contrast, if the consumer were to evaluate the wager along the event utility function in Figure 3.1, they would

---

[3] In chapter 5, some empirical work suggests that the range of income represented by the wager and the typical gambling winnings is too modest for consumers to experience diminishing marginal utility of unearned income. Therefore, an alternative form of event utility as a function of unearned income would be linear.

be unlikely to gamble because the expected cost of the wager (as shown on the dashed extension of the event utility function in Figure 3.1) would exceed the gain from the expected income transfer. Which utility function is used depends on how the consumer views the opportunity cost of making the wager.

Economics teaches that the opportunity cost of any spending is the goods and services that are foregone. According to this theory, the opportunity cost of the wager would therefore be represented by a movement along the event utility function for unearned income alone. If so, gambling would not be done because, with diminishing marginal utility of event income, the expected utility cost of the wager would exceed the expected utility gain from the income transfer. Although this definition of opportunity cost is used in many textbooks because it readily communicates the basic notion of economic scarcity, what economists consider to be the opportunity cost of spending is not limited to the commodities foregone.

One such alternative definition is the labor required to earn the income for the spending. This view of the opportunity cost has long been recognized by economists as an alternative measure of the value of spending. For example, in *The Wealth of Nations*, Adam Smith writes that

the real price of every thing, what every thing really costs to the man who wants to acquire it, is the toil and trouble of acquiring it. What every thing is really worth to the man who has acquired it, and who wants to dispose of it or exchange it for something else, is the toil and trouble which it can save to himself, and which it can impose upon other people. (Smith [1776] 2000, 33)[4]

The opportunity cost of spending is sometimes more generally defined as the cost of any resources used in production that spending. For example, in McConnell, Brue, and Flynn's (2012) venerable introductory economics textbook, the authors explain opportunity costs with the example that there is "no free lunch because the resources used to produce a lunch could have

---

[4] It should be noted that Smith's is a true marginalist theory that relies on the individual's preferences, and is not the same as the labor theory of value that David Ricardo or Karl Marx would later champion. In the latter theory, the value of a commodity is determined by the amount of past labor that was used to make it. In Smith's theory, the value of a commodity is determined by the value that the consumer places on the labor one could "save" if one had the commodity and did not need to buy it, or the value of the labor a seller could "impose upon other people" if they wanted to purchase the commodity.

been used to produce something else" (Parkin 2016, 13). From this alter-native perspective, the opportunity cost of the wager includes the value of the work done to earn the income spent and so the opportunity cost of the wager would best be represented by the movement along the no event utility function for earned income. Evaluation of the wager along an earned utility function would capture both the value of the additional goods and services foregone and the value of the work that had created the income that was spent. If so, the consumer would be more likely to gamble, as Figure 3.1 indicates.

Empirically, what consumers actually consider when evaluating the spending on any commodity is far from standardized. Indeed, it is often psy-chological and appears to be both complex and varied (Thaler 1985). This complexity and lack of uniformity is perhaps best illustrated by the marketing literature (reviewed, for example, by Sanchez-Fenandez and Iniesta-Bonillo (2007) and Boksberger and Melsen (2011)) which describes the various ways that consumers evaluate the spending they do on the various commodities.

Moreover, empirical evidence suggests that consumers often do not regard opportunity cost as the commodities foregone. For example, some studies show that only about a half of all households use a formal budget when making spending decisions, a seeming prerequisite for considering the opportunity cost in terms of consumption forgone (Hilgert, Hogarth, and Beverly 2003; Lin et al. 2016). Other studies show that giving cues to consumers to think of spending in terms of what commodities are foregone changes consumer behavior, suggesting that existing spending decisions made without such cues do not always consider forgone commodities (Frederick et al. 2009; Lowenstein and Prelec 1993). There is also evidence that budgeting is used less in households with greater incomes and that households with greater incomes gamble more (Zelizer 1994). As Thaler observes,

> Of course, there is considerable variation among households in how explicit the budgeting process is. As a rule, the tighter the budget, the more explicit are the budgeting rules, both in households and organizations. Families living near the poverty level use strict, explicit budgets; in wealthy families, budgets are both less binding and less well defined. (Thaler 1999, 193)

In Canada in 2018, for example, as the household income quintile increased from 1 to 5, the prevalence of gambling increased monotonically from 53.8 percent to 71.5 percent (Rotermann and Gilmour 2022). Thus, empirically, the evidence suggests that not all consumers regard the opportunity cost of spending as the commodities foregone.

While the alternative to "commodities foregone" is not specified in these studies, this evidence is nevertheless consistent with the idea that some consumers adopt a more "behavioral" approach to the opportunity cost of the wager. Such consumers might still evaluate a wager by considering the goods and services forgone, but would place this consideration in the context of having (1) income that is derived from an ongoing job, (2) where the income is periodically replenished reliably, and (3) where the income is great enough that there is no need to account for the goods and services forgone in the present pay period. As a result, these consumers would consider the opportunity cost of the wager along the no event utility function and generally be more likely to gamble than those whose income is seen as intermittent, tenuous, or small, and who consider the opportunity cost of the wager as the commodities forgone alone.

Second, variation in the demand for gambling may derive from the extent to which the utility of earned and unearned income captures the same amount of consumption spending. The conventional approach is that all income is fungible, implying that a dollar of income would have the same effect on consumption, regardless of its source. There is, however, ample empirical evidence that income from different sources generates different levels of consumption spending (Zhang and Sussman 2017). Specifically, a number of studies in the behavioral economics literature have found that the marginal propensity to consume (the MPC is the percentage of the last dollar of income that is spent rather than saved) is lower for "regular income" than it is for "windfall income" (Arkes et al. 1994; Shefrin and Thaler 1988; O'Curry 1999; Thaler 1999; O'Curry and Strahilevitz 2001; Milkman and Beshears 2009). In these studies, regular income is income that is predictable and modest, as earned income from a regular job would be. Windfall income is unusual, unexpected, and often large in size, as a bonus at work, a tax refund, or the income transfer from a gambling win would be. These studies, therefore, suggest that a dollar of unearned income received in the form of gambling winnings may have a larger effect of increasing consumption than a dollar spent on a wager out of earned income in reducing consumption. As a result, consumers who are sensitive to this difference may desire a gambling income transfer in order to finance a splurge in consumption.

One illustration of the magnitude of this difference comes from the estimates of the MPC for income tax refunds. Souleles (1999) found that the

MPC for income tax refunds—a type of windfall income—is about 0.64, using data from the Consumer Expenditure Surveys from 1980 through 1991. This compares to Fisher et al. (2020), who found that the MPC for family income after taxes is about 0.08, using a similarly comprehensive spending variable from the Panel Survey on Income Dynamics from 1999 to 2013. To the extent that the unearned income transfer from a gambling win is similar to this type of windfall income, and earned income for the wager is similar to the family income after taxes variable used in the Fisher et al. (2020) study, a comparison of the point estimates suggests that a dollar of gambling winnings would generate about an eight times greater change in consumption spending than would a dollar reduction in earned income from a gambling wager.

According to equation 3.1, the demand for gambling is determined by the difference between the expected utility cost of the earned wager and the expected utility gain from the unearned income transfer. Even though the expected wager and expected income transfer are the same amount of income, they may translate into dramatically different implications for consumption spending. Thus, some consumers who desire a splurge in consumption may gamble in order to obtain the windfall income required for such a splurge. That is, the splurge in consumption might only be "allowed" because the gambling winnings are an unearned windfall. This potentially large increase in consumption may represent an exciting utility-increasing prospect and lead to increase in the demand for gambling. Variation in the demand for gambling may, therefore, occur because of differences in the nature of how consumers perceive the utility from this unearned income. Those consumers who desire a splurge in consumption might exhibit steeper utility functions of unearned (event) income and therefore be more likely to gamble.

Third, variation in the demand for gambles might also be related to whether consumers focus on both the gain in utility from the income transfer plus the savings in labor disutility from not having to work for the income transfer (equation 3.2), or on the gain alone (equation 3.1). In that regard, the more onerous the job or the more difficulty the individual experiences when working, the more likely consumers are to focus on the disutility of labor from the income transfer and include the disutility of labor saved in determining their demand for gambling. That is, having a job that is especially disliked or one that is painful may orient a worker to also considering the labor costs saved from the income transfer in the gambling decision, and therefore increase the demand for gambling.

These same negative job characteristics may also be present with the income earned for the wager, but consumers may discount these factors for the wager because there is less flexibility to change them. Constraints on the types of jobs available in the local labor market or on the length of the workday may lend a degree of inevitability to the job situation and so reduce the ability of the individual to respond behaviorally to a particularly bad employment situation. This discounting may be reinforced by consumer's need for a certain level of income for subsistence, which would compel consumers to find any job in that market or to work a full day in the job they have. Moreover, even though these negative characteristics may be present in a job from the first hour at work, their effects on utility are likely to become more pronounced as the workday wears on, and so negatively affect the range of income represented by the income transfer more than the range of income represented by the wager.

While the three variability factors from the quid pro quo model are all related to economic variables—labor, income, consumption, and the utility of each—there may be a number of more psychological or behavioral factors that influence the demand for gamble. These may include (1) whether the consumer feels lucky, (2) the desire to chase losses, (3) betting in response to the gambler's fallacy, (4) responding to gambling advertisements, (5) the increase in physical attractiveness of a gambling winner, and so on. It should be noted, however, that these psychological or behavioral factors may be important in determining *variation* in the amount of gambling, but they would quickly fade in importance if the fundamental economic basis of gambling did not exist and consumers were required to work for the income transfer when gambling.

By way of summary, it is clear that not everyone gambles. If lottery gambling is excluded, the casino, racetrack, and the other types of gambling that are best explained by the present theory are likely to be done by less than half the population in any given year. Therefore, a theory that would show that gambling is economically welfare-increasing generally for all consumers would clearly be suspect. The quid pro quo theory suggests that even though the utility gain from gambling is represented by the additional income for which the winning gambler does not need to work, this gain would not compensate for the utility lost from paying the wager if consumers adopted the standard view that the opportunity cost was the goods and services forgone. Gambling occurs when consumers instead view the opportunity cost of the wager as including the income from work, and when this income is sufficiently predictable, regular, and large that the utility gain from working acts to discount the utility loss from the commodities forgone. Gambling may also occur when the actuarially fair income transfer implies a much larger increase in consumption than the decrease in consumption from paying the fair wager. And, gambling may also occur when the consumer's job is so bad that, in addition to the utility gained, they consider the utility cost saved from not having to work for the income transfer when contemplating whether to gamble.

Two Complications

A fact that complicates this theory is that, although in most gambling experiences the initial wagers are financed by earned income, once the gambling episode has begun, the winnings from a previous bet are often used to finance the next wager. If so, the wager would be obtained without working and so it could not reflect the initial utility from having a job. Admittedly, therefore, the wagering part of this gambling theory is a more complex than is represented by equation 3.1. Even though subsequent wagers out of winnings cannot reflect the positive initial utility from having a job, they may be regarded as having a similarly smaller opportunity cost than the standard one, and so generate a demand for more gambling.

The quid pro quo theory is based primarily on a utility gain from the income transfer to workers. Nevertheless, the utility gain from differential consumption could apply to nonworkers as well. For example, an heir might gamble because they recognize that the prospect of the consumption splurge from the gambling income transfer that is larger than the consumption lost from the income of the wager. The same story might apply to the retired consumer. In addition, even though not working, both heirs and retired consumers may have reliable, regular, and large sources of income that would contribute to a reevaluation of the opportunity cost of the wager.

Conventional Theory

The conventional Friedman–Savage model of the demand for gambling differs from the quid pro quo model (Friedman and Savage, 1948). Under the conventional theory, the consumer gambles because of a desire for uncertainty or risk. Such a consumer assumes that utility is a function of unearned income, but that utility is increasing with income at an increasing rate.

Figure 3.2 illustrates the conventional theory. Y_0 is original income, Y^* is income after the wager is paid, and Y_1 is income after the gambling winnings of $(Y_1 - Y^*)$. The conventional utility gain would be represented by the gain from uncertainty. As depicted in Figure 3.2, the gain would be captured by the upward-pointing dashed arrow, representing the forgoing of the certainty of Y_0 income in preference for the risk from an uncertain level of income, either Y_1 or Y^*. Expected utility gain from uncertainty of the gamble is $[EU - U(Y_0)]$.

The utility gain using the quid pro quo approach would be the same as the utility gain from the conventional approach, if the same Friedman-Savage assumptions apply. In Figure 3.2, the expected income gain from winning the income transfer is $\pi(Y_1 - Y_0)$ or $(Y_{eit} - Y_0)$, and the expected gain in utility is depicted by the upward-pointing solid arrow. The expected income loss from making the wager is $(1 - \pi)(Y^* - Y_0)$ or $(Y_{ew} - Y_0)$, and the expected loss in utility is the downward-pointing solid arrow. The net

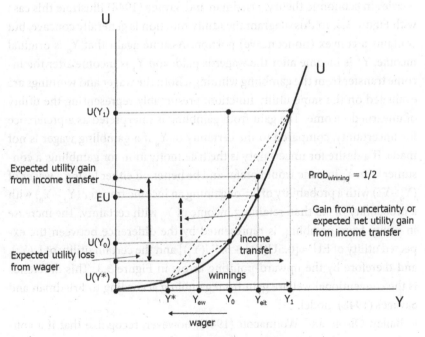

Figure 3.2 Conventional theory of demand for gambles

utility gain is the difference between the upward-pointing solid arrow and the downward-pointing solid one and, given certain characteristics of the utility function, would be of the same magnitude as the upward-pointing dashed arrow. Thus, the quid pro quo theory would show the same utility gain from gambling as the conventional model, if the quid pro quo model assumed that utility was increasing with income at an increasing rate and did not recognize a shift in utility from the disutility of labor. The interpretation of the motivation to gamble, however, would change from a desire for uncertainty to a desire for an income transfer, which, given the form assumed for the utility function, would increase utility more than the decrease caused by the loss of the wager.

Insurance-Purchasing Gambler

Figure 3.2 illustrates the case of the consumer who only gambles, but Friedman and Savage (1948) recognize that many consumers purchase insurance and gamble more or less simultaneously. As a result, explaining the insurance-purchasing gambler has come to represent one of the classic puzzles in economic theory. Friedman and Savage (1948) illustrate this case with Figure 3.3. In this diagram the utility function is generally concave, but contains a convex (nonconcave) portion. Assume again that Y_0 is original income, Y^* is income after the wager is paid, and Y_1 is income after the income transfer from the gambling winnings. Both the wager and winnings are evaluated on the same utility function, presumably representing the utility of unearned income. The gain from gambling is interpreted as a preference for uncertainty, compared to the certainty of Y_0 if a gambling wager is not made. If a desire for uncertainty is the true motivation for gambling, a consumer with Y_0 income would prefer and be better off either losing a wager of $(Y_0 - Y^*)$ with a probability of 0.5 or gaining an income transfer $(Y_1 - Y_0)$ with a probability of 0.5 than retaining income of Y_0 with certainty. The increase in utility from gambling is represented by the difference between the expected utility of $EU = [0.5U(Y^*) + 0.5U(Y_1)]$ and the certain utility of $U(Y_0)$, and therefore by the upward-pointing arrow in Figure 3.3. This difference is the conventional welfare gain from gambling according to Friedman and Savage's (1948) model.

Bailey, Olson, and Wonnacott (1980), however, recognize that if a consumer possessed a utility function like this and two periods were available,

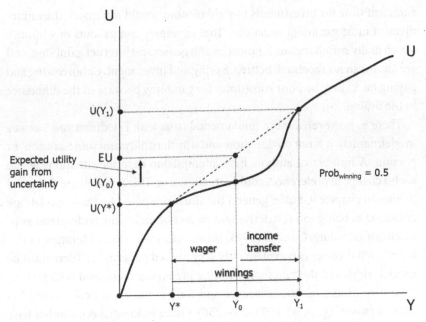

Figure 3.3 The insurance-purchasing gambler from the Friedman-Savage model

it would not be necessary to gamble in order to obtain the conventional theory's gain in utility. Rather than retaining Y_0 in both periods, one could save $(Y_0 - Y^*)$ in the first period and spend $(Y_1 - Y_0)$ in the second. From an *ex ante* perspective, this would represent the certainty equivalent of an expected spending of $0.5U(Y^*) + 0.5U(Y_1)$ over each of the two periods, and the utility of this combination would exceed that of having a certain income, Y_0, in each. Alternatively, the consumer could borrow $(Y_1 - Y_0)$ in the first period and pay $(Y_0 - Y^*)$ back in the second to obtain the same utility gain. So if the consumer exhibits a convex (nonconcave) portion of the utility function, expects to have income somewhere in that range, and can save or borrow over two periods, saving or borrowing could generate the same utility gains as gambling. Indeed, if the consumer's rate of time preference were different from the market interest rate, saving or borrowing might be preferred to a fair gamble.

Hartley and Farrell (2002) are critical of this argument and show that the income levels, the rate of time preference, and interest rate conditions under which it would apply are limited. In addition, the two-period model, with

sufficient time for investments to yield income, would not match the imme-
diacy of most gambling situations. That is, wagers and payouts of winnings
are virtually simultaneous for most casino games and internet gambling, and
are almost so for racetrack betting. Saving and investment, or borrowing and
paying back, may be poor substitutes for gambling because of the difference
in the timing.

There is, however, a more fundamental issue with Friedman and Savage's
model, namely, it is not obvious how and why the utility function has a convex
portion. A number of authors have attempted to describe situations where
such a change in preferences could actually occur. These models are discussed
further in chapter 9, but in general the situations posed by these models are
criticized as being too restrictive and so do not match the widespread popularity of gambling. Conlisk (1993) summarizes the critical literature in this
way: "Such theories can explain only very limited patterns . . . There must be
special wiggles in the functions defining preference combined with just the
right magnitudes for the insurance and the gamble. Such explanations become strained" (Conlisk 1993, 255–256). Other influential economists have
expressed dissatisfaction with the Friedman and Savage (1948) approach
to the insurance-purchasing gambler for similar reasons (Samuelson 1952;
Hirshleifer 1966; Arrow 1974).

Moreover, evidence suggests that those who gamble do not seem to match
Friedman and Savage's assumptions. For example, a 2018 national survey
found that 73 percent of Americans gambled during the last year (National
Council on Problem Gambling 2018). But even though gambling was less
common for Americans at the extremes of income/wealth, still a majority
of Americans in the highest and lowest income/wealth categories gambled.
Figure 3.3 suggests that those in the highest and lowest income/wealth
categories would not gamble.

Finally, in contrast to a number of empirical studies intended to support
the conventional *insurance* theory, there is a complete lack of empirical research in support of the welfare implications of the conventional *gambling*
theory. An empirical study in support of the Friedman and Savage model
of gambling might use some measure the curvature of each respondent's
(convex) utility function and show that increases in the (convex) curvature
cause consumers to gamble more or more often. This evidence might further
be used to estimate the welfare gain that gamblers derive from a fair gamble,
since that is the implication of the conventional model. While such empirical

studies have been attempted with insurance, to my knowledge, no similar gambling study has ever been done.

Direct Utility from Gambling

Next to Friedman and Savage's (1948) model, the theory of the demand for gambling that appears to have captured the most attention (and, perhaps, the most adherents) among economists is Conlisk's (1993) model.[5] Conlisk proposed that gamblers obtain an additional small utility gain directly from the entertainment associated with participation in the gambling experience. Because the amount of money wagered with gambles is typically modest, Conlisk's model assumes that consumers are locally "risk-neutral" over the typical range of gambling wagers, even though they would be risk-averse over larger ranges. As a result of the small stakes and assumed linear utility, it would take only a small amount of gambling fun to overcome an overall aversion to risk, and so to gamble.

Conlisk supports his model empirically by relating it to some experimental studies. Conlisk's model predicts that as the amount of money wagered increases, the underlying risk aversion would become more apparent and fewer people would desire to gamble. This result is borne out in a series of experimental studies (e.g., Hershey and Schoemaker 1980b, 1985; Hershey, Kunreuther, and Schoemaker 1982). In these experiments, subjects were given the choice between a certain gain in dollars and a gamble with one outcome being a larger gain in dollars and the other zero dollars, but with the same expected value as the certain gain. For example, an experimental choice between two options: (a) a certain US$100 and (b) an uncertain 0.5 probability of winning US$200 and a 0.5 probability of winning US$0. The experimenters then varied the size of the stakes across experiments, while keeping the probability of winning the same. As the stakes increased, a smaller and smaller percentage of the experimental subjects opted for the uncertain option, consistent with the prediction from Conlisk's model.

As Conlisk recognizes, these experiments could readily be interpreted by the experimental subjects as the choice of whether or not to gamble: choosing to give up the certain gain would be equivalent to making a wager. Opting for

---

[5] Others have suggested a similar motivation. The earliest proponent of gambling as motivated by entertainment to my knowledge is Suits (1979).

the uncertain gain versus nothing (with the same expected magnitude as the wager) would be the same as making a gamble. However, a small extension of this view would be to assume that mental accounting would also predispose the subject to regarding choice A, the sure gain, as part of the consumer's existing stock of earned income or wealth, and choice B, the uncertain gain, as unearned income or wealth, even though both are artifacts of the experiment. Thus, subjects in these experiments might be interpreting the choices as being consistent with a quid pro quo framework. The expected utility gain could be represented by equation 3.1 and the difference between the upward-pointing and downward-pointing solid arrows in Figure 3.1.

If so, the same prediction regarding (1) decision to gamble and (2) the size of the wager and corresponding actuarially fair gain (holding constant the probability of winning) would prevail: as the wager and the corresponding fair winnings increase, holding constant the probability of winning, the likelihood that a consumer would gamble would fall. Inspection of Figure 3.1 makes this clear: at the given probability of winning, an increase in the size of the gamble (representing an increase in amount of choice A in the experiment and the actuarially equivalent uncertain choice B) would imply a larger utility decrease from paying a fair wager than the expected utility increase from the increase in the expected income transfer. This would make a gamble less likely. Therefore, the results of these same experiments could support the quid pro quo theory of demand for gambling as well as Conlisk's.

Conlisk's model postulates local risk neutrality as the reason why the utility gain from the entertainment of gambling need not be large in order to overcome the general aversion to risk by consumers and motivate gambling. There is, however, another factor that must also be overcome by the utility from entertainment, namely, the unfairness of the gambling prospect. That is, Conlisk assumes a fair gamble, but most gambles at casinos, racetracks, or other such venues have wagers and winning probabilities that favor the house. Unlike the curvature of the utility function, there is no local range of betting that would make these costs from gambling go away. That is, a risk-averse person, or even a risk-neutral person, should simply not be predicted to gamble if the expected income gain is negative (as it is with the standard house take) and there is only a small entertainment value to gambling. In casinos, the house take varies with the game being played and ranges from about a 2 percent average for blackjack, to 5.3 percent for roulette, to an average of about 27 percent for keno (Hannum n.d.). Racetrack betting has a house take of between 10 and 30 percent. Conlisk does not explain how his small direct utility from entertainment could be sufficient to overcome both a natural aversion to risk and a substantial house take.

In contrast, the utility loss avoided from not having to work for an income transfer (for example, the added disutility from working the additional hours or days to earn US$1,000 for a factory worker, a supermarket checkout clerk, or a construction carpenter, compared to receiving US$1,000 without working) can be quite substantial, especially for some jobs and some workers. Moreover, whether the opportunity to work more would exist at all would also vary. Thus, the quid pro quo theory appears to be more robust at explaining gambling because it relies on a possibly large shift in utility functions rather than the addition of a small utility bump to a static utility function that is locally risk-neutral. For some jobs and consumers, such a shift would be sufficiently large to overcome the house take and generate gambling.

Lotteries

Lotteries are gambling opportunities where the winnings are large but the wager is small because of the small probability of winning. Lotteries are popular: the 2018 National Survey on Gambling Attitudes found that lotteries represent the most popular of the gambling games they considered, with 66 percent of American respondents reporting that they bought at least one lottery ticket during the past year (National Council on Problem Gambling 2021). Conlisk (1993) recognized that lotteries were a special case and addressed them by postulating a separate theory: if the probability of winning is small enough, small gains in utility from gambling entertainment would still overcome the consumer's risk aversion regardless of the size of the gain at stake, and allow for the purchase of a lottery (as long as the utility gains from entertainment are not too small).

Like casinos, racetracks, bingo parlors, and similar forms of gambling, lotteries rely on transfers of unearned income to the consumer to generate demand for their wagers. That is, few lottery tickets would be purchased if the winnings had to be earned, so a shift to an unearned income function would also be a prerequisite for the demand for lotteries. However, because the income gain at stake in a lottery is so large, the fact that the consumer would not have to work for the income transfer may have been overlooked in the decision-making process in favor of a focus on the extensive change in the consumer's lifestyle that such a large income transfer would imply. Thus, it may be the change in lifestyle that would be derived from a win that better explains the demand for lotteries.

That the utility of the very large winnings from a lottery is different from that of the smaller winnings from casino gambling, racetrack gambling, and the like is supported by the literature. Clotfelter and Cook (1989) suggested that because the size of the largest lottery prize (the jackpot) is so great, lottery purchasers are in essence buying a dream. The dream would not compare the cost of winning, say, US$1,000, to the cost of earning it at work, but instead fantasize about winning so much money, say, US$10,000,000, that one would never need to work at all. Thus, with lotteries, it is the very large size of the jackpot that generates the demand, rather than a comparison of unearned and earned income (although that is an essential prerequisite). The larger the jackpot, the greater the number of consumers who would be responsive to the dream of this level of wealth, and the more lottery tickets sold.

The relative importance of the size of the jackpot compared to expected payout as a portion of the cost of the ticket was recognized by Adam Smith:

That the chance of gain is naturally over-valued, we may learn from the universal success of lotteries. The world neither ever saw, nor ever will see, a perfectly fair lottery; or one in which the whole gain compensated the whole loss; because the undertaker could make nothing by it. In the state lotteries, the tickets are not worth the price which is paid by the original subscribers, and yet commonly sell in the market for twenty, thirty and sometimes forty per cent advance. The vain hope of getting some of the great prizes is the sole cause of this demand. The soberest people scarce look upon it as folly to pay a small sum for the chance of gaining ten or twenty thousand points; though they know that even that small sum is perhaps twenty or thirty per cent more than the chance is worth. In a lottery in which no prize exceeded twenty pounds, though in other respects it approached nearer to a perfectly fair one than the common state lotteries, there would not be the same demand for tickets. In order to have a better chance for some of the great prizes, some people purchase several tickets, and others, small shares in a still greater number. There is not, however, a more certain proposition in mathematics, than that the more tickets you adventure upon, the more likely you are to be a loser. Adventure upon all the tickets in the lottery, and you lose for certain; and the greater the number of your tickets the nearer you approach to this certainty. (Smith [1776] 2000, 124–125)

Thus, to Smith, the size of the lottery prize was far more important than the fairness of the price of the lottery ticket (in terms of the percentage of the ticket cost paid out in prizes) in determining the demand for lotteries.

The importance of the size of the jackpot in determining demand has been shown empirically. The analysis of demand for lottery tickets has traditionally estimated the quantity of lottery tickets sold as a function of the effective price of a ticket. The effective price of a ticket is usually modeled as one minus the expected payout, as a proportion of the nominal price of the lottery ticket. For example, if the expected payout is US$0.80 for lottery ticket that costs US$1, the effective price of that ticket is $US0.20. A number of empirical studies found a significant demand relationship using this approach (Cook and Clotfelter 1993; Gulley and Scott 1993; Scott and Gulley 1995; Walker 1998; Farrell, Morgenroth, and Walker 1999; Purfield and Waldron 1999; Forrest, Simmons, and Chesters 2002). Because of the assumption that consumers are generally averse to risk, these traditional models typically are based on Conlisk's notion that the lotteries are demanded because the consumer has fun choosing the numbers and anticipating the win.

Forrest, Simmons, and Chesters (2002) found the same significant relationship with the effective price variable in their study. They recognized, however, that the effective price variable was itself determined largely by the rollover of the jackpot winnings to the next game if the jackpot was not won, and thus the size of the jackpot. That is, the more weeks that a jackpot is unclaimed and rolls over, the smaller the takeout as a percentage of the nominal price of a lottery ticket and the smaller the effective price. Thus, the effective price would be so correlated with the size of the jackpot that its interpretation in an empirical study would not be clear. To show this, these authors substituted the size of the jackpot for the effective price in the equations and ran the same two-stage least squares analysis (to deal with endogeneity). They found that the jackpot variables were just as significant as the effective price in explaining the demand for lotteries and that the regression equations with the size of the jackpot variables had a higher adjusted R-square. These authors conclude:

> The two models are based on very different views of bettor behavior. The traditional model has consumers gaining "fun" from the game and, just as with most consumer goods, they choose to purchase more fun when the price of that fun is reduced. The alternative model takes the relevant price as the face value of the ticket (which is fixed) and then represents sales as

responding to any increase in the maximum lotto prize on offer under the conditions of any particular draw. . . . what they are paying for is a dream of being able to spend whatever is the largest sum of money that a ticket could bring them in the particular draw. (Forrest, Simmons, and Chesters 2002, 494)

So, because this alternative motivation seems especially dominant, lotteries would need to be exempted from the quid pro quo theory.

Gambling Motive and Insurance

It should be noted that the insurance payout is also work-free, and this work-free aspect of the income transfer might represent an additional utility gain that reinforces the quid pro quo demand for insurance. That is, compared to the premium, which is typically paid for with income for which the consumer is required to work, the insurance payout does not require work. This difference is not recognized in the insurance models because they implicitly assume that all income (or wealth) is obtained without working for it. Thus, a revised insurance model that distinguishes between premiums earned with regular income and insurance income transfers obtained without working for them, especially if also regarded as windfalls, might generate an additional welfare gain.

Although work-free, the payout is not free of specifying the conditions that trigger it. Insurance fraud is often represented by an attempt to uncouple the payout conditions of insurance from the payout, so that only the work-free aspect of the insurance payout remains. For example, the fraud associated with workers' compensation insurance often appears to be directly related to the work-free aspect of the payout. Governments and insurers have put into place mechanisms to monitor for, detect, and largely eliminate such fraud in insurance contracts. Moreover, insurers often contract to pay for only expenses related to the commodity affected by the triggering event itself, thus eliminating the payment of a lump-sum amount of work-free income that might have represented an increased incentive for fraud. For example, health insurance pays for the actual medical care received by the insured, not a certain fixed amount per diagnosis. The fact that these types of insurance contracts and fraud detection measures exist suggests that the work-free aspect of the insurance payout may contribute to the demand for some insurance as well, at least for some consumers, and that demand for insurance would probably be a greater if these fraud-reducing measures were not in place.[6]

Conclusions

This chapter presents a model of the demand for gambles where the motivation to gamble relies on either (1) gaining a transfer of unearned income for which the expected utility gain exceeds the expected utility lost from paying the wager out of earned income (equation 3.1), or (2) that gain plus the savings of expected disutility from not having to work for the income transfer (equation 3.2). So in both cases of the quid pro quo model, the consumer is motivated primarily by the prospect of gaining an unearned income transfer. This differs from the conventional model that holds that consumers gamble because they desire uncertainty and that by gambling, uncertainty would be achieved regardless of whether they win or lose.

The quid pro quo model of the demand for gambles also differs from the original model of the demand for gambles suggested in Nyman (2004) and Nyman, Welte, and Dowd (2008). In that model, the lone motivation for gambling was the savings of disutility from not having to work additional hours for the winnings. That is, the central gain in utility from gambling in the original model was represented by the *difference* between equations 3.1 and 3.2. That model assumed that the utility cost of the wager would always be captured by the utility function of unearned income, just as it is in the conventional Friedman–Savage (1948) model. Thus, the original theory suggested that the additional expected utility gain from the consumers'

---

[6] Critical care insurance is a relatively new type of health insurance that pays off with a fixed lump sum income payout if the consumer receives any one of a series of medical diagnoses, such as cancer, heart attack, stroke, Alzheimer's disease, kidney failure, coronary artery bypass graft, and others. Critical care insurance is growing in popularity as is evidenced by the growth in the number of insurers that provide it. A critical care contract might, for example, specify initial benefit amounts of $10,000, $15,000, or $20,000, paid in a lump sum and chosen by the beneficiary *ex ante*. This payment would not be a replacement for traditional health or disability insurance, but instead provide a fund for paying copayments, deductibles, and other expenses associated with the health or disability insurance. These payouts are not pegged to the consumer's medical experience, and so the consumer must meet a number of policy and certification requirements set by the insurer in order to receive them. They are sometimes sold by insurers who advertise their worth by calling attention to the new draws on a household's finances when ill to cover additional expenses, such as childcare. They thereby acknowledge the quid pro quo theory that insurance is demanded in part because of the increase in utility and marginal utility of the income that would be used to cover the new demands caused by illness.

recognizing the savings in disutility from not having to work for the income transfer could alone be sufficient to overcome the expected utility loss when the utility function for unearned income is increasing at a decreasing rate (that is, "risk-averse") and used to evaluate both the wager and the income transfer. The original model reasoned that this gain could generate a demand for gambles in itself, especially for those workers who had jobs they did not like or who had difficulty working. This theory, however, had limited applicability because the demand for gambling clearly extends beyond just those who face unfavorable working conditions.

In the present model, a second reason to gamble means that the quid pro quo model would apply to a greater number of consumers. This reason derives from the cost of the wager being evaluated along the (no event) utility function for earned income and compares this cost to the gain from the income transfer evaluated along the (event) utility function for unearned income. The portion of the (no event) utility function of earned income used to evaluate the wager captures both (1) the utility gain from being employed and from the work done during most of a normal workday, and (2) the utility cost from the consumption foregone. That is, there is still a commodity opportunity cost of spending on the wager, but this cost is tempered by the utility gain from being employed. As a result, the utility cost of a dollar spent on a wager is less than the utility benefit of a dollar received from an unearned gambling income transfer, and so represents a second reason to gamble.

To be clear, the reasons for gambling described in the preceding two paragraphs are both related to work, but in different ways. The first explanation suggests that gambling is done because for some, working for additional income at the end of a workday or workweek would be too onerous in terms of the utility cost. This cost is saved if the same additional income were to be won by gambling. A focus on these savings generates a demand for gambles. The second explanation suggests that gambling is done to obtain the same additional unearned income, but that for many, the utility cost of the commodities foregone from spending the earned wager is tempered by the gain from having a job and being employed. This means that (1) the expected utility cost from the earned wager is not as great as (2) the expected utility gain from the consumption generated by the unearned income transfer, and this difference generates a demand for gambles.

While the first explanation no doubt captures the motivation of some specific types of consumers, the second explanation seems to be more broadly applicable to the typical gambler. For example, in Canada, the typical gambler in 2018 was employed in a job with an above-average income (Rotermann and Gilmour 2022). The theory suggests that such a person would seek to spend some of that income on gambling wagers, motivated by the prospect that a winning night at a casino would provide him with the additional unearned income.

This additional unearned income might generate a demand for gambling especially because it finances a splurge in consumption. The additional income won at the gambling table or horse track might be spent with relative abandon and on those goods and services (often luxuries) that the consumer might not normally purchase (O'Curry and Strahilevitz 2001). This additional spending out of unearned income may represent an exciting prospect that generates a substantial portion of the demand for gambling. Although a tax refund, an inheritance, or a bonus at work are all windfalls that would generate the same type of consumption splurge, gambling may represent one of the few ways that consumers can create the prospect of a splurge in consumption entirely on their own.

To my knowledge, no studies have estimated the marginal propensity to consume out of gambling winnings, but anecdotal evidence suggests that it is high. Few cases are more proverbial than that of the gambler who, upon winning a few thousand dollars at the blackjack table or racetrack, spends it quickly on frivolous or unhealthy consumption. The nongambler might look on such spending as unwise because the gambler has "blown through" the winnings with "nothing left to show for it," but that spending may reflect one of the core appeals of gambling. While the origins and exact nature of the appeal of this type of spending must be left to psychologists to explain, economists can at least provide the broad explanatory outlines for this behavior.

This, of course, is all speculation (theory), but there is important empirical support for these explanations. It has been shown that for most workers, the disutility of labor does not set in until the end of the normal workday. Until then, working generally increases utility. This implies a difference between the utility lost from spending the wager and the utility gained from not having to work longer than standard hours to obtain additional income by gambling. Studies suggest that while the prevalence of gambling increases with income, the percentage of households that engage in an explicit budgeting process decreases with income. Studies of the marginal propensity to consume out of windfall income suggest a difference in the consumption costs from spending earned income on a wager and the consumption gains from receiving unearned income from the gambling winnings. Additional studies reviewed in chapter 7 show that the desire for additional income is the main motivation for most gamblers. Studies reviewed in that chapter also show that employment difficulties are associated with increased gambling, consistent with the theory in equation 3.2. Admittedly, this is meager evidence on which to base the quid pro quo theory of gambling. On the other hand, there is very little, if any, empirical evidence supporting the explanation that consumers gamble because they desire uncertainty, and much to the contrary, as is described in chapter 5.

The quid pro quo model also differs from the Conlisk (1993) model that motivates gambling by the entertainment value of the gambling experience. In chapter 7, a number of studies are reviewed that show that not only is additional income the main motivation for most gamblers, but that even though entertainment is viewed by many as another important motivator, the entertainment aspect of gambling is critically related to the ability of the gambling to produce additional income. For example, playing a slot machine for meaningless tokens is less entertaining than playing a slot machine for real income, if it is entertaining at all. This suggests that entertainment is motivator secondary to the main one: the prospect of winning additional income for which the gambler does not need to work.

Chapter 9 reviews a number of the alternative explanations of the behavior of the consumer who purchases insurance and gambles at the same time. Rather than a puzzle, this chapter suggests that the widespread existence of the insurance-purchasing gambler should, more than anything, be viewed as a reason for scrapping the Friedman–Savage model (1948). In comparison, the quid pro quo model implies no inconsistency if the consumer purchases insurance and gambles at the same time.

4

Insurance and Gambling Supply

Introduction

While the motivation of the individual consumer's demand for insurance and gambling is focused on transferring income into a state of the world where it is either more valued (insurance) or less costly to obtain (gambling), the motivation for the supply side of this market is focused on making business profits and making them more predictable. Commercial insurers and gambling houses are firms that owe their very existence to taking on risk, so they are hardly averse to it. At the same time, these commercial enterprises desire to make their profits more predictable, and so engage in behaviors designed to reduce the risk of unexpectedly large expenditures. In both cases, however, the firms' perspectives regarding risk are subsumed in and secondary to their primary goal of maximizing profits.

Both types of firms make profits because of a difference between the money they receive from consumers in the form of either premiums or wagers, and the money they are obligated to pay out in the form of either payments for covered "losses" or gambling winnings. As the two previous chapters have suggested, these firms are able to make profits because consumers experience a net utility gain from fair insurance or fair gambles. This net utility gain means that firms can charge premiums and set wagers at levels that exceed the amount that firms expect to pay out to consumers. In this way, these firms can cover their administrative costs and make profits from their revenues.

The amounts of money that commercial insurers and gambling houses must pay out to consumers are a major part of their business costs, and these costs determine their profits. These costs, however, are uncertain. Business profits are almost always uncertain, but profits in these industries are doubly so because the firms rely on chance to keep these expenditures small. That is, firms are only required to make payouts to those consumers who meet certain conditions, such as to those who have become ill or to those who have bet on a certain roulette number. These conditions are largely stochastic. The firm's expected costs are determined by the amount of the payout they

A Theory of Insurance and Gambling. John A. Nyman, Oxford University Press. © Oxford University Press 2024.
DOI: 10.1093/oso/9780197687925.003.0004

have obligated themselves to pay, weighted by the probability that the payout would occur. However, even though positive profits might be expected on average, they are not assured because of the stochastic nature of the payout. These firms are, therefore, further motivated to make sure that these profits actually do materialize. They do this by selling such a large number of similar insurance policies or gambles that their uncertain expenditures become more predictable. Thus, the essence of their behavior is that they use (1) probability to estimate their expected costs and (2) the law of large numbers to increase the likelihood that their expenditures will be such that their expected profits will actually exist.

One way to understand better the connection between probability and the law of large numbers, on the one hand, and the behavior of firms selling insurance and gambling opportunities, on the other, is to review the history of the development of the insurance and gambling industries. This history is revealing because it documents how these businesses established themselves in their nascent and most basic form, and so it allows for a clearer understanding of the motivations for their behavior. This history describes the firms' adoption and use of the concepts of probability and diversification of risk, concepts so important to the supply of insurance and of gambling opportunities.

This history is admittedly Eurocentric, and perhaps unfairly so. The European focus is intentional, however, because it also provides an historical context and likely antecedence for the formal mathematical treatises on probability and the law of large numbers that were written about first by Europeans. It is also interesting to review the development of these industries in Europe in order to understand how the environment may have contributed to this thought.

For the insurance industry, the focus is on the development of shipping underwriters because the insurance industry developed in shipping far in advance of any other type of insurance (de Roover 1945). Moreover, the focus is on the development of this insurance industry in Italy. During the late medieval period and early Renaissance, Italian financial markets were among the most advanced in Europe, and Italian business owners were first to develop the modern type of premium insurance. The practices that the Italians developed in maritime insurance were exported, along with their cargoes, to other parts of the Mediterranean area, then to France, the Netherlands, England, and other parts of northern Europe, and from there to the New World and elsewhere. Likewise, the development of a gambling industry is also

Eurocentric and focuses on Italy. Although the first legally state-sanctioned European casino was established in Venice in 1638, the development of a gambling industry in that Italian city predates that event and has parallels to the development of maritime insurance (Walker 1999; Schwartz 2006). Thus, Italy figures prominently in the development of both industries.

Once the history of the development of commercial insurers and gambling houses has been reviewed, the story of the formal mathematical and statistical discoveries is recounted. It seems clear that the development of the insurance industry in Italy and the methods the industry employed for estimating and reducing risk occurred far in advance of when the formal mathematical thought on these subjects was written down and became generally known in society. This is also true for the gambling industry, although the timing of that development occurred later. This means that, if the mathematicians who developed the theories of probability and the law of large numbers had lived two or three centuries earlier and had been able to discuss their theories with the average Genovese maritime insurance underwriters of the mid-1300s or the average card dealer who ran a *bassetta* table of one of the *ridotti* in Venice a century or so later, they probably would not have been telling these Italian businessmen anything they did not already know, or at least intuitively suspected.

Development of an Insurance Industry

Insurance is a concept as basic to human society as agreements, often implicit, among village households for mutual help in putting out a house fire, or among villages for mutual assistance in the event of war or invasion. The insurance concept of mutual assistance is one of the main advantages to belonging to a family or a clan. Evidence of formal insurance contracts dates back to ancient times. In perhaps the earliest known historical reference, Hammurabi set down the requirements for insurance-type arrangements as part of the legal codes he established for Babylon around 2250 BCE (Vance 1908; Ungarelli 1984). For example, one of Hammurabi's laws stipulated that filing a false claim of a loss was illegal and would be punished by the state.

As far back as ancient Roman times in Italy, sea loans or *foenus nauticum* were commonly used as a type of proto-insurance contract to cover the merchant's risk of losing a shipping cargo on a sea voyage (de Roover 1945; Nelli 1972). With sea loans, an investor lent money to a merchant, who would use it to finance a shipment of goods, and who would typically travel with their cargo to the ship's destination port and back. The loan would need to be repaid only if the cargo arrived safely at its destination port, and if the ship and merchant returned to the port of origin with the proceeds of the sale of the cargo to repay the creditor. Thus, sea loans represented a way for the merchant both to finance the cargo and to transfer the risk of the sea voyage to creditors. In return, the creditors would be repaid with an amount that exceeded the amount of the loan, the excess representing both the interest payment for the use of the money and payment for accepting the risk of the sea voyage (de Roover 1945).

These financial arrangements for transferring sea risk to others were an improvement over the efforts that the traders could employ to manage the risk on their own. The cargo and the ships used to transport the cargo to distant ports were at the mercy of uncertain events like storms, fire, piracy, and naval capture during wartime (Kingston 2014). Overland traders, of course, faced many of the same risks, and had developed methods for managing them, such as joining together in caravans, employing armed escorts, or stopping for the night in walled towns or guarded oases. Some of these same measures could be used by maritime traders. For example, to deal with piracy, traders might try to organize a convoy of ships that were all headed to the same destination port. This meant, however, a potential problem with coordination of preparations and sailing times for a number of independent ship captains and merchants as well. Moreover, the increased supply of goods from a convoy of ships, all arriving at a port at once, would depress selling prices of the exported goods and increase buying prices of the supplies and the commodities destined for the return shipment to the home port (Barbour 1929). Maritime traders could also divide their goods into smaller parcels and use a variety of vessels bound for a number of different receiving ports. This strategy, however, was not ideal either because the traders would then need to find a number of ships that were each going to a different port and contract with each ship separately. Moreover, because they could no longer accompany their cargo on a single voyage, they would need to entrust their shipments to others—sea captains, of course, but also agents in distant ports who would be asked to sell the cargo and use the proceeds to buy goods for the return voyage. The trustworthiness of these captains and agents might not always be apparent (de Roover 1945).

Instead of managing their risk directly, many merchants sought to manage it financially by transferring their risk to others by using a sea loan. At the same time, the creditors who issued sea loans to the merchants could use financial methods to manage and diversify their own financial risk. Rather than loaning an amount to cover the loss of an entire shipment, a number of creditors would each loan only a portion of the value of the cargo and would then do the same thing for a number of different shipments, thus diversifying their investment and reducing their risk of a total loss. The splitting up of the financing among various creditors was an easier and more efficient so-lution than the splitting of the cargo among different ships. Thus, the *founds nauticum* form of sea loan contract became a common means of managing sea risk in Italy and some other parts of Europe during this period. The *founds nauticum* was used until about the 1200s, when it was replaced by another type of sea loan contract called the *cambium nauticum,* which specified fur-ther conditions for repayment, but functioned similarly (de Roover 1945).

Sea loans, however, suffered from two major shortcomings. First, the mer-chant might not need to borrow the money, but might be compelled to do so anyway, because these loans represented the only way the merchant could contractually transfer the sea risk of shipping to others (de Roover 1945). Second, the Catholic Church had condemned the practice of usury, and so the sea loan contracts were often written in ways that would obscure the in-terest payments on the loan. For example, some contracts specified that the creditor would initially sell the merchant's own cargo to the merchant (a fic-titious sale), but would buy it back only if it were lost and lying at the bottom of the sea. The backward language and tortured logic, however, meant that these contracts were not completely reliable because some of the provisions were open to interpretation (Piccino 2016).

During the early Italian Renaissance, however, trade became so common that the practice of merchants accompanying their cargo to the destina-tion port was replaced by the practice of merchants remaining at home and paying agents to receive the goods in distant ports, sell the goods, and broker deals for the return shipment of goods. This meant that traveling merchants were gradually replaced by sedentary merchants. By remaining in a home port, sedentary merchants could do far more business than was possible by traveling with each shipment. At the same time, financial markets were be-coming more efficient and bills of exchange were replacing sea loans as a way of raising money. Bills of exchange were formal debt instruments issued by the merchant to obtain money to finance a shipment. Unlike sea loans, bills of exchange were negotiable and could be resold to other investors. The dis-advantage for the borrower was that they were payable in any event, often on demand after an interval of time had passed. Thus, they were pure loans and did not cover sea risk because the merchant was liable for the repayment regardless of whether the cargo had made it to port and had been sold, or not. There was, therefore, the need for a second type of contract that would allow the sedentary merchant to remain in port yet insure the sea risk of the cargo, since most merchants simply could not honor the bill of exchange unless all had gone well with the shipping (de Roover 1945).

By the mid-1300s, modern insurance contracts with premiums and conditions for coverage of cargoes for specific shipping voyages were being written in Italy as an alternative to the sea loans and bills of exchange (Nelli 1972). De Roover (1945) provides an illustration of one such contract that was concluded in the year 1350:

A Genoese merchant, Leonardo Cattaneo, underwrote or insured (*assecuravit*) a shipload of wheat, belonging to one Benedict de Protonotaro of Messina, up to the amount of fl. 300 [300 florins] for a voyage from Sciacca, on the island of Sicily, to Tunis. Leonardo Cataneo declared that, from the time of the ship's sailing from Sicily until its safe arrival in Tunis, he would assume all risks arising from an act of God or of men and from the perils of the sea (*omni risicum, periculum et fortunam Dei, maris et gentium*). The sum of fl. 300 was due one month after receiving "certain" news of the cargo's loss. If the loss was only partial, the insurer's responsibility would be commensurate with the extent of the damage. The premium was 54 florins or 18 per cent. It was clearly stated that the contract was concluded for purposes of insurance (*ex causa assicurationis*) and that the underwriter had received from the insured the 54 florins "for that insurance" (*pro qua securitate*). (de Roover 1945, 189)[1]

By the end of the 1300s, insurance contracts like this one with premiums, set payoff amounts, and coverage limitations were widely used in Italian sea trade (de Roover 1945). Italian merchants traded throughout the Mediterranean Sea and soon brought these practices to cities in Catalonia in the west and in the Christian Levant in the east. As the Atlantic trade opened up, Bruges and Antwerp became insurance centers, and when the intercontinental trade with the Americas and Asia boomed in the 1500s, insurance centers were established in the port towns of Bilbao, Rouen, Bordeaux,

---

[1] The original documents in Italian can be found in Zeno 1936.

Nantes, and finally, Amsterdam and London (Addobbati 2016). By the time coffee had replaced beer and wine as the drink of choice for European breakfasts, and Edward Lloyd had converted his famous coffeehouse on Tower Street in London into an insurance brokerage center in 1686, the European insurance industry was already well established.

Probability and Diversification in Insurance

Italian maritime insurance underwriters were aware of the concepts of probability and the law of large numbers or, if they were not, they behaved as if they were when pricing their insurance policies and managing their sea risk. Italian underwriters recognized that voyages were not all equally dangerous, and so it was common practice to charge different premiums depending on the riskiness of the voyage and implicitly on the different probabilities of having to pay for damages. For example, premiums would increase with the length of the voyage because more could go wrong with more time at sea. Premiums also varied with the seasons with winter voyages costing more because they were more treacherous. Premiums could decrease with the size and the seaworthiness of the transporting ship. Indeed, shipping on the sturdy and powerful vessels owned by the Italian city-states was considered so reliable that the merchant might not purchase any insurance at all for cargo transported on these ships.

Even more important than the risk represented by nature was the risk of human hazards, namely, of a ship being intercepted by pirates, privateers,[2] or state navies. Privateering and the state confiscation of ships and their cargos was a risk when the state of the merchant at the originating port was at war with another state located on the way to the destination port. Interception by pirates, however, was almost always a risk. Variation in risk from human hazards would also be factored into the specifics of the contracts. If there were reports of the presence of pirates or privateers in the ship's intended sea lanes, premiums would be larger. If the underwriter or his agent was able to bribe a politician with connections to a one of these actors, or if the privateers, naval

---

[2] Privateers were privately owned ships which, during time of war, purchased from the home country's sovereign the right to capture and seize the ships and cargoes of merchants from hostile countries. It was a common way for the sovereign to raise money for the war effort.

captains, or pirates could be bribed directly for an assurance of safe pas-
sage, premiums might be lower. After years of such experience, insurers and
merchants became able to evaluate these risks and thus refine the premiums
the insurers would charge. As de Roover writes, "The merchants could hardly
fail to learn from experience that goods arrived safely in most instances and
that only a small percentage of all cargoes was lost. It was, therefore, possible to measure the risk with a fair degree of accuracy" (de Roover 1945,
180). Thus, premiums that were correlated with the likelihood of a loss meant
that both merchants and insurance underwriters were aware of the concept
of risk, if not of the actual calculation of probabilities, as early as the 1300s
and likely before.

Merchants, sea loan creditors, and insurance underwriters also behaved
as if they understood the law of large numbers because they typically sought
to take on a large number of small ventures, rather than a small number of
large ones. As mentioned, merchants would sometimes divide their cargoes
among multiple shippers bound for the same or different ports (Kingston
2013) or a sea loan creditor might agree to be responsible for only a small
percentage of the total sea loan (de Roover 1945). After the introduction
of formal insurance contracts, underwriters would often pledge to cover
only a fraction of the total value of the cargo in each contract and would
sign on to a number of insurance contracts. For example, records show that
one underwriter claimed to have concluded over 1,000 such contracts (de
Roover 1945).

An insurance contract of the time might work like this. A merchant who
needed insurance coverage for a specific cargo and voyage would identify an
underwriter who would act as a broker for the insurance contract. The broker
might then have such a contract drawn up by a notary with the specifics of
the cargo, what risks were covered, and the premium, usually determined as
a percentage of the insurance coverage that was underwritten. The contract
would then be circulated among the known underwriters, many of whom
were other merchants because merchants tended to be most knowledge-
able about the risks of a sea voyage, to see to what portion of the value of the
cargo each would subscribe. Some small shipments might have only a few
underwriters sign on and large ones might have ten or more. Depending on
the particulars of the contract and the premium percentage, it might take
some time to find sufficient subscribers to cover the value of the entire cargo
(de Roover 1945). Once the contract was fully underwritten, the merchant
could ship the cargo with relative confidence.

Centuries later, mathematicians would show formally that these diversification measures reduced risk because they made the insurance underwriter's costs more predictable. This, however, was something that these early maritime insurers probably knew intuitively because of their experience. That is, the advantage that maritime insurance held over other forms of insurance was that the marine merchants, and those who financed sea loans, had had a keen business interest in keeping track of this shipping information and in looking for patterns not only based on their own experience, but also on the experience of any other traders they knew of who used similar ships, sea captains, sea lanes, ports, and so on. Early shipping insurance underwriters who used this information to determine premium rates and to diversify by signing on additional underwriters were more successful than those who did not, and their competitors could not help but notice this. So the marine insurance underwriters were simply carrying on a data-gathering tradition established earlier by the sea loan creditors and the merchants themselves.

In contrast, other forms of insurance were much slower to develop because similar sources of corresponding information were not as readily available. For example, with life insurance, no one during the early Renaissance had a similar level of interest in keeping track of deaths, except perhaps for the clergy, and they probably did not have the same level of interest in identifying patterns. Life insurers, therefore, had to develop their information-gathering infrastructure anew, without the aid of a cadre of business owners who were already collecting this information. As a result, the life insurance industry and other forms of insurance would need to be developed more intentionally, along with the structure for gathering the appropriate information and the formal mathematics required to assess and reduce the risk. Again, in de Roover's words, for maritime insurers, the gathering anew of "elaborate statistical information was not necessary, and it is not surprising that the underwriting of marine insurance became a sound business long before actuarial science gave the same standing to life insurance" (de Roover 1945, 180). Thus, there was an information-based reason why insurance was developed in the shipping industry first.

Development of a Gambling Industry

Like insurance, gambling has been an aspect of human behavior from time immemorial. Although the true origins of gambling remain shrouded by time, excavations of the ancient city of Mohenjo Daro of India have found primitive dice—made from astragali, the anklebones of hooved animals—that date perhaps from 6000 BCE (Basham 1954). Gambling is mentioned (and lamented) in the Rig Veda religious texts from perhaps 1500 BCE (Basham 1954). China, where playing cards were used as early as the tenth century CE, has had a long history of fascination with gambling (Schwartz 2013). In contrast, playing cards did not appear in Europe until around 1350 CE (David 1962). While informal gambling among acquaintances has long been practiced, commercial establishments selling gambling opportunities as businesses appear to be more recent. In Europe, the first legally state-sanctioned casino dates from the opening of *The Ridotto* in Venice in 1638, although informal gambling houses had existed in Venice, and no doubt elsewhere, before this.

The astragali that were used in ancient gambling were also commonly used in Medieval Europe and even into the modern era (David 1962). Astragali were only roughly cubical; they were instead oblong, with two opposite sides that were wider than the other two, and two ends that were rounded, so an astragalus would never come to rest on either of the rounded ends. The sides were often distinguished by a numbering. For example, in Roman times various combinations of the numbers from casting four astragali simultaneously would mean either a contribution of money into a common gambling pot or the winning of money from that pot. Even in ancient times, however, the more familiar six-sided dice with relatively uniform sides were also used. In Europe, these dice eventually supplanted the astragali, but never completely (David 1962). It was apparent from the objects themselves that the intent of many early artisans was to make dice look beautiful, but not necessarily fair. Indeed, the dice were often intentionally made unfair in ways that only the owner would know (Lanciani 1892). This unfairness, and thus the lack of consistent experience by gamblers, may have been one of the reasons that the calculation of probability—how to calculate, say, the likelihood of a six throw on a six-sided die—took so long to grasp.

Even after tooled dice with uniform sides and weights became common, the concept of the probability of a six on a given toss was not immediately recognized. David (1962) suggests a number of reasons for this delay. First, even though as early as the first century BCE, the Roman writer Cicero was aware of the relative probability of certain throws of the dice and that a rare dice throw would occur only if there were a prolonged number of successive throws, these ideas were apparently lost to Europe in the intervening years.

With the advent and eventual dominance of Christian thinking in Europe, all events were seen as minutely controlled by the will of God, so the randomness that gave rise to the concepts of probability and the law of large numbers was not even a theoretical possibility. Second, experimentation was not practiced much in Europe before the Italian Renaissance and the scientific investigations of Leonardo da Vinci popularized the practice among the free thinkers of Italy in the late 1400s. Before Leonardo, it simply did not occur to others to start throwing a die and record how many times a six appeared in a certain number of throws. Third, dice were not only used in gambling, but also in religious ceremonies of divination or sortilege—foretelling the future—and sometimes by members of the Christian clergy. Many of the investigations into the frequency of dice throws were designed to find ways to make the dice show the intended sign, rather than to determine the likelihood of a certain sign at random. Finally, because of its religious connection, it was considered sacrilegious, or at least impious, to seek to know too much about how the outcomes of dice came about.

Despite its prohibition by the Church, gambling was widely practiced in much of Christian Europe before the Renaissance, as the frequency with which priests warned parishioners against its evils in their sermons attests. By the time of the Italian Renaissance, the frequent gambler probably had some intuitive empirical understanding of the probabilities involved in gambling games like hazard, one of the earliest dice games mentioned in the literature and one that the Crusaders probably brought back to Europe from the East. Indeed, by around 1600, experienced gamblers could distinguish between the *relative* likelihood of some gambling events, even the outcomes of certain throws of multiple dice which were 1/100 more likely than others, but they could not explain why (David 1962).

Many informal and some formal gambling houses in Venice preceded the state sanctioning of *The Ridotto* in the San Moise Palace in 1638, although the precise history of their development remains unclear. The development a gambling industry in Venice may have been more advanced than in other cities of Europe because of the permissiveness of Venice's popular Carnival season. Carnival attracted out-of-towners who were interested in entertainment of all types and who could participate anonymously because of the common practice of wearing a mask during this holiday season. Gambling venues would spring up in various neighborhoods overnight to take advantage of the Carnival trade (Walter 1999). Much of what is known about gambling in Venice comes from descriptions of court prosecutions of violations of gambling laws. Although gambling was not illegal in Venice during the Renaissance, it was heavily proscribed, and stringency of the rules varied with the times (Walter 1999).

Probability and Diversification in Gambling

Venetian gambling was done on an informal basis in private residences—the *ridotti* or private rooms—so named to emphasize the desire to keep these places unknown by the authorities. *Ridotti* could be in someone's home, but they could also be in a more public place like a tavern, inn, barber shop, house of prostitution, or even certain streets or *piazzi* with a reputation for attracting gamblers. By 1590, *ridotti* in Venice had evolved into formal gambling establishments, with larger clienteles who paid the owners for the opportunity to gamble, as is evidenced by the owner of one who was prosecuted for requiring a cut of the money in play (Walker 1999). Another type of gambling house, the *casini*, were originally the social clubs of the nobility that often provided a venue for gambling for their membership, sometimes employing dealers and charging for the use of decks of cards. *Casini* also evolved into commercial gambling establishments where gamblers played against the house instead of playing against other gamblers (Walker 1999).

These commercial gambling houses in Venice made money either by taking a cut of the stakes or by playing games—such as the card game, basset—that were run by an employee dealer and where the probabilities and payouts favored the house (Schwartz 2013). The exploitation of favorable odds by the house was not confined to the gambling houses of Venice. For example, roving German knights, *Landsknechte*, set up their gambling businesses in the towns as they passed through and played a game with odds that favored the knights (Schwartz 2013). Because of this commercialization of gambling, there was also perhaps a growing awareness of the concept of probability.

There might also have been a growing realization that a greater number of gambles meant that the house's take and profits were more predictable. As gambling transitioned from private social clubs to larger and commercially dedicated casinos, other changes were made to increase the volume of betting. The games played in the *casini* became more efficient as the rules were simplified and the durations of the games shortened so that more gambling events could take place in a shorter amount of time (Schwartz 2013). New games were introduced that could accommodate a greater volume of betting. For example, basset—originally a game where participants gambled against the house, one at a time—was replaced by games like faro—another card game, but where both the participants and observers could bet against the house (Schwartz 2013). Although increasing the number of bets would have had the effect of increasing the amount of profits, it also had the effect of making the profits more likely. That is, the predictability of casino profits became more reliable by their increasing the volume of betting and thus implicitly exploiting the law of large numbers.

Lotteries

In chapter 3, the demand for lotteries was separated out as being different from the demand for common casino games, such as roulette or blackjack. Lotteries were deemed to be different because their demand was derived predominantly from the attractiveness of the fantasy associated with winning such a large amount of money that it would change the gambler's life completely. This fantasy was deemed more important than the fact that the winnings would be obtained without the need to work for them, thus removing the demand for lotteries (and lottery winnings) from being directly or solely due to the disutility of labor. Lotteries were often used by early governments to raise revenues. They were common in many parts of Europe during the early modern period of the 1500s and 1600s, including France, the Netherlands, the German states, England, and Poland (Welch 2008).

In Italy, too, various municipalities used lotteries to raise money. Even in the 1500s, the lure of the private fantasy of winning large amounts of money or valuable prizes was recognized as an effective demand-side motivator. It was, however, criticized by some because of its ability to extract money from the poor. For example, in 1537 the satirist Pietro Aretino send a letter to Giovanni Manenti, the man responsible for running Venice's lottery, bemoaning the lengths that poor citizens of Venice would go to, and what they would be willing to part with, in order to participate in the state lottery. The attractiveness of the lottery was recognized by this observer to include the motivation of not having to work: "A peasant, having chanced along to see the draw and hearing that six *marcelli* were enough to win, sold his cloak and bellowed that he would never touch a spade again, even if it were the one Christ used when he appeared as a gardener" (Aretino 1537, in Welch 2008, 102). But this observer also describes the allure of the lottery fantasy: "Another . . . imagines himself grasping one of the jewels or the necklaces and placing it on his finger or round his neck . . . One sets his heart on getting money, another land and another houses" (Aretino 1537, in Welch 2008, 102). Thus, even at this early period, lotteries were understood by some to have a unique motivation.

Probability

Probability is the percentage of times a particular outcome is expected to occur on average given a series of similar and independent events. While this concept seems so fundamental to most of us today, it was not until after the discovery of the printing press in 1436 and the ferment of the Renaissance crisscrossed Europe that this concept became more widely known among the European populace. The impetus for understanding the concept seems to have come mainly from the trying to further understand gambling, and especially games with dice.

Girolamo Cardano is credited with writing the first treatise on the rules for calculating probability in his book, *Liber de Ludo Aleae* (*Book on Games of Chance*) (Bernstein 1996). Cardano was homeschooled in mathematics by his father, a lawyer, who also lectured in mathematics at the University of Pavia (Bellhouse 2005). The young Cardano later graduated from the University of Padua in medicine and became better known during his lifetime for his doctoring and his obsession with gambling than for his contributions to mathematics (Muir [1961] 1996; Bernstein 1996). From the references internal in *Liber*, it appears that the manuscript version was published in 1564 or later, but a print version did not appear until 1663 (Bellhouse 2005).[3] Therefore, it is unclear how influential his analysis would have been on public thinking about probability during the intervening years (Bernstein 1996).[4] Moreover, because some of the text mirrors a discussion of probability in an anonymous thirteenth-century elegiac comedy, *De Vetula*, the

---

[3] Hacking (2006) thinks Cardano's treatise was written "around 1550."
[4] Hacking (2006) suggests that because he was a popular lecturer, his ideas might have nevertheless been disseminated through word of mouth.

level of originality to ascribe to Cardano's work is also unclear (David 1962; Bellhouse 2005).

Most of the probability analysis in the book concerns dice outcomes, but there is some treatment of the card games that were popular at the time, too. The book also addresses cheating and how the various games would need to be played so that the outcomes are a reflection of the underlying probabilities alone (Bellhouse 2005). For example, Cardano suggested that the amounts that two people should bet on the occurrence of any event (one betting that the event occurs, the other that it does not occur) is the ratio of the probabilities of the two (mutually exclusive) events occurring, or the odds ratio. Wagers of any other size, he argued, should be regarded as unjust.[5]

Cardano explains how to measure probability of rolling a one on a six-sided die, and the probabilities of a number of more complex situations. In his analysis, he explains that, although only eleven outcomes were possible when rolling two six-sided dice (2, 3, . . . 12), there were actually 36 different combinations possible, and so each of the eleven outcomes has a different probability of occurring. This was useful practical knowledge in games of chance and one would think that this information should have gained widespread popularity immediately. Hacking (2006), however, has argued that it was not until about 1660 that the knowledge of how to calculate probabilities became suddenly and widely known among the general public. While this may be true, it is, however, likely that the *relative* probabilities of different rolls of the dice and card draws were in fact understood long before that, and even before the theory was formally written about by Cardano in the mid-1500s. As Bernstein explains, "The facts in the book about the frequency of outcomes were known to any gambler; the *theory* that explains such frequencies was not" (Bernstein 1996, 49).

Law of Large Numbers

Understanding probabilities was important for both insurers and those who owned or ran casinos because probabilities represented the essential information needed to calculate the business expenses that were to be expected by these firms (Eadington, 1999). The difference between the wager and the

---

[5] Shafer (1996) suggests that it was not until the writings of Jacob Bernoulli that the study of probability transitioned from an inquiry regarding equity to an inquiry of numerical calculation.

expected payout represented the expected profits of a game played against the house in the *casini*. Similarly, the amount of the insurance coverage of a cargo weighted by the probability of its loss during a sea voyage determined the insurance underwriter's expected expenditures for damages, with the difference between the insurance premiums and these expected expenditures being the firm's expected profits. The problem, however, was that these were *expected* expenditures and so the profits were *expected* as well. Whether profits actually materialized or not, however, was dependent on chance. That is, risk had been taken on by casinos and insurers for a profit, but there were (as yet) no others onto which the risk could be further transferred. The owners of these businesses were the ultimate risk bearers because that was their business model. Yet it became clear to those who underwrote maritime insurance and to those who ran gambling houses that the more frequent the insurance contract or the wager, and the smaller the possible payouts per contract or wager, the more predictable their expenditures would be. Thus, insurers and gambling houses practiced behavior consistent with the law of large numbers long before the law of large numbers was ever explained mathematically.

The law of large numbers holds that as the number of incidences of some uncertain event increases, the observed average value of those incidences becomes ever closer to the expected value. For example, as the number of throws of a fair six-sided die increases, the observed average of the number of dots facing up on those throws approaches 3.5, the expected value. In practice, for those insurance underwriters with a limited amount of capital, this meant that insuring a smaller portion of a larger number of similar shipments would increase the predictability of their insurance settlements, which was exactly what the early insurance underwriters tried to do. With gambling, this meant increasing the number of bets by simplifying the rules, making the game less complex so that more games could be played in a given amount of time, and allowing many gamblers to bet simultaneously on the same game together would all increase the predictability of the winnings paid out. These changes describe how gambling changed with the advent and development of casinos.

Jacob Bernoulli is credited with being the first to write formally on the law of large numbers. Jacob was born in Basel, Switzerland, in 1654 and came from the same family of mathematicians and thinkers responsible for number of important of mathematical and statistical discoveries. He was the uncle of Daniel Bernoulli, who developed the concept of utility (see chapter 2), and was a contemporary of both Isaac Newton in England and Gottfried Wilhelm Leibniz in Germany, with whom he corresponded (David 1962). Jacob Bernoulli's book, *Ars Conjectandi* (*The Art of Conjecturing*), which contained the theory of the law of large numbers, was written between 1684 and 1689, but it was not published until 1713, eight years after the author's death, by his nephew, Niklaus Bernoulli (Shafer 1996).

The book contained both the formal mathematical proof of the law and an application of the law to determine the number of observations necessary to achieve a specific level of confidence that an observed value was sufficiently close to the expected value. In motivating the proof, Bernoulli observed that the law was so intuitively obvious that most people would really require no formal proof of its veracity, and so he posed what might be considered a straw man argument to motivate need for the proof anyway. He suggested that, even though the sample mean might appear to approach the expectation for increases in small samples, there might be a limit or asymptote for large samples that was different than the expectation. Thus, the need to prove that the sample mean approached the expectation as the size of the sample increased, rather than a number close to it.

His practical application of the law was first to define a range for the observed values that contained and that was centered on the expected value. Then, he determined the number of observations necessary for the probability that the observed value was within this range to be a certain multiple of the probability of it being outside this range. In his example, if the expected value were 30/50 and the range were 29/50 to 31/50, for the probability that the observed value is within that range to be 1,000 times greater than the probability that the observed value is outside this range, the minimum number of observations would need to be 25,500. For a smaller range and the same probability, or for a more precise probability within the original range, a larger sample of observations would be needed. Statisticians today use a variation of this approach, but usually start with a given number of observations from a sample of the population and a level of error that would be tolerated, then determine the range of observed values—the confidence interval— that would be likely to contain the true expectation (Cummins 1974). As is well-known, the level of error typically tolerated today is 5 percent—the 5 percent significance level—which means that 95 percent of the confidence intervals computed will contain the actual parameter or the true expected value. The 1-in-1,000 ratio of probabilities that Jacob Bernoulli used was a considerably more precise criterion than the 1-in-20 criterion that is used today. Bernoulli's development of the formal law of large numbers was the first attempt to derive statistical measures from information on individual probabilities (Newman 1956).

Motivations of Firms

What were the motivations regarding risk of those early merchants who purchased insurance and those early underwriters who sold insurance? The conventional assumption in economics is that such firms are profit maximizers, and this motivation would appear to apply to both the merchants who purchased insurance and the underwriters who sold it. The merchants may have been motivated to purchase an insurance contract to shed their risk, but at the same time, they had chosen to pursue profits in a business—the import/export trade of the fourteenth century—that was renowned for its riskiness. Similarly, the insurance underwriters took on the risk of the merchants in order to make profits, but at the same time they charged greater premiums to insure riskier voyages and diversified their risk by insuring only a portion of a ship's cargo and by spreading their financial commitments over a larger number of shipments and voyages. Is this evidence of an underlying risk seeking or risk aversion?

The owners of the casinos who supplied the gambling opportunities are also assumed to have been profit maximizers. They were taking on risk by selling gambles, but at the same time, they were also diversifying their risk by establishing their businesses in halls that were large enough to accommodate a large number of gamblers, by simplifying the games and thus speeding up the frequency with which games were played, and by moving to games that would accommodate betting by both participants and observers. What does that say about the desire of the early casino owners regarding risk?

It seems clear that, were it not for the profits, these early business owners would be much less interested in exhibiting any of the behaviors regarding risk that were observed in the development of the insurance and gambling industries. That is, the insurance underwriters did not simply prefer the uncertainty they would experience by covering the expected expenses of the merchant for an actuarially fair premium. The insurers were interested in charging premiums that were larger than their expected expenditures and desired to make those profits more predictable by the diversification of the contracts. Similarly, why would a casino owner agree to cover such a large

number of wagers—most of which the owner could not possibly participate in or experience personally—if it was simply for the risk that could be
obtained by making fair bets? Were it not for the profits that such an operation could generate for the firm, the firm's owner would not go to the trouble
and expense both to make the gambles available and to take measures to diversify the risk in order to make the profits more predictable. The business
owners may have had preferences regarding risk, but these preferences must
have been secondary, at best, to their preferences for profits.

Unlike the merchants, insurers, and casino operators, consumers are not
in the *business* of buying and selling risk in order to make profits. Therefore,
their behavior regarding insurance and gambling may be motivated more directly by their attitudes toward pure risk itself, since their livelihoods do not
depend on it. This is the basis of the conventional theory. However, their behavior might alternatively be motivated by factors that are unrelated to risk
preferences, such as the desire for an income transfer when the increase in
income is either more valuable or less costly to obtain. This is the quid pro
quo theory.

In order to understand better the role of risk in the demand for insurance, we next turn to the empirical studies that determined to what extent
consumers who purchase insurance are actually as averse to the risk of loss,
as they are assumed to be according to the conventional theory. Similarly,
we will also turn to empirical evidence to understand how risk enters the
consumer's decision to gamble. Because a relatively large number of such
empirical studies have investigated this issue, we have a reasonably good understanding of how preferences regarding risk enter these decisions. We turn
now to a review of those studies in chapter 5.

5

Evidence on Risk Preferences and the Role of Prospect Theory in Insurance

Introduction

The theory presented in this book represents a rethinking of the demands for insurance and for gambling, and a transition from theories that are based on risk preferences to theories that are based on the desire for additional income and the consumption that would be derived from that income transfer. The problem with attempting to explain the demand for insurance or gambling with income is that both these types of economic transactions possess the unusual characteristic that the income payoffs—the *quos* in the quid pro quo transactions—are uncertain.[1] Because of the unusualness of this feature in economic transactions, it would seem that preferences regarding uncertainty should be salient when explaining the demand for insurance and gambling, with the desire for additional income either ignored or placed in the background to serve as the context from which to analyze preferences regarding uncertainty. This is how conventional theory has approached the understanding of these demands.

The quid pro quo theory presented in chapters 2 and 3 suggests instead that uncertainty plays a much different role in the demand for insurance and gambling than is assumed in conventional theory. Uncertainty under the quid pro quo theory serves as the multiplier of the premium or wager to determine an often much larger income transfer for the consumer. This additional income is desired because it arrives either in a state of the world where

---

[1] Indeed, in the present model, the consumer's premium and wager payments—the *quids*—are also uncertain, because they are paid only if the triggering event does not happen. Otherwise, if the triggering event were to happen, they would have been paid and then are implicitly returned to the consumer as part of the insurance payout or winnings, implying no change in income. The *quid pro quo* approach is intended to focus attention on the importance of an augmented income transfer in explaining demand.

A Theory of Insurance and Gambling. John A. Nyman, Oxford University Press. © Oxford University Press 2024.
DOI: 10.1093/oso/9780197687925.003.0005

it is more valuable than the state in which the premium is paid, or in a state where it is not necessary to work for the additional income compared to the state where such additional income would normally need to be earned.

The role of uncertainty in the *supply* of insurance or gambling opportunities is similar, but as shown in chapter 4, has just the opposite effect: instead of multiplying the income received, uncertainty reduces the firms' expenditures. With insurance, the uncertainty reduces the firms' contractual obligations to only that portion of insured consumers who satisfy a specific condition, such as having an automobile accident or becoming ill. Similarly, with gambling, the uncertainty reduces the firms' implicit obligations to pay out winnings to only that portion of wagers that meet the criteria for winning in a casino game, and thereby reduces the firms' costs and increases their profits. For the firms, the economic analyses have generally not focused on preferences regarding uncertainty because of the overriding assumption that insurers and gambling houses seek to maximize profits, and because as business entities, the firms in themselves do not have preferences.

Not so with the demand side. When explaining the demand for insurance or gambling, almost all economic analyses have focused on the consumer's preferences for risk, as displayed by the shape of the utility function. With regard to insurance, perhaps the one exception is de Meza, already discussed in chapter 2 in reference to the existence of moral hazard derived from a normal income effect (de Meza 1983). De Meza's insurance model focuses on the effect of uncertainty in reducing the premium's present consumption costs of the income transfer to consumers. His model shows that, because of uncertainty, an insurance premium (that would be needed to generate a certain amount of payout) would require foregoing far less consumption in the present period than either the savings or borrowings required to generate the same amount of income transfer. The quid pro quo analysis of insurance agrees with de Meza's analysis but places its emphasis instead on other side of the transaction: the ability of uncertainty to generate an augmentation of income as represented by the payout. The augmented payoff is the important focus of quid pro quo model because the event that triggers the income payout can also shift the utility function so that the income is evaluated in a state that is different than the state in which the premium (or wager) occurs. It is both this increase in income and change in state that explains demand according to the quid pro quo model. In addition, this multiplication of the income transfer may allow for a level of increased consumption which would not have been possible otherwise, even with saving or borrowing.

Thus, in the present model, uncertainty does not directly motivate insurance or gambling demand behavior, but instead acts primarily as a mechanistic determinant of the quid pro quo relationship between the premium and the insurance coverage payout, or between the wager and the winnings. Given a level of uncertainty, the consumer evaluates the insurance contract based on the differences between the utility expected to be lost from paying the premium and the utility expected to be gained from receiving the larger payout after the triggering event has occurred in the *ex post* period. Similarly, given a level of uncertainty, the consumer evaluates the gambling opportunity by comparing the utility expected to be lost from making the wager to the utility expected to be gained from receiving the larger winnings after the triggering event has occurred in the *ex post* period. The preference for additional income in these *ex post* periods represents the consumer's enticement for purchasing insurance and for gambling. Thus, preferences for certainty may exist, but they in themselves contribute little, if anything, to the utility gained by these transactions, and so are largely irrelevant.

This does not mean that uncertainty is ignored. Differences in outcomes are weighted by the probabilities with which they occur, just as they are with expected utility theory. It is just that the shape of the no event utility function does not override the effect of the probabilities. This distinction was made famous in an early paper by Samuelson (1963) on how the law of large numbers affects expected utility maximization. Samuelson tells of the time he asked a colleague whether he would accept a coin toss bet where the colleague loses US$100 if heads and wins US$200 if tails. His colleague rejected the bet, but said he would accept 100 similar independent bets, relying on the law of large numbers to make the outcomes more predictable. Samuelson (1963) says that his colleague would have made a mistake to reject the single bet but take the 100, if he were maximizing expected utility. This is because his utility function is still risk-averse, as was revealed by his response to the offer of the single bet, so he should also reject the 100 similar bets, even though the probabilities have changed.[2]

---

[2] Samuelson (1963) writes that, if instead the colleague had said he would have accepted 100 bets of a US$1 wager for US$2 in winnings, this would have been consistent with expected utility theory because "the utility function's curvature becomes more and more negligible in a sufficiently limited range around any initial position" (Samuelson 1963, 112).

According to the quid pro quo model, the change in the expected loss due to the reduction of its probability should be recognized by consumers and it might legitimately lead to a change in behavior. With regard to Samuelson (1963), Rabin (2000) notes that the expected US$50 income transfer (my term) from each of the 100 independent bets totals (US$50*100 =) US$5,000, but the probability of losing any money at all has dropped from π = ½ in the original single bet case, to a negligible π = 1/2,300 for the hundred US$100 wagers. The probability of losing more than US$1,000 would be truly negligible at only π = 1/62,000. Thus, the loss of US$100 (what Samuelson's colleague is apparently most concerned about in rejecting the initial bet) has become so much less likely with the multiple wagers and has so reduced the expected loss that it would (and should, according to Rabin) change the colleague's behavior. In contrast to Samuelson's view, this revised expected gain and the reduction in the expected loss because of the change in probability would also be legitimate considerations with the quid pro quo theory. Thus, the quid pro quo theory lies firmly within the standard expected utility framework.

The intent of this chapter is to review the empirical evidence regarding the role of risk preferences in the demand for insurance and gambling, and then to review the empirical evidence in support of a quid pro quo approach to the demand for insurance. Accordingly, the rest of this chapter has three parts: Part 1 summarizes the evidence that risk preferences are exactly opposite to those suggested by Friedman and Savage (1948) in their model; Part 2 focuses on the relationship between prospect theory and insurance; and Part 3 shows how the prospect theory diagram can be transformed into one that shows the demand for insurance under the quid pro quo theory. There is also a concluding summary section.

Part 1: Evidence on Risk Preferences

This part consists of three sections that summarize the evidence on risk preferences and show that risk preferences are exactly opposite to those suggested by Friedman and Savage (1948) in their model. This part also describes the alternative theory of risk preferences—prospect theory— suggested by these studies and the standard interpretation of this theory that concludes that insurance should not be purchased and that gambling should not be done.

Experiments That Contradict Risk Preferences

According to Friedman and Savage (1948), consumers are expected utility maximizers, and so when given a choice to purchase insurance or not, prefer to pay an amount (the premium) with certainty, rather than face the prospect of an uncertain uninsured loss of the same expected magnitude. Insurance is chosen because expected utility is greater if insured. Consumers demand gambling opportunities because they prefer uncertainty, and so they prefer the uncertainty of an income gain or loss, to having an actuarially equivalent amount of income (the wager) with certainty. In the case of gambling, the expected utility of the uncertain gamble is greater than the utility of the certain wager, even though both also have the same expected magnitude. Thus, risk preferences represent the motivation for the demand for insurance and gambling under conventional expected utility theory.

Perhaps the most troubling aspect of conventional theory's reliance on risk preferences to explain the demand for insurance and gambling is that empirical evidence finds that just the opposite is true. That is, the results of behavioral experiments done by Kahneman and Tversky, their students, and others show that, contrary to conventional insurance theory, most consumers prefer an uncertain loss to a certain one of the same expected magnitude (Kahneman and Tversky 1979; 1984; Tversky and Kahneman 1981; 1988; 1991; 1992; Fishburn and Kochenberger 1979). Similarly, these studies find that, contrary to conventional gambling theory, most consumers prefer a certain gain to an uncertain gain of the same expected magnitude. These results are diametrically opposed to the conventional explanations of the motivations to purchase insurance and gambling contracts, thus they contradict conventional theory.

The empirical findings supporting prospect theory are often dramatic. For example, in one of their most famous experiments, Tversky and Kahneman (1981) posed the following choice to their subjects, students at Stanford University and the University of British Columbia. The number of students queried and the percentage who preferred each program are indicated:

Problem 1 [N = 152]: Imagine that the US is preparing for the outbreak of an unusual Asian disease, which is expected to kill 600 people. Two alternative programs to combat the disease have been proposed. Assume that the exact scientific estimates of the consequences of the programs are as follows:

If program A is adopted, 200 people will be saved [72 percent].

If program B is adopted, there is a 1/3 probability that 600 will be saved, and 2/3 probability that no people will be saved [28 percent].

Which of the two programs would you favor? (Tversky and Kahneman 1981, 453)

Kahneman and Tversky find that significantly more subjects preferred the certain gain (72 percent) to the uncertain one (28 percent). Then, they rewrote the programs so as to frame the choices as between losses instead of gains, and reran the same experiment:

Problem 2 [N = 155]:

If program C is adopted, 400 people will die [22 percent].

If program D is adopted, there is a 1/3 probability that nobody will die, and a 2/3 probability that 600 will die [78 percent].

Which of the two programs would you favor? (Tversky and Kahneman 1981, 453).

The authors find that, even though the choice between programs C and D corresponded exactly to the choice between programs A and B, reframing the wording from a gain to a loss reversed the preferences: 22 percent preferred the certain loss and 78 percent preferred the uncertain loss. So when expressed as a gain, certainty is preferred, but when expressed as a loss, uncertainty is preferred. Because insurance is conventionally modeled as a choice between a certain loss and an uncertain one of the same expected magnitude, the risk preference results of these experimental studies would predict insurance should not be purchased. Likewise, gambles should not be purchased because certain gains are generally preferred to uncertain ones.

More Evidence on Risk Preferences

The evidence against risk preferences as a source of motivation for the purchase of insurance extends beyond the experimental work by Kahneman and Tversky and their students. A large literature has now developed that correlates the actual purchase of insurance with characteristics of the individual that measure risk preferences. This literature is too broad to review in this book, but one study, Eling, Ghavibazoo, Hanewald (2021), might serve to provide both a summary of that literature and an example of the evidence that risk preferences are not a reliable motivator for the demand for insurance, at least not in the way that is predicted by conventional theory.

Eling, Ghavibazoo, Hanewald (2021) investigate the relationship between self-reported willingness to take on financial risks, and the purchase of either life insurance or long-term care insurance. Using data from the almost 34,000 respondents to the 2013 Survey of Health, Ageing and Retirement in Europe (SHARE) from 14 such countries, these authors use as the measure of risk aversion the respondent's answer to this SHARE question:

When people invest their savings they can choose between assets that give low return with little risk to lose money, for instance a bank account or a save bond, or assets with a high return but also a higher risk of losing, for instance, stocks and shavers. Which of the statements on the care comes closest to the amount of financial risk you are willing to take when you save or make investments?
1 Take substantial financial risks expecting to earn substantial returns
2 Take above-average financial risks expecting to earn above-average returns
3 Take average financial risks expecting to earn average returns
4 Not willing to take any financial risks. (Eling, Ghavibazoo, and Hanewald 2021, 4)

In a probit analysis of whether or not the individual participant has purchased each of three types of insurance—long-term care insurance, term life insurance, and whole life insurance—the participant's response to each mutually exclusive answer to this question is entered as a separate dummy variable, with the risk-averse response (answer 4) as the excluded variable. The analysis is done using equations both with and without additional explanatory variables. These researchers find that those who characterize themselves as preferring investments at any of the three levels of risk are more likely to purchase each of the three types of insurance than those who are averse to risk, contrary to the conventional theory. The coefficients were all positive, and are statistically significant for 11 of the (2 equations * 3 risk levels * 3 types of insurance =) 18 coefficients. The authors would have liked to have performed the analysis using panel data, but there was an insufficient number of repeated responses across the waves of the SHARE to conduct such an analysis. This meant, however, that they did not employ a statistical fix for the possibility of endogeneity and that all the relationships should be regarded as associations.

As one robustness test, the analysis was replicated using whether the respondent owned stock, as the negative measure of risk aversion. Again these researchers found that stock ownership was positively and significantly associated with ownership of each of all three types of insurance. As a second robustness test, the authors performed the same original probit analysis on a different wave of the SHARE survey that contained the responses of participants to whether they had purchased supplementary health insurance. Again, the authors found that that respondents who are averse to risk do not purchase supplementary health insurance, contrary to conventional theory.

Eling, Ghavibazoo, Hanewald (2021) include in their study a review of 26 other studies that regress ownership of either long-term care insurance or life insurance on a measure of risk aversion. These studies find a mix of results, with six studies showing that those who are risk-averse are significantly more likely to purchase these types of insurance, eight concluding that those who are risk-averse are significantly less likely to purchase these types of insurance, and 12 studies finding no significant relationship at all. Considering both these authors' convincing results and the lack of a clear and consistent signal from the literature, this study also suggests that risk preferences are in themselves unlikely to motivate the purchase of insurance.

Prospect Theory

Kahneman and Tversky summarized the findings of the experimental studies in their prospect theory (Kahneman and Tversky 1979). The preferences for uncertain losses and certain gains were translated into a value function that is increasing at a decreasing rate for gains from the status quo, and decreasing at a decreasing rate as losses increase from the status quo. Furthermore, in their studies they found that the aversion to losses was stronger than the attraction to gains of similar magnitudes. This "loss aversion" result meant that the value function is steeper for losses than for gains. Finally, they also found that their subjects reinterpreted very low probabilities to be greater than their actual mathematical meaning, and high probabilities to have a reinterpretation that is lower than their actual mathematical meaning. Although these findings from their experiments represent the three main tenets of prospect theory, their theory also suggests that changes in income are more important than levels of income in explaining decisions under uncertainty.

The prospect theory value function is illustrated in Figure 5.1 as V(y). Figure 5.1 shows the implications of prospect theory for the purchase of insurance. The status quo would occur under conventional theory at the origin with y_0 income. A loss of $(y_0 - y_1)$ occurs with a probability π so the expected income loss if uninsured is $\pi(y_0 - y_1)$. Full insurance coverage of the loss can be purchased for an actuarially fair premium $(y_0 - y^*) = \pi(y_0 - y_1)$. The expected loss of value if uninsured, EV, is smaller than the value of the certain loss if fully insured, V(y*), and implies that insurance should not be purchased. A similar analysis could be presented for gambling, only using the positive portion of V(y) lying to the right of the origin. This analysis would show that a certain gain would generate a greater value than an uncertain one of the same expected magnitude, suggesting that gambling should not be done.

Kahneman and Tversky (1979), however, suggest that prospect theory might still predict the purchase of insurance for coverage of those events that

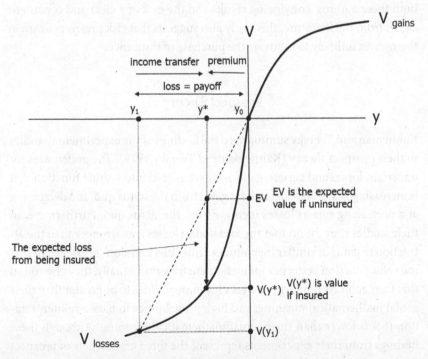

Figure 5.1 Prospect theory value function and demand for insurance

are very rare. This is because people interpret very low probabilities of loss to be greater than they actually are. If consumers weight probabilities in this way, it would mean that insurance premiums based on actual probabilities may seem to be a bargain for those who interpret the likelihood of a loss to be higher than it actually is. As a result, consumers would be willing to pay more for insurance than, say, the actuarially fair premium that an insurer charges reflecting the true probability, and thus buy insurance. The problem with this explanation is that one of the classic puzzles in insurance economics is that people underinsure low probability events with large losses, seemingly just the type of event that would generate the most demand if such a reinterpretation of the probabilities were commonly taking place (Schmidt 2016). For example, Kunreuther et al. (1978) and Kunreuther and Pauly (2004) note that disaster insurance covers costly losses with a very low probability of occurring, but disaster insurance is not generally purchased. This is even more puzzling because some types of low-probability disaster insurance, such as flood insurance, are also subsidized in the US by the government, but still not widely purchased. Other researchers have found this tendency not to purchase very low probability insurance in experimental studies (e.g., Slovic et al. 1977). Although this reinterpretation of low probabilities might apply to some special cases, there is little evidence that it is behind the demand for insurance generally.[3] Thus, the main implication of the experimental evidence supporting prospect theory is that, if risk preferences are the motivation, insurance should not be purchased (Nyman 2001a; 2003).

With regard to gambling, prospect theory finds that a certain gain is preferred to an uncertain one of the same expected magnitude and that, when evaluated on that portion of the value function for gains, the value of a certain gain is greater than the expected value of an uncertain one from a fair gamble. This, too, is exactly opposite to the Friedman–Savage (1948) theory that consumers gamble because an uncertain gain generates greater utility than a certain gain of the same expected magnitude, which in turn is explained by the a portion of their otherwise concave utility function that is

---

[3] There appears to be a growing interest in the analysis of probability weighting—the notion that consumers reinterpret the probability of both low and high probability events—in determining the demand for insurance (Barberis 2013; Barseghyan et al. 2013; O'Donoghue and Somerville 2018). Some of the studies of the demand for insurance acknowledge this factor, but assume that it is irrelevant to their analyses in order to concentrate on other aspects. This book takes a similar approach and assumes that probability weighting might matter at the margin in determining the extent of the demand for insurance for various types of coverage, but it does not explain why the demand for insurance or gambling exists, nor does it provide insights regarding whether demand is derived from risk preferences or from the desire for income transfers.

convex (nonconcave).[4] Instead of convexity, prospect theory finds that the value function for gains is generally concave, as represented by the portion of the consumer's value function that covers gains from the origin in Figure 5.1. Thus, prospect theory predicts that consumers should not gamble.

Again, very low probabilities of winning may be reinterpreted by the consumer as being higher than they actually are. As a result, low probability gambles may appear to be a bargain when comparing the consumer's expected winnings to the actual wager required, but this would not be the general case.[5] If based on risk preferences, the experiments that generated prospect theory would suggest that neither insurance nor gambles should be widely purchased. This contradictory evidence raises the question of whether risk preferences really matter in the motivation to purchase insurance or to gamble.

Part 2: Insurance and Prospect Theory

This part focuses on insurance and consists of five sections that look at the evidence from a series of empirical and theoretical studies to determine whether the conventional interpretation is actually how prospect theory should interpret the demand for insurance. That is, these five sections review a series of issues and empirical results that would refine the interpretation of prospect theory so that it is consistent with the quid pro quo demand for insurance.

Is Insurance a Standard Gamble Choice Between Certain and Uncertain Losses?

Because of its use by Friedman and Savage (1948), but also because of its use by von Neumann and Morgenstern (1947) in their path-breaking new method

---

[4] Markowitz (1952) points out a number of issues with utility functions that are generally convex but have concave portions, as Friedman and Savage (1948) had suggested was the case in order to explain the demand for gambles. His objections are summarized in chapter 7.

[5] Lotteries are gambles with exceedingly small probabilities of winning and are also popular. Thus, it may be true that the overweighting of the probability of winning contributes to their demand. Lotteries, however, have already been excluded from the quid pro quo analysis in chapter 3 because, although lottery winnings are not earned by working, the additional motivation generated by the vivid imaginings of possessing the winnings seems to dominate.

of measuring utility, conventional economic analysis held that the insurance decision represents the same type of decision as a standard gamble. Using the standard gamble approach meant that risk preferences seemed to be at the forefront of any decision. Purchasing an insurance contract—as represented by, say, the payment of a certain US$100 premium versus the uncertainty of a US$1,000 loss that occurs with a 10 percent probability or a US$0 loss with a 90 percent probability—was thus assumed to be the same operationally to consumers as a standard gamble choice between the certainty of a US$100 wager versus the uncertainty of a gamble where US$1,000 payout is made with a 10 percent probability or US$0 payout with a 90 percent probability. It appeared that purchasing insurance therefore meant opting for the certainty over uncertainty because that seemed to be the only difference between the two options.

Early on, however, researchers recognized that consumers think differently about insurance than they do about the standard gamble. For example, Slovic, Fischoff, and Lichtenstein (1988) presented their 208 subjects with two sets of choices: (1) between a 0.001 chance of losing US$5,000 and a certain loss of US$5, and (2) between a 0.25 chance of losing US$200 and a certain loss of US$50. Sometimes these situations were framed as a standard gamble choice, and sometimes the purchase of insurance. The proportions opting for the purchase of insurance were 66 and 65 percent, for the 0.001 and 0.25 probabilities of loss questions, respectively. However, the proportions opting for the certain loss dropped to 39 and 20 percent, respectively, when the choice was presented in the standard gamble context. Studies by Schoemaker and Kunreuther (1979), Hershey and Shoemaker (1980), and Hershey, Kunreuther, and Schoemaker (1982) found similar differences. Thus, consumers tend to view insurance as being different from the standard gamble choice. This raises the question: In what way do consumers regard insurance as different? To my knowledge, only one study has attempted to explain the subtleties of how the insurance decision differs from the standard gamble.

Connor (1996) wanted to determine what type of decisions are most like the purchase of insurance to consumers. He therefore presented his subjects—154 MBA students from the University of Minnesota who had all had training in expected utility theory—with choices using the following five frames (summarized from Connor 1996, 43–45):

1. A: You will lose $40 on your next trip.
   B: You have a 2 percent chance of losing $2,000 on your next trip.
2. A: You will lose $40 on your next trip. In addition, you will have a 2 percent chance of losing $2,000 on your next trip AND getting an unexpected $2,000 gift the same day from a distant relative.
   B: You have a 2 percent chance of losing $2,000 on your next trip.
3. A: You will lose $40 on your next trip. In addition, you will have a 2 percent chance of losing $2,000 on your next trip AND recovering $2,000 the same day by searching.
   B: You have a 2 percent chance of losing $2,000 on your next trip.
4. A: You have a 2 percent chance of losing $2,000 on your next trip. You buy $2,000 in travel checks for $2,000 plus a $40 fee which will let you recover the $2,000 loss the same day if it occurs.
   B: You have a 2 percent chance of losing $2,000 on your next trip. You do not buy travel checks.
5. A: You have a 2 percent chance of losing $2,000 on your next trip. You buy travel insurance for $40 which will reimburse you for this $2,000 loss the same day if it occurs.
   B: You have a 2 percent chance of losing $2,000 on your next trip. You do not buy travel insurance.

Frame 1 is the standard gamble and is intended as the choice between certain and uncertain losses, reflecting conventional insurance demand theory. Frame 5 is the purchase of insurance, where the premium is paid in exchange for an income transfer, a quid pro quo transaction. Connor includes frame 2 to capture that notion that a prior loss colors how the consumer views a subsequent but unconnected gain, perhaps, through indirect mental accounting (Thaler and Johnson 1990). Frame 3 is included to test the effect of being able to overcome and control environmental hazards by your own effort (Lopez 1987; Langer 1980). Frame 4 is a quid pro quo exchange like the insurance frame 5, but stated without using the word "insurance." This frame reflects the possibility that "people may place extra value on the reversal of something bad when the reversal is caused by a prior investment or precautionary saving" (Connor 1996, 42).[6] Thus, the author suggests that the consumer's recognition that an initial payment is able to generate a larger payment that reverses an uncertain loss may increase the demand for the option of the certain loss and thus represent the motivation behind the demand for insurance.

Connor uses (1) the loss of money on a trip as one of the contexts for his set of five items, and also (2) the loss from a burglary at home and (3) a business loss as alternative contexts in formulating the five questions. Altogether, (3 contexts * 5 questions =) 15 items were asked and completed by each of his 154 subjects. The subjects were asked to tell which of the two choices each preferred, and also gauge the intensity of their preferences as represented by their responses on a 13 point scale ranging from "strongly prefer A" to "indifferent between A and B" to "strongly prefer B".

Connor (1996) found that his subjects tended to prefer the uncertain choice B or be indifferent in frames 1, 2, and 3, and to prefer the option A with frames 4 and 5. Choice A in frame 4 was represented by (1) the US$40 purchase of traveler's checks, (2) the $40 rental of a burglar alarm, or (3) the $40 rental of a computer program, and each $40 price being paid explicitly so that $2,000 could be received back if $2,000 were lost, but without using the word "insurance." Choice A in frame 5 was the payment of a $40 premium for travel, home, or business insurance, which paid back $2,000 in the event of a $2,000 loss. The respondent's preferences for the quid pro quo exchange in the frame 4 contexts closely matched the respondent's preferences for purchasing insurance in frame 5. Connor concluded that "rather than suffer a single loss to avoid a negative situation, people prefer to invest in something that offers them the opportunity to salvage something positive from a negative situation" (Connor 1996, 50).

This study suggests that the purchase of insurance is not viewed as a standard gamble choice between certainty and uncertainty, but more as a quid pro quo transaction or investment against a loss: income is paid or invested in the form of a premium in order to obtain a return of income, but a return of income that happens to coincide with a loss. And, regarding the reinterpretation of prospect theory to explain the demand for insurance, this study suggested that consumers regard the evaluation of the payment of the

---

[6] A number of others have hinted that recognizing the potential loss might be a factor in determining the demand for insurance, but do not go on to represent the effect that a loss by a shifting out of the *ex post* utility or value functions (Slovic et al. 1977; Kunreuther 1978; Kahenman and Tversky 1979; Schoemaker and Kunreuther 1979; Hershey et al. 1982; Kunreuther et al. 1985).

premium as being separate from the evaluation of the income transfer from insurance.

Do Premiums and Insurance Payouts Have the Same Reference Points?

Both parts of the conventional insurance problem represent losses from the reference point of the status quo—the loss of a US$100 premium if insured or the prospect of either a US$1,000 loss or a US$0 loss if uninsured. Under the original Friedman and Savage (1948) theory, the status quo was assumed to be a point on a positively defined concave risk-averse utility function, the first interpretation of Figure 2.1. But because these options were both losses, prospect theory would measure both from the status quo at the origin of the value function and evaluate them on the "risk-seeking" or convex portion of the prospect theory value function, as in Figure 5.1. The prospect theory analysis would thus indicate that insurance should not be purchased.

One way to accommodate the purchase of insurance under prospect theory is to redefine the reference points. For example, Slovic, Fischhoff and Lichtenstein (1988) suggested that, rather than insurance representing losses from the status quo, the insurance decision might be made by a consumer who assumes that insurance has already been purchased. Thus, instead of a choice between a 25 percent chance of losing US$200 or a certain loss of US$50, both from the reference point of the origin as the status quo, the choice would be between already having spent US$50 on insurance, and either (A) keeping the insurance for a US$0 gain from the status quo origin, or (B) forgoing insurance and accepting the gamble of a 75 percent chance gain from not having to pay the US$50 insurance premium if healthy or a 25 percent chance of incurring a US$150 loss, from losing US$200 but getting to keep US$50 that would have been paid in premiums if ill. The authors reason that under prospect theory, because consumers are more sensitive to losses than gains and because smaller probabilities tend to have greater weights, the individual would prefer to remain insured.

Different reference points can dramatically alter the expected gains and losses from purchasing insurance, but whether it is reasonable for analysts to assume that consumers adopt these alternative reference points is not clear. Some of the redefinitions of reference points for the insurance decision seem so contrived that they surely cannot accurately represent how consumers view the insurance decision. In the above example, do consumers really assume that they have already purchased insurance when the insurance salesman comes to call? Already having purchased insurance might represent the perspective of the household who must make the decision of whether to renew an insurance policy, but it would hardly represent the perspective of a household that is making the decision regarding purchasing insurance anew. Purchasing insurance anew must be the perspective that is addressed in determining the theory of the demand for insurance.

As an alternative approach, Schmidt (2016) proposed that, while the premium could be evaluated as a payment loss on the negative portion of the value function, the insurance payout could be evaluated as a gain on the positive portion of the value function. Because the loss of income (or wealth) that is generated by the triggering event is not really a part of the insurance transaction, it would be incorporated into the prospect theory diagram as having already occurred. Thus, the loss would be modeled as having changed the reference point from which the insurance payoff gain is evaluated. The intuition behind this approach, according to Schmidt (2016), is that paying the premium from the status quo reference point would represent a loss of value from the regret experienced if the insured event does not occur (regret is discussed further in chapter 6), and receiving the insurance payoff would represent a gain after the loss from the insured event had occurred and the change in status quo had been taken into account.

Schmidt further conducted a quantitative analyses of this approach to determine whether the parameters of the value function suggested by Tversky and Kahneman (1992) would produce net gains. Schmidt (2016) found that, if these parameters—especially the effect of loss aversion in evaluating the payment of the insurance premium—are used, insurance would only be purchased for loss probabilities in excess of 0.5, which would exclude the purchase of insurance for all realistic cases. Thus, applying Schmidt's reinterpretation of the insurance problem to a prospect theory context could generate the purchase of insurance, but only if the parameters that were found in the experimental prospect theory studies—and especially the loss aversion parameter—did not apply.

Do Insurance Premiums Have the Same Effect on Utility as a Prospect Theory Loss?

To be consistent with prospect theory, the quid pro quo approach from chapter 2 would use the same reference points and directions for the income changes as Schmidt (2016) does. This is because the emphasis in the quid pro quo approach is on the exchange of the premium for the expected income payout, rather than a choice of types of losses. Any income (or wealth) loss generated by the triggering event is not a part of the insurance transaction and would determine the context, and thus the reference point, from which the income payout occurs. In contrast to Schmidt (2016), however, this re-interpretation would assume that the premium is simply the payment of a market price, not a surprise loss for which the consumer does not plan, as would be suggested by prospect theory.

Such an intentional payment for the insurance contract would be similar to most other purchases that a consumer makes and so would not be evaluated from the perspective of loss aversion. Regarding whether to view the premium payment as a prospect-theory-type loss, Kahneman and Tversky (1984) write that loss aversion is "unlikely to play a significant role in routine economic exchanges. . . . Payments made by consumers are also not evaluated as losses but as alternative purchases. In accord with standard economic analysis, money is naturally viewed as a proxy for the goods and services it could buy" (Kahneman and Tversky 1984, 348–349). Thus, these authors are clear that loss aversion does not (or should not) apply to payments in market transactions, such as the payment of a premium for an income transfer in an insurance contract.

In an empirical study, Novemsky and Kahneman (2005) investigate whether consumers regard the willingness to pay (WTP) to purchase a commodity as exhibiting a prospect theory loss aversion. This paper summarizes the data and findings from eight separate studies where a total of 1,007 students from universities in Canada, California, and New York were queried about how much they valued chocolates, pens, or mugs. Some subjects received these items up front and others did not. The willingness to accept (WTA) was measured as the minimum price that sellers demand to give up the good and WTP as the maximum price that buyers are willing to pay for the good anew. In addition, some subjects were given a choice to receive the good in question or an amount of money. This choice equivalent (CE) option was defined as "the minimum amount of money for which choosers prefer to receiving the good" (Novemsky and Kahneman 2005, 121). The CE was regarded as a measure of the true transactional value of the good. The authors found that WTA > CE, but that WTP = CE. Thus, although they also found evidence of an endowment effect, WTA > WTP, they did not find that the WTP is regarded differently than its transactional value, CE. This implies that payments in market transactions, like a premium payment for an insurance contract, do not elicit a loss aversion reaction when paid.

In a separate study that was viewed as an "adversarial collaboration" by including Kahneman in a team of researchers from the University of East Anglia, this same issue was tested using another data set (Bateman, Kahneman, et al. 2005). These authors requested the same type of WTA and WTP information from 320 undergraduates at the University of East Anglia in Norwich, England for an amount of chocolate. In addition, they requested information on the equivalent gain (EG), defined as the minimum amount of money that the individual would be willing to accept in place of a gain of one unit of the good, a concept very near (identical?) to the CE used by Novemsky and Kahneman (2005). Bateman, Kahneman, et al. (2005) found that sometimes WTA = EG and sometimes WTA > EG, but that EG > WTP, and significantly so. Thus, although they find evidence of an endowment effect, WTA > WTP, they also find that the WTP is regarded differently than its transactional value, EG, and that it represents a loss of money that the subjects were apparently averse to incurring. Thus, in this study, there is evidence of loss aversion in the payment of the *quid* in a standard quid pro quo market transaction.

Taken together, the ambiguous results from these two studies (and additional findings discussed in chapter 6) may mean that consumers differ with regard to whether they view the payment of an insurance premium as part of a standard market transaction or as an uncertain loss to be avoided, and that these differences may be caused by subtle differences in consumers that are unrecognized in these experiments. Importantly, these results might further suggest that those who view the premium payment as a transaction are more likely to purchase insurance than those who view the premium as an unplanned or surprise loss.

Is the Utility Function Curved Reflecting an Aversion to Risk?

The conventional analysis of the demand for insurance was presented in chapter 2 and illustrated using Figure 2.1. The demand for insurance was represented by the gain in utility as measured by the difference between expected utility of the uninsured loss compared to the certain level of utility when paying the premium with insurance. This gain in utility depended on and would increase with the curvature of a risk-averse utility function.

A measure of the curvature of the utility function was developed independently by Arrow (1964; 1965) and Pratt (1964). If $U(y)$ is the utility function for income, the now standard Arrow-Pratt absolute risk aversion measure is calculated as $-U''/U'$, the negative of the ratio of the second derivative of the utility function to the first derivative. The relative risk aversion measure, $\rho = -yU''/U'$, is the absolute risk aversion measure multiplied by the level of income at which the function was evaluated. The second derivative, U'', is assumed to be negative because of the risk-averse shape of the utility function, and so the Arrow-Pratt risk aversion measure would be positive for a utility function that is increasing at a decreasing rate. As the curvature of the function, as measured by an increase in either of these measures, increases, the utility derived from insurance would also increase, according to the conventional theory, holding other things constant (Mossin 1968). The same Arrow-Pratt calculation could also be used to calculate the degree of risk aversion implied by positive portion of the prospect theory value function. Thus, the prospect theory evaluation of the demand for insurance would be generated by the same curvature of the value function that motivated demand under conventional theory.

Studies by Hanson (1988) and Kandel and Stambaugh (1991), and most prominently by Rabin (2000), however, recognized that almost any concave function, even one that shows very little risk aversion over modest amounts of money, leads to unreasonable implications regarding consumer behavior if the same function were applied to large stakes. For example, Rabin (2000) calculates that if a person were to turn down a 50–50 gamble of either losing US$10 or winning an income transfer of US$11(that is, to turn down a bet of US$10 to win US$21 with a 50 percent probability), the curvature of the utility function that is implied by such a risk-averse choice should also lead the consumer to reject a 50–50 gamble to either lose US$100 or win an infinite amount of money (that is, bet US$100 to win an infinite amount of money with a 50 percent probability). This implies that for modest-sized losses—that is, insurance coverage of monetary losses in the hundreds or even thousands of dollars—the utility function would need to be virtually linear in order to be reasonable. This would mean that the curvature of the utility function and risk aversion could no longer explain the purchase of insurance. According to Rabin (2000), the curvature of the utility function and risk aversion could still explain the purchase of insurance against large-scale losses, but modest scale losses would require an alternative theory.[7]

There appears to be, however, a substantial demand for modest-stake insurance coverage anyway. Consumers often purchase modest-stakes insurance contracts, such as extended warranties on consumer durables such as washing machines, automobile service contracts, and lower deductibles in automobile insurance (Pashigian, Schkade, and Menefee, 1966). Sydnor's (2010) study of the purchase of lower deductibles for home insurance coverage of theft, accidents, and weather-related losses is a rare empirical analysis showing the extent of the misattribution of insurance demand to risk aversion. Using a sample of over 50,000 insurance contracts from the same insurer in an undefined post-2000 year, Sydnor finds that the large payments that new policy holders are willing to pay to reduce their deductibles from US$1,000 to either US$500, US$200, or US$100 imply degrees of risk aversion that are absurdly high. For example, the payment that the median consumer purchasing a US$500 deductible was willing to make implied a lower bound of the Arrow-Pratt relative risk aversion measure of 1,839 and an upper bound of 5,064. This is compared to Chetty's (2006) estimate of the Arrow-Pratt relative risk aversion parameter derived from labor supply elasticities, which is at most 2, or to Gourinchas and Parker's (2002) estimate derived from a study of consumption over the life cycle, which is somewhere in the range of 0.5 to 1.4. Thus, while there is a clear demand for insurance coverage of modest-stake losses, risk-aversion as measured by the shape of the utility function, simply cannot explain it.

---

[7] If the standard risk aversion motive is not responsible for the purchase of insurance coverage modest scale losses, Rabin and Thaler (2001) point to mental accounting and loss aversion as the most likely alternative explanation. Mental accounting is the idea that consumers evaluate different expenditures based on the mental accounting categories to which the expenditures are implicitly assigned (Thaler 1985; 1999). Here, these authors focus on the consumers' accounting of each risk of loss they face as being presented to them in isolation and separately from the other risks they face. Therefore, they purchase insurance when, if they looked at the big picture, they might not purchase this insurance. Loss aversion is addressed more completely in chapter 6.

Are Insurance Buyers Sufficiently Sophisticated?

Are insurance buyers sufficiently sophisticated to purchase insurance because of the reasons suggested by prospect theory, given the modifications and ambiguities found in the empirical studies? Ambiguity regarding the effect of paying the premium on utility was reflected in the diametrically opposed findings from the two empirical studies of the way that consumers view the insurance premium (Novemsky and Kahneman, 2005; Bateman, Kahneman et al., 2005). Ambiguity regarding how the income transfer would enter the analysis was reflected in the observation that some of the stakes in insurance or gambling contracts could be so modest that risk preferences, as manifested by the curvature of the utility or value function, could not plausibly explain the demand (Rabin 2000). Nevertheless, prospect theory represented a way of accommodating the ambiguity in both these issues through the variability of the reference points from which various insurance or gambling contracts are regarded.

Kőszegi and Rabin (2007) develop a model to show how the demand for insurance is dependent on the consumer's beliefs about the reference points from which the insurance decision would be evaluated. Like Barberis and Huang (2001) and Barberis, Huang, and Santos (2001) before them, Kőszegi and Rabin (2007) specify a utility function that is composed of two parts: consumption utility, which may have the conventional risk-averse shape for gains, and a gain-loss utility that reflects the loss aversion parameter of the prospect theory value function. For modest stake losses, the consumption utility is virtually linear, and so the gain-loss utility from the prospect theory value function alone determines the demand for insurance. If so, the demand for insurance would depend on the reference points that the consumer expects to occur with respect to the particulars of the insurance contract under consideration. Sometimes the difference between a reference (or expected) monetary amount and an actual monetary amount is planned, as would be the case with the purchase of a commodity, and so would generate no utility gain or loss. However, if the difference were unplanned, any surprise shortfall of money from the expectation would be evaluated according to the loss aversion parameter of prospect theory and generate a commensurate reduction in utility. For large stakes, these gain-loss utility differences are too small to matter, and so the demand for insurance depends almost entirely on the risk aversion of the consumption utility, reflecting the conventional theory. These authors give the following examples:

To illustrate implications for modest-scale risk, where consumption utility is approximately linear, consider a person's decision on whether to pay $55 to insure a 50 percent chance of having to pay $100. If she had expected to retain the status quo of $0, our model makes the same prediction as prospect theory: because of diminishing sensitivity, she does not wish to insure the risk. If she had expected to pay $55 for insurance, however, paying that amount generates no gain or loss, while taking the gamble exposes her to a fifty-fifty chance of losing $45 or gaining $55. With a conventional estimate of two-to-one loss aversion, she strongly dislikes this gamble and buys the insurance. Yet, if a person had been expecting risk to start with, paying $0 instead of $100 can decrease expected losses, and paying $100 might just decrease expected gains, so the gamble is less aversive. When the ex ante expected risk is the gamble itself, this decreased risk aversion can be interpreted as an endowment effect for risk. When the ex ante expected uncertainty is very large, $100 cannot much change the extent to which money is evaluated as a loss rather than a gain, so the person is close to risk neutral. (Kőszegi and Rabin 2007, 1048–1049)

Thus, by varying the reference points and the assumptions regarding the expectedness of the "loss," these authors are able to accommodate the ambiguous utility effects for both paying the insurance premium and receiving the insurance payoff.

Kőszegi and Rabin (2007) further illustrate their model by posing a series of gambles, and then showing (in their Table 1) how the different possible (expected) reference points would determine the different willingnesses to pay for insurance to cover the gamble. They use a specific risk-averse utility function for large stake insurance and specific gain-loss utility functions for modest stake insurance, assuming that the gain-loss component of demand reflects unplanned (surprise) differences. The authors show that for modest stakes, the willingness to pay for insurance against a gamble varies with the reference point expectation according to the gain-loss portion of utility alone. However, for large-stake gambles, even though both the consumption and gain-loss aspects of utility are included, the gain-loss aspect is so limited that demand for insurance is dominated by the risk aversion assumption from consumption utility. This means that for large scale stakes, Kőszegi and Rabin's model essentially devolves into the conventional theory, where only risk preferences, as manifested by diminishing marginal utility, matter.

For modest-stake insurance, their model has the advantage that it is flexible, but this is also a disadvantage because it can accommodate almost any behavior depending on the assumptions regarding the consumer's assumed reference point—or more accurately in their model, the assumptions regarding the consumer's distribution of expected reference points—and whether the consumer views the premium as a planned or unplanned expenditure. That is, the model can provide an explanation of any behavior depending on what is assumed about the consumer's expectations. Because the consumer's expectations are difficult to observe, making and testing predictions with this model is also difficult.

Even more fundamentally, for modest stakes, the specification of a consumer's expected reference point is critical, but one must then consider whether consumers have the sophistication to possess the expectations—and strong enough ones—to reasonably generate the demand for insurance under Kőszegi and Rabin's model. Indeed, it appears that the level of sophistication in understanding what to expect with insurance is not particularly great for a large portion of the insurance-buying population. Kunreuther et al. (1977) describe the low level of understanding that typical consumers in flood- and earthquake-prone regions have regarding premiums, deductibles, probabilities, likely monetary damages, and other information necessary to make an informed decisions regarding flood and earthquake insurance. Loewenstein et al. (2013) describe the limited numeracy and understanding of health insurance, finding, for example, that only 14 percent of respondents were able to choose the correct definition of deductibles, copays, coinsurance, and maximum out-of-pocket payment from multiple choice survey questions. Only 11 percent were able to understand such factors clearly enough to correctly answer a question about the effective cost of a hospitalization. Such a lack of consumer sophistication is apparent in the results of other studies of the understanding of health insurance that these authors review. If this lack of understanding is generally the case for all insurance, to move beyond simply regarding insurance as paying a premium in the status quo for additional income—or for the additional specific consumption which such income could buy—when some triggering event occurs would seem to require a level of sophistication that few among the insurance-buying public possess. In other words, the Kőszegi and Rabin (2007) model can explain the demand for insurance in a way that makes sense to economists, but it requires actual consumers to go beyond the standard quid pro quo transaction, an approach that the consumer would have become accustomed to after a lifetime of purchasing other commodities. For many if not most prospective consumers of insurance, such a departure from custom would seem unlikely.

Finally, in their theory, Kőszegi and Rabin's model the impact of the triggering event on insurance demand as being limited simply to specifying the probability with which the event occurs. There is no recognition that the event itself might alter the way in which an income transfer from insurance is evaluated. There is, for example, no recognition that becoming ill might alter the utility derived from the income intended for the consumption of medical care, or that becoming disabled might increase in the value of income that could now be obtained without having to work for it, or that becoming homeless through a house fire might increase value of income because of the new expenses for housing that are now added to the budget. Despite these issues and important omissions, the Kőszegi and Rabin (2007) model probably represents the current state-of-the-art manifestation of the conventional model of the demand for insurance.

Part 3: Quid Pro Quo Diagram

This part consists of one section that shows how the prospect theory diagram can be transformed into one that shows the demand for insurance under the quid pro quo theory.

The Quid Pro Quo Reinterpretation of Prospect Theory

Two diagrams represent the respecification of the quid pro quo model and parameters into the prospect theory context. These diagrams are capable of showing the demand for insurance for all three cases described in chapter 2: (1) an income transfer where there is no loss (e.g., health insurance), (2) an income transfer to cover a loss of income (e.g., unemployment insurance), and (3) an income or wealth transfer to cover the loss of an asset (e.g., homeowners insurance). These diagrams show the exchange of a certain premium payment for an expected total income payoff, rather than the exchange of an expected premium for an expected income transfer, and so include the payment and repayment of the premium through the insurance payoff, if the event occurs. In other words, they capture the comparison

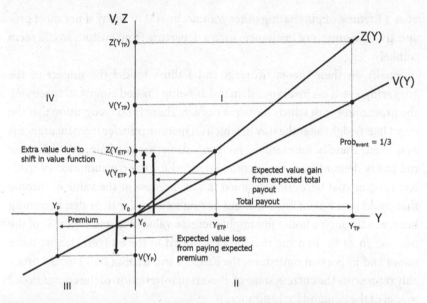

Figure 5.2 Demand for insurance with a linear value function of income

found in equation (2.8), which gives a complete accounting for the gain from insurance when the triggering event shifts utility.

In both Figures 5.2 and 5.3, the no event value function is represented by $V(Y)$ and the event value function by $Z(Y)$. Figure 5.2 represents the case of a modest increase in income where the value function is linear. Figure 5.3 represents the case of a large income transfer where the positive portion of the value function is increasing at a decreasing rate. In both cases, the premium is assumed to represent the same reduction of value as any planned consumer purchase. Also in both cases, the demand for insurance is captured by comparing the loss of value from paying the premium to the expected gain from the total insurance payout as evaluated by Z.

The insurance premium represents a loss of value, but one that would match a commensurate gain of value for income used for normal transactional purposes. Thus, the premium payment paid in the *ex ante* state is evaluated by an extension of the no event value function, V, into quadrant III of Figure 5.2. That is, the value function for the premium mirrors the portion of V in quadrant I that would be used to evaluate gains in income used in the purchase of normal commodities. The reduction of income to pay for the premium from the status quo, $(Y_P - Y_0)$, translates into a loss of value of $[V(Y_P) - V(Y_0)]$.

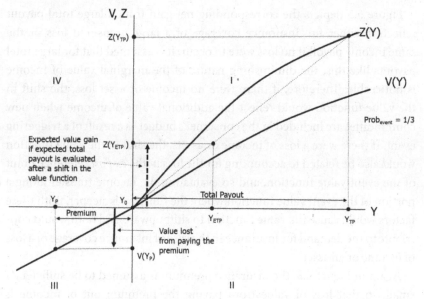

Figure 5.3 Demand for insurance with a curved value function for income

In Figure 5.2, if either a loss of income or a loss of an asset occurs, it is assumed that the insurer would pay the consumer a full-coverage payment to cover the entire uninsured loss, $(Y_{TP} - Y_0)$. This same income payoff is also assumed if no loss of Y occurred, as in the case of health insurance or an annuity. Y_0 can therefore represent either the status quo reference income, if insurance that does not involve a loss, or a reference point on the event value function after a loss is accounted for, if insurance involves a loss of either income or wealth. Note that even if there were an increase in value because of an event, a Z value function would still be based at the origin, consistent with the prospect theory tenet that only changes from the reference point matter.

Gains from the income payoff in the *ex post* period are evaluated by the event value function, Z. The expected income gain from the total insurance income payout is $\pi(Y_{TP} - Y_0)$, the same as the premium payment, $(Y_P - Y_0)$, for this assumed actuarially fair insurance. The expected value gain is $[Z(Y_{TP}) - Z(Y_0)]$. Because the expected value of the gain from the income payoff with insurance is greater than the value loss from paying the premium, $[Z(Y_{TP}) - Z(Y_0)] > |[V(Y_P) - V(Y_0)]|$, insurance would be purchased. The additional expected value from evaluating insurance after the triggering event has shifted the V function is represented by the upward pointing dashed arrow.

Figure 5.3 depicts the corresponding net gain from a large total payout reflecting either full insurance coverage of a large uninsured loss or the same income payoff if no loss were to occur. It is assumed that for large total payouts like this, the diminishing nature of the marginal value of income is noticeable. Therefore, if there were no income or asset loss, the shift in the value function would reflect the additional value of income when new commodities are included in the consumer's budget as a result of a triggering event. If there were a loss of income or assets, the shift in the value function would also be related to accounting for the loss in the *ex post* reference point of the event value function, and so evaluating the income transfer along a portion of the event value function where the function is steeper. Both these factors would cause the value function to shift upward and both would contribute to the demand for insurance in the case of insurance coverage of a loss of income or an asset.

Again in Figure 5.3, the insurance premium is assumed to be sufficiently small, so that loss of value from paying the premium out of income is represented by a function with no apparent curvature. Therefore, the loss of value from paying the premium is similar to the loss of value as was shown in Figure 5.2.

In Figure 5.3, because the expected value of the gain from the total income payout with insurance is greater than the value lost from the payment of the premium, $[Z(Y_{ETP}) - Z(Y_0)] > |[V(Y_p) - V(Y_0)]|$, insurance would be purchased. The upward pointing dashed arrow represents the expected value generated by the expected income payout after the shifting in the value function. This length of this arrow exceeds the length of the downward pointing solid arrow representing the loss of value from paying the premium.

Summary

In this chapter, the experimental work supporting prospect theory was reviewed to show that risk preferences worked exactly opposite to the way they were assumed to work under the conventional theory. This and other empirical work on the relationship between measures of risk preference and the actual purchase of insurance raises the issue of whether risk preferences matter at all in understanding the demand for insurance. This is important because in comparison, the quid pro quo theory generates a demand for insurance without any motivation from risk preferences.

Also in this chapter, prospect theory was introduced. Prospect theory is important because it is the basis for most of the recent revisions of the conventional model of the demand for insurance. For example, Kőszegi and Rabin's (2007) model of the demand for insurance is built on a combination of Friedman and Savage (1948) risk aversion, prospect theory value function parameters, and prospect theory reference points. In addition, their model also incorporates the assumption that the value function could be linear for modest income payoffs. Kőszegi and Rabin's (2007) work is important because it appears to represent the current state of the art reformulation of the conventional model.

While their model may make sense to economists, it seems unreasonably complex as a description of how consumers would actually think about the decision to purchase insurance. This is because it assumes that insurance buyers have in mind a distribution of possible reference points and that these reference points would interact with various assumptions regarding how the premiums and insurance payouts are evaluated to generate a distribution of demands for insurance. Given what we know about the level of knowledge and sophistication possessed by the typical purchaser of insurance, it seems unlikely that consumers would generally be able to manage such an approach.

In this chapter, the quid pro quo theory is presented in the context of the prospect theory diagram and is shown to be much less complex. It assumes that, if insurance is purchased, the insurance premium would be evaluated in the same way that the consumer would evaluate any planned purchase of a consumer commodity. The income payoff could be modest and so the consumer might not recognize its value as diminishing. If so, the demand for insurance would be attributed entirely to the increase in the marginal value of income now that the demands for new commodities are included in the consumer's budget. Alternatively, the payoff could be so large that the consumer would recognize that the value of additional income is diminishing. If so, the demand for insurance would be attributed the same new commodity demands, plus a possible change in the basis from which the function is evaluated, if the triggering change in state also implied a loss of income.

A quid pro quo approach is more likely to reflect how consumers actually view the purchase for insurance because it is similar to the way consumers purchase most other commodities in a market economy. That is, consumers are accustomed to transactions where they weigh the costs they pay, against the value of what they receive. With insurance, the cost is the premium, and the payoff received might be in terms of either commodities (for example, a medical procedure or a car repair) or dollars (for example, income, in the case of unemployment insurance). The key extension represented by the quid pro quo model is that the consumer would evaluate these new commodities or additional dollars of income as being received in the state of the world that triggered their payment.

Admittedly, evaluating contingent commodities accurately is, in many cases, difficult. Can the consumer really imagine the value of all the various healthcare procedures covered by health insurance in the event of the various illnesses? Nevertheless, it seems clear that the broad implications of the changes in states can be understood by consumers and are likely to be factored into whether and how much consumers would value medical procedures, car repairs, unemployment payments, or any of the other insurance payoffs that are contingent on the occurrence of an important, and often dramatic, change in state. The effect of this change in state on the value of the insured commodity is missing from the conventional insurance demand model or any of the models that have been modified according to prospect theory. This suggests that the quid pro quo approach provides a more complete understanding of the demand for insurance.

There remain two other potential sources of value that could increase the demand for insurance. One is loss aversion, and this source of additional demand is addressed next in chapter 6. The second source is related to the difference between an insurance payoff in income, compared to the recovery of a specific commodity that the consumer had voluntarily purchased. This issue is addressed in chapter 8 when the impact of insurance on the consumer surplus is more broadly discussed.

6

The Role of Loss Aversion in Insurance

Introduction

One of the important findings from the empirical work in support of prospect theory is the result that losses are more important than gains to the consumer. This finding is reflected in value functions that show diminishing sensitivity for both gains and losses, but that are steeper for losses than for gains. In chapter 5, the impact of loss aversion on the insurance premium was considered. It was suggested that, if insurance is actually purchased, those consumers who purchase insurance are unlikely to have viewed the premium as a prospect theory loss with loss aversion. Thus, variation in the demand for insurance may be due to whether consumers view the premium payment as an unexpected loss or as the planned or expected payment of a *quid* for some *quo* in a standard market transaction.

It was also suggested that, because insurance is viewed more like a quid pro quo exchange than a standard gamble choice, the loss associated with some insurance contracts may be instrumental in increasing the value of the income payoff. That is, additional income that is paid in the context of a loss or perceived loss may be more valued by consumers than it would be without such a loss. This effect would be in addition to the effect of the loss in changing the reference point from which the income payoff is evaluated. In this role, loss aversion could contribute to the demand for insurance.

In the present chapter, empirical evidence is reviewed to determine whether loss aversion has had an effect on the demand for insurance, either negatively through the payment of the insurance premium or positively through the income payout. However, before reviewing these studies, this chapter lays out the context of this research by reviewing (1) the empirical and theoretical evidence that shows that loss aversion is distinct from risk aversion, (2) the theoretical papers that suggest various reasons for the existence of loss aversion, and (3) the studies that describe the ways in which loss aversion has been measured.

A Theory of Insurance and Gambling. John A. Nyman, Oxford University Press. © Oxford University Press 2024.
DOI: 10.1093/oso/9780197687925.003.0006

Loss Aversion Versus Risk Aversion

The concept of loss aversion is part of prospect theory, and as was shown in Figure 5.1, is captured in the relative steepness of the loss portion of the prospect theory value function, compared to the gain portion. Assuming that the value function is represented by the following form,

$$V(Y) = \begin{cases} -\lambda Y^\alpha, Y < 0 \\ Y^\alpha, Y \geq 0 \end{cases} \tag{6.1}$$

the parameter, λ, represents the loss aversion coefficient. From their empirical work, Tversky and Kahneman (1979) estimate these parameters as $\alpha = 0.88$ and $\lambda = 2.25$. This means that the effect of an unexpected loss of $100 in reducing value is over twice as great as the effect of a gain of $100 in increasing value. Thus, losses and gains have profoundly different effects on value.

The other parameter that Tversky and Kahneman (1979) estimate, α, captures the "diminishing sensitivity" characteristic of the both sides of the prospect theory value function. This parameter represents an estimate of the diminishing marginality of the two parts of the value function and, in conventional theory, is the sole source of the demand for insurance from risk aversion. However, for modest losses, Rabin (2000) and others suggest these functions must be linear, and so diminishing sensitivity cannot generate risk aversion and a demand for insurance. This raises the question whether loss aversion can generate a demand for insurance independently of risk aversion.

For this to be the case, it must be clear that loss aversion and risk aversion are different phenomena. One way to investigate this issue is to determine whether loss aversion exists in both riskless and risky situations. In their study investigating the value of the premium, Novemsky and Kahneman (2005) also test whether there is a difference between the experimental subject's willingness to accept in the sale (representing a loss) of a commodity when the queries are presented to subjects in a risky frame or a riskless frame. They find that there is little difference between the payment consumers are willingness to accept to make a risky sale of a commodity and the payment consumers are willingness to accept to make a riskless sale of the same commodity. Thus, they conclude that "there is no risk aversion beyond loss aversion" (Novemsky and Kahneman 2005, 123). They caution, however, that this finding is dependent on the amount of income payment (representing the loss) being relatively modest in size. Similarly, in the companion "adversarial collaboration," Bateman, Kahneman, et al. (2005) also find no significant differences between the payments that consumers are willing to accept for losses of commodities that are either certain or uncertain.

Gächter, Johnson, and Herrmann (2022) investigate the same issue using a random sample of 660 Austrian, German, and Swiss nonstudent car purchasers. Their study design asks respondents to complete a questionnaire regarding their willingness to accept and willingness to pay for a low-value commodity (a toy car) in both riskless and risky frames. They find that 82 percent of their respondents exhibited an endowment effect when presented with a riskless choice, and 71 percent exhibited one with the risky choice. Their estimates for the median loss aversion coefficients were $\lambda = 1.73$ for the riskless frame, and between $\lambda = 1.15$ and $\lambda = 1.50$ for the risky frame. These coefficients were positively correlated across the two frames. Although there are differences, the authors conclude that these findings again suggest that risk preferences are largely irrelevant in explaining the consumers' aversion to losses.

Tversky and Kahneman (1991) investigate the existence of loss aversion in a riskless model of consumer behavior and describe how loss aversion can shift indifference curves and utility functions. As an ultimate justification for the existence of loss aversion, they write, "The asymmetry of pain and pleasure is the ultimate justification of loss aversion in choice. Because of this asymmetry a decision maker who seeks to maximize the experienced utility of outcomes is well advised to assign greater weight to negative than to positive outcomes" (Tversky and Kahneman, 1991, 1057). Thus, for these authors, loss aversion is a primal human emotion that is independent of risk aversion.

In a quid pro quo transaction like the purchase of an insurance contract, the consumer could experience loss as either (1) the premium required to purchase the contract or (2) the loss that triggered the income transfer. The impact of loss aversion on the former would diminish the demand for insurance while the impact of loss aversion on the latter would likely increase demand. The issue with the theory of demand for insurance, therefore, is understanding where loss aversion has the greater impact. To better understand where this impact might be greatest, it is also important to understand the theoretical sources that have been suggested for loss aversion.

Theoretical Sources of Loss Aversion

In addition to the asymmetry of the utility from pain and pleasure, a number of specific behaviors have been identified to explain the consumers' aversion to losses. Some researchers have focused on an *endowment effect* as a manifestation of loss aversion (Thaler 1980; Knetsch and Sinden 1984; 1987; Knetsch 1989; Kahneman, Knetsch, and Thaler 1990; 1991). The endowment effect is demonstrated in studies that find that the amount consumers are willing to accept when selling a commodity is greater than the amount consumers are willing to pay when buying the same commodity. One of the early studies of the subject gave the following example:

> A wine-loving economist we know purchased some nice Bordeaux wines years ago at low prices. The wines have greatly appreciated in value, so that a bottle that cost only $10 when purchased would now fetch $200 at auction. This economist now drinks some of this wine occasionally, but would neither be willing to sell the wine at the auction price nor buy an additional bottle at that price. (Kahneman, Knetsch, and Thaler 1991, 194)

The above example may also reflect another interpretation of the same phenomenon—a *status quo bias*—which suggests that consumers have a preference for remaining in their current situation and therefore have a bias against both buying and selling. The status quo bias was first identified by Samuelson and Zeckhauser (1988), and has now been studied by others in a number of different situations (e. g., Hartman, Doane, and Woo 1991). Both the endowment effect and the status quo bias suggest that consumers have a more intense emotional or psychological reaction to losses than to gains.

The desire to avoid *disappointment* may also contribute to a consumer's aversion to losses (Bell 1985; Loomes and Sugden 1986). Disappointment can be thought of as "a psychological reaction to an outcome that does not match up to expectations" (Bell 1985, 1). The more desired are the expectations, the greater is the disappointment. Disappointment can motivate the same behavior as has been explained traditionally using conventional risk-aversion theory. As Bell writes,

> If you accept a 50–50 gamble between $0 and $2,000, there is a chance that you will be disappointed when the lottery is resolved. You may prefer to swap the lottery ticket for a sure $950 not so much because of arguments

about decreasing marginal value, but because doing so removes the possibility of disappointment. (Bell 1985, 1)

The desire to avoid *regret* was identified a few years earlier by the same two
pioneering research groups (Bell 1982; 1983; Loomes and Sugden 1982) and
is similar to disappointment. The difference is that regret is not caused by
comparing an outcome to expectations, but by comparing a choice that was
made to the actual outcome that occurred. In the earlier example, if the consumer had chosen the 50–50 lottery over the $950 and the outcome of the
lottery was $0, the consumer would regret not having chosen the $950. The
desire to avoid disappointment or regret may make potential losses more im-
pactful than gains, and reinforce the demand for insurance.

Hsee and Kunreuther (2000) suggest that there can be extraordinary
feelings of attachment to inanimate objects, thus making their loss especially
aversive. As an early illustration of this effect, Adam Smith observed:

> A man grows fond of a snuff-box, of a pen-knife, of a staff which he has long
> made use of, and conceives something like real love and affection for them.
> If he breaks or loses them, he is vexed all out of proportion to the value of
> the damage. The house which we have long lived in, the tree whose verdure
> and shade we have long enjoyed, are both looked upon with a sort of respect
> that seems due to such benefactors. The decay of the one, or the ruin of the
> other, affects us with a kind of melancholy through we should sustain no
> [financial] loss by it. (Smith [1759] 1966, 136–137])

In their experimental study, Hsee and Kunreuther (2000) find evidence
that the demand for insurance increases when this effect is present in the
insured commodity and call this an *affection effect*. In a subsequent piece,
Kunreuther and Pauly (2005) point to affection, along with disappointment
and regret, as generating an "adjusted value" of the loss that would increase
the demand for insurance. According to these authors, factors such as these
would lead to a search for insurance policies with greater or more complete
coverage. They suggest that "in effect, this approach attaches an additional
value to the object and asks what would be rational insurance purchasing
when the loss of the object means more than just the loss of its monetary
value" (Kunreuther and Pauly 2005, 86). Thus, their adjustment for loss aversion appears to include a parameter for loss aversion that would change the
function itself.

The psychology literature identifies a number of additional factors that might either cause loss aversion or cause a moderation of the effect of loss aversion if it exists. Some studies attribute loss aversion to factors such as memory, attention, or selective information processing. These factors seem similar in origin to the framing differences found to be important in some of the original experiments conducted by Kahneman and Tversky (1979). For example, Johnson, Häubl, and Keinan (2007) show that what an individual thinks of first in a transaction may determine the value that they place on a good. Those who possess a commodity may tend to think first of value-enhancing considerations and thus the negative consequences of not having the good. Those who do not possess the commodity may think first of the value-reducing considerations, such as the alternative commodities that could be purchased with the same money. This would lead those who possess a commodity to place a higher value on it than those who do not possess it.

Mrkva et al. (2019) review the psychological motivations for loss aversion, and the ways in which these motivations can be modified, if they exist. These authors suggest that providing more information on the commodity, or educating the consumers and sellers on the characteristics of the commodity, can modify loss aversion. In their empirical analysis, they find that individuals who have less knowledge or experience with a commodity are more loss aversive. They also find that older and less educated respondents are more loss aversive. These authors conclude that how consumers view the insurance decision matters importantly in determining the demand for insurance.

The motivation to cancel or avoid a loss could manifest itself in either the insurance income payout or the premium. For the income payout, these theories suggest that, because of factors like endowment, status quo, disappointment, regret, and affection, the acquisition of additional income that occurs in the context of a loss may generate additional demand for insurance than the acquisition of additional income without a loss. For the premium, these theories suggest that the payment of the premium itself might be subject to loss aversion through the endowment, status quo, or affection effects. The premium might, however, be less responsive to regret or disappointment effects because the loss could only be imagined in the *ex ante* period when the premium is being paid and before the *ex post* outcome is known.

Measuring Loss Aversion

If the parameter, α, measuring the degree of diminishing sensitivity in equation 6.1, is the same for both the negative and positive portions of the prospect theory value function, then the parameter, λ, measures the sole difference between these portions of the value function. As indicated earlier, this parameter has been estimated to be λ = 2.25 by Tversky and Kahneman (1992), which means that on average, consumers generally are over twice as averse to losses as they are attracted to gains. Consumers, however, may differ with regard to their level of loss aversion. Thus, the greater the value of λ is for a consumer, the greater would be the consumer's reaction to losses compared to the consumer's reaction to gains.

Fehr and Goette (2007) derive a measure of loss aversion based the assumption of a risk-neutral prospect theory value function, that is, one where α = 1 in equation 6.1, consistent with Rabin's (2000) contention that the utility function for small stakes gambles is, for all practicable purposes, linear. They present their subjects with a choice between accepting gamble A: win Y = CHF8 (CHFs are Swiss francs) with probability 0.5 or lose Y = CHF5 with probability 0.5; or rejecting gamble A. If their subjects reject gamble A, they receive CHF0. Assuming that the reference points for both changes are the status quo, the respondent's expected value (V) if they reject the gamble must be consistent with:

$$0.5[V(-5)] + 0.5V(8) \leq V(0) \tag{6.2}$$

According to equation 6.1, this simplifies to

$$0.5(-5\lambda) + 0.5(8) \leq 0 \tag{6.3}$$

$$\lambda \geq 8/5 \tag{6.4}$$

Thus, the consumer would reject the gamble if his or her loss aversion parameter, λ, were greater than or equal to CHF1.6. That is, because the consumer who rejects this gamble would be giving up a chance for an expected gain of CHF1.6, it shows that the effect of loss aversion on his or her value function must be at least 1.6 or higher.

In their study, Fehr and Goette (2007) also present their subjects with a similar choice between accepting gamble B: 6 independent repetitions of gamble A; or rejecting B. If their subjects reject gamble B, they receive CHF0. Using the 7th row of Pascal's Triangle to determine the probabilities for the 7 different binary combinations of wins and losses possible after 6 repetitions, Gamble B would be rejected if

$$(1/64)[V(-30)] + 6/64[V(-17)] + (15/64)[V(-4)] + (20/64)V(9)$$
$$+(15/64)V(22) + (6/64)V(35) + (1/64)V(48) \leq V(0) \qquad (6.5)$$

which simplifies to

$$(1/64)(-30\lambda)] + 6/64(-17\lambda) + (15/64)(-4\lambda) + (20/64)(9)$$
$$+(15/64)(22) + (6/64)(35) + (1/64)(48) \leq 0 \qquad (6.6)$$

$$\lambda \geq 4 \qquad (6.7)$$

This means that respondents' loss aversion can be classified according to whether they would accept or reject these 2 gambles. The consumers with the greatest loss aversion are those who reject B (it is assumed that if you reject B you would also reject A because A has a smaller expected value than B), a middle category of loss aversion is represented by those consumers who accept B but reject A, and the consumers with the least loss aversion are those who accept A (again it is assumed that if you accept A, you would also accept B because B has a higher expected value than A). So those who reject neither have a loss aversion parameter between 0 and 1.6 (that is, $0 \leq \lambda < 1.6$), those who reject A and accept B have one between 1.6 and 4 (that is, $1.6 \leq \lambda < 4$) and those who reject both have one greater than 4 (that is, $\lambda \geq 4$). Thus, with the answers to these two questions, three categories of loss aversion can be distinguished in consumers. Note that this method determines a range of values, rather than a single value, for λ for each respondent.

This method has been used to construct loss aversion parameters that vary according to a series of gambles and that do not necessarily assume that the value function is linear. For example, Gächter, Johnson, and Herrmann (2021) pose the following question to their subjects along with the information in Table 6.1:

In the following table you find a list of coin tosses with different payoffs. The payoffs differ in how much you lose if the coin turns up heads. For each row you need to indicate whether you want to toss the coin or not. To determine your payoff, one of the six rows will be randomly selected by rolling a six-sided die. If you have determined that for the randomly selected row you want to toss the coin, then the coin will be tossed, and you will be paid accordingly. (Gächter, Johnson, and Herrmann 2021, np)

These authors use the answers to these questions and the methods of Fehr and Goette (2007) to generate a table of median values for λ, based on various assumptions regarding diminishing sensitivities and also probability weighting. Their weights, corresponding to the assumptions of a linear value function with no probability weighting, are listed in Table 6.2.

Table 6.1 Questionnaire from Gächter, Johnson, and Hermann (2021)

	I don't want to toss the coin	I want to toss the coin
1. If the coin turns up heads, then you lose €2; if the coin turns up tails, you win €6.	( )	( )
2. If the coin turns up heads, then you lose €3; if the coin turns up tails, you win €6.	( )	( )
3. If the coin turns up heads, then you lose €4; if the coin turns up tails, you win €6.	( )	( )
4. If the coin turns up heads, then you lose €5; if the coin turns up tails, you win €6.	( )	( )
5. If the coin turns up heads, then you lose €6; if the coin turns up tails, you win €6.	( )	( )
6. If the coin turns up heads, then you lose €2; if the coin turns up tails, you win €7.	( )	( )

Table 6.2 Loss aversion weights from Gächter, Johnson, and Herrmann (2021)

Acceptance choices	Max acceptable loss	λ from the last acceptable loss before switching to reject	Loss at midpoint of range	λ
Reject all lotteries	< 2€	> 3.00	< €2	> 3.00
Accept 1, reject 2–6	€2	3.00	€2.5	2.40
Accept 1–2, reject 3–6	€3	2.00	€3.5	1.71
Accept 1–3, reject 4–6	€4	1.50	€4.5	1.33
Accept 1–4, reject 5–6	€5	1.20	€5.5	1.09
Accept 1–5, reject 6	€6	1.00	€6.5	0.92
Accept all lotteries	€7	≤ 0.86	≥ €7.0	≤ 0.86

This approach appears to represent a promising way to measure independently the consumer's aversion to losses.

An alternative measure of loss aversion that is more straight-forward is the ratio of the willingness to accept to the willingness to pay, or WTA/WTP (Mrkva et al. 2019). As this ratio increases across individuals, the degree of loss aversion would also increase. Such a parameter would require that WTA and WTP data exist for the same individuals. One advantage of this measure is that it cannot be conflated with preferences for risk since it is not constructed from data on whether gambles with uncertain outcomes would be accepted.

Loss Aversion and the Demand for Insurance

The quid pro quo model suggests that, instead of risk preferences, the demand for insurance more likely depends on how the consumer regards changes in income. In the quid pro quo model, changes in income are represented by both payment of the insurance premium and receipt of the income payout. As mentioned earlier, the aversion to losses can manifest itself either as an aversion to the loss (payment) of the insurance premium itself, or as the context with which the income payoff from the insurer is received, that is, whether it is received in the context of a loss or not. In chapter 5, it was shown that whether the consumers tend to regard the premium as an aversive loss or as a normal payment in a transaction is not clear (Novemsky and Kahneman 2005; Bateman, Kaheman et al., 2005). And, as indicated above, some have suggested that loss aversion might increase the demand for insurance either by altering the perception of the gain from the income transfer (Kunreuther and Pauly 2005 or by some other mechanism (Sydnor 2010; O'Donoghue and Somerville 2018).

In this section, we turn to the empirical studies to see if there are any dominant trends to how loss aversion might affect the demand for insurance. We investigate both how loss aversion impacts the demand for various types of insurance, and whether the way in which the insurance transaction is presented to the consumer—whether it emphasizes the gains or the losses—affects demand. This is a fledgling literature, so it would be easy to overstate the importance of its findings. Nevertheless, it provides some notable clues to the relationship between the aversion to losses and the demand for insurance. The first five studies reviewed—two empirical and three theoretical—investigate the direct effect of the consumer's loss aversion on their demand for insurance.

Nagy et al. (2020) investigate the effect of loss aversion on the purchase of *life insurance* using a sample of 364 Romanian and Hungarian adults in 2018. The dependent variable was a likert scale indicating how determined the respondent was to purchase a life insurance contract in the next year. Loss aversion was constructed from information on whether the respondent would accept a series of 50–50 wagers where the gain if heads was fixed at 6 euros and the loss if tails varied from 7 euros to 1 euro. The respondents were asked to accept or reject each wager and the authors then use the gain (G) and loss (L) of the first accepted wager to construct a loss aversion parameter, λ, for each respondent. They used the parameters from Kahneman and Tversky (1991) in their calculation:

$$\lambda = 0.933 \, (G/L)^{0.88} \tag{6.8}$$

The authors find that an increase in this loss aversion variable significantly decreased the likelihood of purchasing life insurance, holding constant other variables, suggesting that loss aversion works mainly through the premium. In their analysis, the authors include a *risk* aversion variable, which had a much smaller coefficient in their regression equation and was never significant. They conclude from their analysis that "loss aversion appears much more significant than risk aversion in the insurance decision" (Nagy et al. 2020, 978).

Huang (2021) also investigated the relationship between loss aversion and demand for insurance. This author used the RAND American Life Survey, where just over 600 respondents in 2012 and 2013 also completed questionnaires that contained the questions on whether the respondent would accept a series of gain or loss coin-toss wagers (Carvalho, Meier, and Wang 2016). These data were then used to construct a measure of loss aversion parameter based on the Fehr and Goette (2007) approach. Huang found that this variable was negatively and significantly associated with the demand for (that is, the ownership of) both *long-term care insurance* and *supplemental disability insurance*. For *automobile insurance*, however, this variable was positive but not significant, no doubt reflecting the mandatory nature of this demand. Because long-term care and supplemental disability insurance are owned by less than 10 percent and less than 20 percent of the American Life Survey respondents, respectively, this assumed aversion to premium losses may help to explain at least some of the lack of demand for these types of insurance.

A number of simulation studies show the effect of loss aversion on hypothetical insurance demand. The conclusions of these modeling studies, unlike the empirical ones, depend on the assumptions that the authors incorporate in their models. In the case of *annuities*, because there is no asset loss to consider and instead a large premium investment that could be considered a loss if the policyholder died early, Hu and Scott (2007) find that "loss aversion always reduces the attractiveness of annuities" (Hu and Scott 2007, 75). Regarding the voluntary acceptance of higher deductibles in *health insurance* in the Netherlands, Van Winssen, Van Kleef, and Van de Ven (2016) consider the reluctance of Netherlanders to voluntarily accept higher deductibles, even though they would benefit from it financially. They assume that loss aversion can only be a factor when the premium is viewed as a loss and the income transfers from the insurer as a gain. However, because consumers are also assumed to consider the deductible an aversive loss, they find that "loss aversion is only expected to make insured [consumers] forego voluntary [higher] deductibles" (Van Winssen, Van Kleef, and Van de Ven 2016, 1065). Thus, loss aversion is associated with greater insurance coverage because of increasing the value of the income payoff. Babcock (2015) finds, using a Monte Carlo analysis, that the presence of loss aversion reduces the expected gain from *crop insurance*, compared to when loss aversion is not present. Not surprisingly, this analysis found that, when the insurance premium is regarded as a sunk cost and so not considered, loss aversion increases the demand for crop insurance dramatically.

These studies seem to indicate that the presence of loss aversion is mostly associated with a decrease in the demand for insurance because the consumer does not want to lose the premium payment. This last study also raises the question of whether the loss aversion is subject to a framing effect. That is, does providing the consumer with additional information on how the loss is or should be treated in insurance influence the demand for that insurance? This issue has been addressed in four existing studies.

Brown et al. (2008) observed that few consumers in the US convert their retirement savings into *annuities*, and investigated how changing the frame of the insurance problem would affect the experimental choice between purchasing an annuity and purchasing one of the consumer's other financial options with actuarially equivalent payoffs. Some of their 1,342 internet-based respondents were presented with a description of the annuity using an investment frame, where the $100,000 payment for the annuity had the potential to be lost upon death so that the return on the investment was uncertain, and others using a consumption frame, where $100,000 was paid in order to receive a certain level of consumption over the consumer's remaining lifetime. Comparing the choice between an annuity and a savings account with actuarially equivalent returns, only 21 percent chose the annuity when presented with the investment frame, but 72 percent chose the annuity when presented with the consumption frame.

In interpreting their findings, the authors focus on the difference between the annuity generating *risky* investment returns and annuity generating *predictable* consumption. Because there is risk in both frames, an alternative loss aversion explanation seems just as reasonable and, perhaps, more likely. That is, in the investment frame, the annuity represented a $100,000 investment that could be lost if the consumer died, while in the consumption frame, the annuity was a transaction that cost $100,000 but paid out a certain amount of income every year of subsequent life until death. An aversion to losses might have weighted the initial $100,000 payment more than the benefit from the income gain in the investment frame, but weighted the income gain in the event of a loss more than the possible loss of a $100,000 premium in the consumption frame. Thus, loss aversion might contribute to the demand for insurance depending on how the transaction is framed.

Kunreuther and Pauly (2018) designed an experiment where the impact of loss aversion on demand for insurance is direct and obvious. In the experiment, subjects are asked to decide whether to purchase *home insurance* for a low probability, high consequence event, like the possible property loss from a hurricane. The subjects decide to purchase insurance or not in each of 10 periods, and the subjects are told up front that they have a 1/25 chance of a loss of US$50,000 damage in every period. About one-third of the subjects are told that they experienced a loss in period 2 and another third in period 8. The rest did not experience a loss. Of the 1,346 subjects, 60 percent said they would purchase insurance in all 10 periods, and 9 percent said they would never purchase insurance. For the 31 percent that switched, a higher percentage of those who experienced a loss in periods 2 and 8 switched to insurance than those who did not experience a loss in periods 2 and 8. This suggests that the reluctance to purchasing insurance may be related to being able to visualize or understand the benefits of insurance against a loss. If so, loss aversion would contribute positively to the demand for insurance.

Gottlieb and Mitchell (2019) note that the take up rate in the US for private *long-term care insurance* is only about 8 percent, and investigate whether a consumer's responsiveness to how decisions are framed affects their demand for this insurance. Using a special version of the 2012 Health and Retirement Survey (HRS), they use a question similar to the classic prospect theory question used by Kahneman and Tversky (1979) and described in chapter 5 to investigate impact of framing on the preference for solutions to the presence of a new Asian disease. Those who gave different and loss aversive answers for the two frames were regarded as "narrow framing" consumers, compared to those who gave consistent answers. It was predicted that narrow framing consumers would have lower demand for insurance through a presumed aversion to losses. In an alternative analysis, the authors included a risk aversion variable that had been collected in the HRS in 2006 and before (Barsky et al. 1997), but doing so reduced their sample from 1,699 to only those 514 who were also in the HRS at that time. The authors included loss aversion variables constructed using the Fehr and Goette (2007) approach. These variables were entered as seven dummy variables that were increasing in loss aversion compared to the excluded (and lowest) loss aversion level.

Gottlieb and Mitchell (2019) found that narrow framing respondents— those who chose to avert losses but embrace gains, even though they represented the same result, and were deemed to be loss aversive as a result— had significantly smaller demand for long-term care insurance, compared to those respondents who viewed the two frames consistently. The loss aversion variables tended to be significant and negatively predictive of the demand for long-term care insurance at low levels of loss aversion (compared to the lowest), but positively predictive and insignificantly so at the higher levels of loss aversion (again, compared to the lowest). Both the framing and loss aversion findings suggest that loss aversion was influencing the demand for insurance mostly through emphasizing the premium cost.

Lampe and Würtenberger (2020) present an analysis of a randomized control trial where a portion of 941 farmers in India were provided education about insurance and others were not. Whether the farmers actually purchased *index insurance* was the dependent variable representing insurance demand. Index insurance is a type of crop insurance that pays off if rainfall is too low in the farmer's area. The authors want to explain why the take-up rate for this insurance is so low, at about 20 percent. They hypothesized that those who received education about how insurance worked would be more likely to overcome any loss aversion (with regard to the premium) and purchase insurance because they would not regard insurance as an investment and be disappointed if they did not receive an indemnity payment if a loss did not occur. They construct a loss aversion variable from information on a series of Binswanger (1980) lotteries, where the least loss averse option is a coin toss where the respondent wins INR25 (INRs are Indian rupees) if heads and INR25 if tails, and the other gambles represent possible lower gain/higher gain combinations.[1] The loss aversion coefficient is constructed according the Fehr and Goette (2007) methods. They find that loss aversion is negatively and significantly related to the demand for index insurance, but when the dummy education variable is interacted with loss aversion, the coefficient becomes positive and significant.

These studies suggest that, while loss aversion initially plays a demand-decreasing role, the addition of framing and "education" can, however, work to convert loss aversion into a demand-increasing factor. Thus, loss aversion can play both negative and positive roles in determining the demand for insurance. None of these studies have attempted to evaluate the importance of loss aversion compared to the other factors that have been used to explain the demand for insurance. The next two studies attempt to both show the effect of loss aversion on demand and evaluate it compared with other demand motives.

In an experimental study, Jaspersen, Ragin, and Sydnor (2022) presented 1,730 subjects with risk and loss attitude questions and choices over insurance products. Regarding the risk and loss attitudes, they collected information on each of their subject's preferences for various lotteries and used that information to calculate the following prospect theory parameters: (1) curvature of the positive portion of the value function (their variable UC+), (2) curvature of the negative potion of the value function (UC–), (3) probability weighting of the positive portion of the value function (PW+), (4) probability weighting of the negative portion of the value function (PW–), (5) the loss aversion factor (LA), and (6) a measure of the preference for certainty (CP). For each subject, they then determined coverage levels that would be purchased for 12 different insurance products.

---

[1] Binswanger lotteries are those where the respondent cannot lose. An example would be a coin-toss lottery where the respondent wins €3 if heads and €6 if tails. The advantage of such lotteries is that, because the respondent never actually loses, they can be used to elicit preferences of poor people.

Jaspersen, Ragin, and Sydnor (2022) regressed the insurance coverage levels chosen by their subjects on the six explanatory and a number of other variables in a fixed-effects analysis. They found that the loss aversion (LA) variable increased demand for insurance and was consistently significant across both their nonparametric and parametric specifications, indicating that loss aversion probably worked through reinforcing the value of the income payout. The risk-related variables showed mixed results. Consistent with probability weighting theory, the PW- variable was correlated with insurance demand at both the low and high probability levels, and the PW+ variable decreased demand significantly for high probabilities, but was not significant at low probabilities. The degree of curvature in the positive portion of the value function, UC+, significantly increased demand, but only in the parametric specification.[2] The variables measuring a preference for certainty, CP, and the curvature of the negative portion of the value function, UC−, were not significantly predictive of the demand for insurance.

These authors note, however, that all the estimated significant coefficients are modest in scale. Interestingly, even though this study is conducted thoughtfully and carefully, these authors also go on to suggest that the experimental approach to determining risk preferences is unreliable. They conclude: "Our results are consistent with the message that, while some underlying component seems to exist, insurance choices are not obviously governed by a simple model of risk preferences" (Jaspersen, Ragin, and Sydnor 2022, 67).

It should be pointed out that a number of similar studies come to similar conclusions regarding the instability of risk preferences and their lack of importance in determining demand for insurance, although they do not specifically investigate the role of loss aversion on insurance demand (e.g., Barseghyan, Prince, and Teitelbaum 2011; Harrison and Ng 2016; Collier et al. 2022).

Finally, surveys of the motives for purchasing insurance are rare, and those that pose questions consistent with the alternative motives suggested by economic theory are even rarer. A recent survey of insurance-purchasing

---

[2] The important differences between the parametric and nonparametric approaches were that in the parametric approach, (1) 454 of the 1,730 subjects who did not seem to be attentive based on an earlier question were excluded (which did not seem to matter) and (2) the parametric structure imposed a nonlinear transformation on the data (which apparently did seem to matter). The latter transformation was not used in the nonparametric analysis where the variables used to determine the curvature of the value function were only related to the riskiness of the lottery that was chosen by the subjects.

respondents from six European countries asked them to indicate which of a series of general reasons for purchasing each of six different types of insurance was most important. The types of insurance were home, motor (referring to comprehensive automobile), car rental, travel, add-on (referring to insurance for a consumer item that is purchased at the same time as the purchase of the consumer item—a mobile phone, washing machine—itself), and home assistance (referring to home healthcare). The number of respondents ranged from 1,548 purchasers of the home insurance to 268 purchasers of home healthcare insurance.

Of the answers, "It provides me with peace of mind" was the almost always the most popular response with percentage of endorsers of this motive ranging from 29 percent for home insurance to 62 percent for home healthcare insurance. The only exception was home insurance, where "It's important to cover the risk" was the most popular at 51 percent. It is, however, not clear whether "cover the risk" refers mostly to the risk (uncertainty) or the coverage (income). However, "peace of mind," according to the authors of the report,

> is linked to loss and regret aversion. Consumers may fear a potential loss to an extent that makes them willing to pay a high premium to insurance against it. Moreover, they may fear the regret they would feel in case they did not purchase the insurance cover and a claim arose. (Suter et al. 2017, 81)

Thus, this survey points to loss aversion as an important motive in increasing the demand for many types of insurance for those who have purchased these types of insurance, but it is interpreted as either detracting from or contributing to the demand for insurance.

Taken together, these studies suggest that loss aversion is a motivator of the demand for insurance, but that it may work initially as a negative motivator through an aversion to the loss of paying the premium and so reduce the demand for insurance. It may be that, only after some level of education has taken place or experience has been gained, the payment of the premium becomes like the *quid* of any other quid pro quo transaction: a payment for a commodity, which in the case of insurance is an income payout from the insurer that often occurs in the event of a loss. After education or experience, loss aversion still exists, but its effect would be to increase the value of the income obtained from insurance after a loss occurs. Thus, loss aversion can be part of the motivation that generates the demand for insurance.

Conclusions

Loss aversion is now considered by some to be an important alternative to risk aversion for explaining the demand for insurance, but the mechanism by which loss aversion increases the demand for insurance is not well understood (O'Donoghue and Somerville 2018). On the one hand, the consumer may regard the premium payment as a loss and at the same time may not recognize the benefit from the income transfer in cancelling or overcoming a loss, when insurance covers one. So consumers who have an aversion to losses might tend *not* to purchase insurance, as has been observed in a number of empirical studies. This seems to be most likely for the case of annuities where the premium commitment is large, or for the case of consumers who have a naïve understanding of the benefits of insurance. On the other hand, if consumers are educated, understand how insurance works and how they benefit from it, or have sufficient experience with losses and can therefore view the insurance payoff as cancelling and overcoming a loss, then loss aversion could act to reinforce and augment the demand for insurance. With this interpretation, demand for the income payout in insurance exists in part because of aversion to losses. Such a demand-increasing effect, however, is not often observed in experimental or empirical studies.

As was suggested in chapter 2, the demand for insurance coverage is derived from the demands for new commodities that are added to the budget by the triggering event and that make income dearer. If losses occur, demand may also be reinforced because the loss of income reorients the evaluation of the insurance payout to a steeper portion of the utility function. In the present chapter, loss aversion is now added as a potential third reason why the value function could have shifted upward, but this would depend on whether the loss aversion tended to effect the evaluation of the premium or the insurance income payout.

Some losses of assets, however, do not exhibit a demand for additional consumption commodities and so may not make existing income dearer for that reason. Instead, they represent a simple loss of wealth. Examples might include insurance coverage of art collections, jewelry, some consumer durables, and so on. In such a case, it might be more appropriate to drop this book's desire for consistency across all types of insurance and to model the demand for such insurance using utility or value as a function of wealth. A quid pro quo analysis of this insurance would base the demand for insurance coverage of these assets on a concave utility or value function of wealth, to the extent that one exists, and on evaluating that function on a steeper portion, after the loss has occurred. This chapter suggests that loss aversion could also increase the demand for insurance coverage for these assets.

As mentioned, there remains, however, one last potential source of value from insurance that could reinforce the other factors in increasing the value of an income payout after a triggering event. This source is addressed in chapter 8.

7

Empirical Evidence for Gambling

Introduction

Under Friedman and Savage's (1948) model, the demand for insurance is motivated by an aversion to risk, but the demand for gambles is motivated by a desire for risk. According to this model, gamblers seek risk, and so a risky experience is the essential commodity sought through gambling. By paying the house's take to the casino as the price and participating in a gambling experience, gamblers are able to purchase this commodity, regardless of whether they win or lose. This is the conventional theory.

Among economists, perhaps the most widely held modification of this model is that the utility from entertainment is overlain on the utility from risk, and the utility from entertainment generates the demand for gambles (Conlisk 1993). The utility function assumed in this model generally exhibits diminishing marginal utility, but because betting stakes are typically so modest, the utility function is virtually linear over the range of most gambles. This view is consistent with the observation of Rabin (2000) and others that the curvature of the utility function cannot possibly explain the demand for modest-stake insurance because it would mean that consumers would not accept large-stake gambles with winnings that are excessively favorable, given the corresponding wagers and probabilities. As a result of the assumption that the utility function is linear for gambling stakes, Conlisk (1993) argued that it would take only a small utility gain from entertainment to generate demand for gambles. As noted in chapter 3, however, Conlisk (1993) does not address the ability of such a small increase in utility to overcome the house take, which in casinos and other gambling venues is substantial.

Conlisk's theory builds on the conventional theory because it assumes that those with diminishing marginal utility of income would not gamble because of aversion to risk. It also assumes that whether the gambler wins or loses does not matter: it is the participation that is important. This is an important and distinguishing implication of the conventional theory.

A Theory of Insurance and Gambling. John A. Nyman, Oxford University Press. © Oxford University Press 2024.
DOI: 10.1093/oso/9780197687925.003.0007

The quid pro quo theory, in contrast, holds that gamblers desire something much more concrete than either uncertainty or entertainment: they
desire the additional income that would be transferred to them in the event
of a gambling win. This additional income differs from the income that
individuals experience in their work-a-day lives because they do not need
to work to obtain it. Moreover, the unearned nature of this income often
"permits" gamblers to spend a larger portion of it on consumption than they
otherwise would, had they earned the same amount of income by working.
Thus, compared to earned income, a gambling win shifts the consumer's
utility function for the additional income upward and represents the core
motivation for gambling (equation 3.1). A consumer who also acknowledges
the savings of labor disutility from not having to earn the additional income
may have an even larger demand for gambling (equation 3.2).

In the quid pro quo model as described in equation 3.1, the price of this
(expected) income transfer is the (expected) wager, which the gambler typically earned through working. The model assumes, however, that the gambler generally derives positive utility from having a job and working initially,
so that the utility cost of paying the expected wager out of earned income is
smaller than the utility benefit from receiving the expected income transfer
in unearned income. For the gambler, this difference is sufficient to cover the
house take that is part of the costs of supplying the gamble and included in
the wager price, and therefore to gamble.

Uncertainty plays an important role in the original conceptualization of
the quid pro quo transaction because both the wager and the income transfer
are uncertain. Uncertainty, however, is not the motivation for the transaction.
Instead, it simply allows there to be an income-related incentive to gamble. The
level of uncertainty allows gamblers to take a relatively small amount of their
earned income, wager it, and convert it into a multiple of that wager if they win,
and for casinos and other gambling venues to stand ready to make that happen.
Without the uncertainty, such an augmentation of the wager would not be possible. For example, in the absence of uncertainty, no gambling establishment
could long pay out US$1,000 with certainty to anyone and everyone who pays
them a US$100 wager. The consumer's ability to convert a small wager into a
large income transfer is due to the uncertainty of the gambling win.

A number of other motivations for the demand for gambles have been
observed and often discussed in the psychology or gambling research literature. It is well known that gambling addiction may motivate some
people to gamble. This pathological or disordered gambling differs from

the recreational gambling that is addressed in this book.[1] Alternative motivations for recreational gambling include (1) fantasizing what could be done with the winnings (as was mentioned in chapter 3 with regard to the motivation to purchase lotteries); (2) seeing gambling as the only way to obtain the level of income sufficient to purchase a certain indivisible commodity that is presently unaffordable (discussed in chapter 2 as a feature of insurance as well); and (3) believing that you personally have a better chance of winning than is reflected by the true risk (feeling lucky). Motivations for *continuing* to gamble include (4) the psychological effect of a large initial win or the intermittent reinforcement from winning; (5) the "gambler's fallacy" that holds that, after a series of the same outcomes, an alternative outcome is more likely;[2] and (6) the "chasing" of losses, that attempts to cover past losses with the winnings from another gamble. According to the quid pro quo theory, these motivations and others all exist, but are secondary to or derived from a more basic motive, namely, to obtain additional income that requires no work. That is, the theory proposed in this paper attempts to model the motivation that would create a demand for gambling in the absence of any of these alternative motives.

That work-free income is the fundamental motivation for gambling becomes clear if one considers how much gambling would be done if, instead of winning an "additional US$10,000," the *quo* of the quid pro quo gambling contract were instead defined as winning "additional work at one's current job until US$10,000 was earned." If there were no difference between normally having to work for additional income in a market economy and not having to work for it in gambling, few consumers would be motivated to gamble, regardless of the other attractions. In essence, the present theory points to the underlying scarcity of economic resources in the economy as the fundamental reason for gambling and models this scarcity by theorizing that consumers gamble because they recognize, perhaps implicitly, the gain in utility from not having to work for gambling winnings.

---

[1] Indeed, it appears that most studies of the determinants of gambling focus on the nonrational motivations; only a few studies have empirically investigated the reasons for recreational gambling behavior.

[2] It is not clear whether the motivation for gambler's fallacy behavior is based on the incorrect assumption that after a number of specific outcomes has occurred the probability of a certain alternative outcome increases, or on the correct assumption that a long series of specific outcomes is unlikely and the gambler is constrained by the game to bet on the series by making marginal wagers. The distinction is explained in more detail in an appendix to this chapter.

Existing Explanations of Gambling

Conventional theories of the demand for gambling have been based on a number of assertions. Each of these assertions, however, quickly runs into difficulties when compared with the available data. This section briefly reviews some of the main assertions of the convention theory of the demand for gambling and the challenges of each.

In Figure 3.2, Friedman and Savage assert that although utility is generally increasing at a decreasing rate, there may be a portion of the utility function that is convex (nonconcave). This "wiggle" is the portion of the utility function that would generate the demand for gambling under conventional theory. Markowitz (1952) appealed to common knowledge about the types of gambling that are typically done in order to challenge this assertion. Markowitz (1952) notes that, if the consumer exhibited preferences according to Figure 3.2 and possessed income at Y_0, about half-way in between Y^* and Y_1, this diagram would predict that such a consumer would desire to make symmetric fair bets: for example, winning or losing US$100 with a coin toss. He notes, however, that this sort of betting is not often observed in practice. For someone with income just less than Y_1, the diagram implies that the consumer would be "willing to take a small chance on a large loss to obtain a large chance of a small gain" (Markowitz, 1952, 152). Again, this type of betting is not observed. Finally, he notes that Friedman and Savage's diagram would also rule out gambling by those who are very rich or very poor, but gambling by those at the extremes of the income or wealth distribution is widely practiced.[3]

Friedman and Savage (1948) assert that consumers who gamble seek an uncertain gain instead of a certain one. This assertion represents the key

---

[3] It should also be noted that Markowitz's critique of Friedman and Savage (1948) anticipates the loss aversion of prospect theory, noting that because people generally avoid symmetric bets, "this suggests that the curve falls faster to the left of the origin than it rises to the right of the origin" (Markowitz, 1952, 154). He illustrates this case with a prospect-theory-like value function diagram. Markowitz (1952) anticipates Conlisk's (1993) model by more than 40 years by noting that the demand for gambling is sometimes explained by its entertainment value, but that the entertainment motive, like the risk motive, is a motivation that is independent of whether the gambler wins or loses. He also anticipates one of the main arguments of this book by more than 70 years by observing that an entertainment motive does not really make sense because "if people like participation but do not like taking chances, why do they not always play with stage money?" (Markowitz 1952, 153). The unstated implication is that, without the possibility of obtaining a transfer of real income—additional income that can be used to purchase valuable commodities—gambling would lose much of its entertainment appeal. Thus, the demand for gambles must be more than just a demand for the fun of participation.

motivation for gambling under the conventional theory. In contradiction, however, Kahneman and Tversky and others find that consumers generally seek certainty when gains are at stake (Kahneman and Tversky 1979; 1984; Tversky and Kahneman 1981; 1988; 1991; 1992). It is generally when losses are at stake that consumers seek uncertainty. This empirical evidence means that, if a gamble is modeled as the choice between a certain gain and an uncertain gain of the same expected magnitude, as Friedman and Savage (1948) do, the certain choice not to gamble would lead to greater utility. Thus, viewing gambling as a choice between certain and uncertain gains would lead to the conclusion the consumers should not gamble.

Alternatively, it could be asserted that a gamble is a transaction, that is, an exchange of loss (wager) for a gain (the winnings), as might be consistent with the gain and loss axes of a prospect theory diagram. If a prospect theory value function were applied and the gamble occurs from the reference point of the status quo, then the wager would be evaluated on the negative portion of the prospect theory value function and the income transfer would be evaluated on the positive portion from the implicit reference point of having paid the wager. Because of the loss aversion parameter of prospect theory, however, the reduction in expected utility from making the wager would be larger than the increase in expected utility from the income transfer, so again gambling would not be done. Thus, none of the assertions from conventional theory are sufficient to provide an explanation of the demand for gambles.

Labor Market Context

The quid pro quo model of gambling (as described in equation 3.1 and Figure 3.1) suggests that the gambler desires an increase in income and that the state of the world in which the additional income is received differs from the state of the world that the consumer faces usually when additional income earned. That is, it is assumed that the utility of labor changes from positive to negative at around the end of the workday. This means, on the one hand, that a positive utility of labor is present in the no event state when most of the income destined to finance a wager is being earned, thus reducing the cost represented by the wager. More importantly, it also means that a disutility of labor would be present in the no event state for the last dollar of earned income at the end of the workday. Thus, compared to the utility from this last dollar of earned income, winning additional income through gambling would represent a gain in utility.

Gambling may also produce a utility gain to the extent that the disutility savings from not having to work for this additional income are explicitly considered as well (that is, to the extent that equation 3.2 replaces equation 3.1). This would be the case if, because the disutility from additional labor is so great that the utility of earned income becomes negative at the end of the workday, consumers also consider the savings in disutility associated with the unearned income transfer. This suggests that those who work in jobs that are disagreeable, dangerous, or arduous, or those workers for whom work is difficult or painful to do, or is hard to come by, may be more likely to focus on the disutility saved and gamble (or would gamble more money or with greater frequency) than those whose jobs are pleasant or for whom working for additional income is relatively pleasurable. Thus, the quid pro quo theory suggests that the demand for gambling is related to characteristics of the job and the characteristics of the individual that bear on his or her facility or ability to do work.

Nyman, Welte, and Dowd (2008) investigate this issue empirically. They begin their analysis by relating the gain from gambling to the standard labor supply problem and diagram. Utility, U, is a function of leisure, l, and income, Y. At wage rate, w, the individual faces a constraint based on the total time available for work or leisure. If total time is normalized to unity, the individual's problem is:

$$\max U = U(l, Y) \text{ subject to: } Y = w(1-l), 0 <= l <= 1 \qquad (7.1)$$

Figure 7.1 shows the individual is optimally working at point A and achieving U_1 level of utility. Giving up sufficient leisure to achieve the level of income at point C would normally reduce utility to U_0 because the extra work is not worth the additional income. However, if the same amount of additional income could be gained without giving up leisure, say, by winning that amount by gambling, the individual would achieve utility level U_2. Thus, the utility gain from obtaining $(Y_1 - Y^*)$ without working is either $(U_2 - U_1)$ or $(U_2 - U_0)$, depending on whether the consumer regards the gain by comparing the new utility to the original utility, or by comparing the new utility to the level of utility that would take into account the disutility from working for the additional income, respectively.

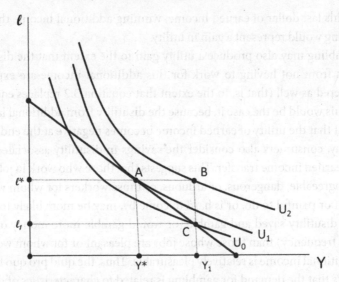

Figure 7.1 The Utility Gain from Unearned Income

Nyman, Welte, and Dowd (2008) hypothesize that gamblers desire "something for nothing," meaning that gamblers desire an income transfer without having to incur the utility cost of working for it. These utility cost savings are greater for some workers than others, suggesting that those with greater utility costs of obtaining income are more likely to gamble, because the savings from the disutility of labor are greater. This hypothesis was tested using the Survey of Gambling in the US, a random-digit-dial telephone survey of the US population conducted in 1999 and 2000. The survey questions included 13 items from the Diagnostic Interview Schedule, which allowed the authors to identify 28 respondents who were deemed to be pathological gamblers according to the standard criterion. After pathological gamblers were excluded, a total of 2,603 respondents were available for the analysis. These observations were weighted by the gender, race, and age composition of the US population in 2000 in the analysis.

Three dependent variables, and alternative forms of two of them, were specified (1) whether or not respondents gambled; (2) the average amount of money won and lost during the last time respondents played various games or (2') the same average amount of money won or lost as a proportion of the respondents' salary; and (3) the frequency with which respondents gambled or (3') the logged frequency. In part because professional gamblers are so rare, it was assumed that the characteristics of the job and the worker were reasonably exogenous and represented determinants of gambling behavior, rather than the reverse. Among the significant findings, the analysis showed that working or having ever worked is significantly predictive of any gambling, compared to those respondents who had never worked at all, holding constant other variables including age, gender, and variables capturing religious orientation. An increase in the amount of wagering was significantly predicted by (1) attaining fewer years of education, (2) being nonwhite, (3) being in poor or fair health, or (4) living in an area with a higher unemployment rate, holding constant the income of the respondent, the income of the respondent's household, and the respondent's age and gender. An increase in the frequency of gambling was significantly predicted by (1) attaining fewer years of education, (2) working in the demanding construction or an extraction industries, (3) being nonwhite, (4) being obese, or (5) living in an area with a higher unemployment rate, again holding constant income, age, and gender.[4] These results, and especially the significant relationship between ever having worked at all and gambling, suggest that the gamblers view their gambling decisions from an implicit labor market context.

Nyman et al. (2013) tested the same hypothesis using the National Epidemiological Survey of Alcohol and Related Conditions (NESARC) from 2001. After eliminating 202 observations that were deemed to represent pathological gamblers according to the DSM-IV (*Diagnostic and Statistical Manual of Mental Disorders*, 4th edition) and 14 observations with no census track information, the data set consisted of 42,877 observations. Two dependent variables were used. The first was whether the respondent had "ever gambled 5+ times in any year" or not, and the second was a variable constructed from the DSM-IV responses and was intended to measure the degree of gambling engagement. The DMS-IV contained 14 items measuring 10 possible indicators of persistent or maladaptive gambling behavior. Endorsement of 5 or more of these was used to eliminate the 202 pathological gamblers, but for those nonpathological gamblers, endorsement of 1 through 4 items was used to represent increasing engagement with gambling, in the same way that these endorsements had been used in other studies (Currie et al. 2006; 2008; Welte et al. 2004; Fisher 2000; Gerstein et al. 1999).

---

[4] Consistent with description of the typical Canadian gambler in chapter 3 (Rotermann and Gilmour 2022), higher salaries for these individuals was significantly associated with greater frequency of gambling and higher household incomes significantly associated with greater amount of gambling.

Therefore, the number of endorsements, 0 through 4, was used as a proxy measure of increasing gambling involvement.

Regarding the logit analysis of the variable measuring ever having gambled at all, if a respondent had ever had the experience of working, this variable was positively and significantly associated with ever having gambled, compared to those who had never worked, holding constant income, age, gender, and a number of other variables that described the respondent's job or ability to work. In addition to (1) ever having worked, those who had (2) less education, (3) poorer health, (4) pain that interfered with work, (5) trouble at work, and (6) an ongoing financial crisis all were significantly more likely to gamble than the corresponding excluded categories. Those who (7) lived in an area with greater unemployment were also significantly more likely to gamble. Regarding the ordered logit analysis of the degree of gambling engagement, as measured by the DSM-IV endorsements, (1) those with poor or fair health, (2) those with pain that interfered moderately with work, and (3) those who were in a financial crisis were the only variables with significant coefficients. The authors, however, viewed this measure of gambling engagement as a limitation of the study.

The authors were testing multiple relationships simultaneously, which meant the analysis could not accommodate any of the standard corrections for selection bias. Nevertheless, these authors argued that the explanatory variables were largely exogenous and that the findings were consistent with the hypothesized causal relationships. For example, the authors note that it is simply not plausible that gambling would cause a respondent to have "physical pain that interfered with work," or that there was a missing unobserved third variable correlated with both. Thus, the authors had confidence in their interpretation of the findings, namely, that demand for gambling was likely to be causally related to whether or not the individual had any work experience, and that the job and the personal work-related characteristics in the analysis acted to generate the demand for gambling.

There are other studies that link gambling to work, but not many. For example, Orford et al. (2010) use the 2007 British Gambling Prevalence survey to investigate the relationship between measures of gambling frequency and amount wagered, on the one hand, and the respondents' occupational category and the extent that they live in areas with deprivation (with respect to income, employment opportunities, health and healthcare, education, housing, crime, and environment), on the other. They found that, for example, the frequency of gambling was significantly predicted by the tendency to work in technical or routine jobs (as opposed to other, perhaps less tedious occupations and professions) and by living in areas of increasing levels of deprivation, holding constant income, variables capturing pathological gambling characteristics, and a possible genetic disposition to disordered gambling. Binde and Romild (2020) use the 2015 Swedish population study on gambling and health (Folkhälsomyndigheten 2016) and find that blue collar occupations (especially those engaged in monotonous work or mobile working conditions) are more inclined to gamble (compared to other occupations). These studies are intended to investigate relationships other than the effect of job and worker characteristics on the amount of gambling, and so they are less informative. Nevertheless, they reinforce the conclusion that the amount of gambling and its frequency are determined at least in part by the consumer's employment conditions and opportunities.

Although this literature is sparse, a number of themes emerge. First, the significant relationships found between whether the respondent has ever worked and whether the respondent gambles suggests that consumers view the gambling decision from a labor market or job perspective. Second, the significant variables associated with the desire for additional income (a poor job market, being in financial crisis) suggest that the demand for gambling is motivated by the desire for additional income. Third, those characteristics of the job and the worker that were found to be significant predictors of gambling in these studies were factors that would make working additional hours undesirable. They suggest that the consumer considers the disutility saved by not working for the additional income when considering whether and how much to gamble. These themes are all consistent with the quid pro quo model.

Demand for Gambles Revisited

In chapter 3, the demand for gambles was explained using a diagram, Figure 3.1, consistent with conventional theory. According to Figure 3.1, the wager produced an expected loss of utility that was smaller than the expected gain in utility from the income transfer and the shift in utility caused by obtaining the additional income in the state of the world where it was not necessary to work for it. In chapter 5, the demand for insurance was illustrated using a modified prospect theory value function diagram, Figure 5.3. A similar diagram can now be used to illustrate the demand for gambles. In chapters 3 and 5, the model of the demand for insurance transitioned to one that included the payment and repayment of the premium if the event occurred as part of the net gain. To be consistent, the demand for gambles now also transitions to one that also accounts for the payment of the wager and its receipt in the winnings in the event of a win. Thus, the demand for the wager is represented by

$$\Delta EU_{complete} = [V(Y^*) - V(Y_0)] + \pi[Z(Y_1) - Z(Y_0)] \qquad (7.2)$$

where the probability of winning is π, original income is Y_0, Y^* is income after the wager $(Y^* - Y_0)$ is paid, and Y_1 is the income after the winnings $(Y_1 - Y_0)$ are received. The wager is assumed to be actuarially fair so that $\pi(Y_1 - Y_0) = (Y_0 - Y^*)$. The wager is evaluated according to $V(Y)$, the value function for earned income and the winnings are evaluated according to $Z(Y)$, the value function for unearned income. Equation 7.2 represents the complete net gain from a gamble and corresponds to the equation representing the complete demand for insurance, equation 2.8.

Figure 7.2 shows the demand for gambles using a modified prospect theory diagram that corresponds to the demand for insurance Figure 5.3. The wager, $(Y^* - Y_0)$, is evaluated as the payment in a quid pro quo transaction and so,

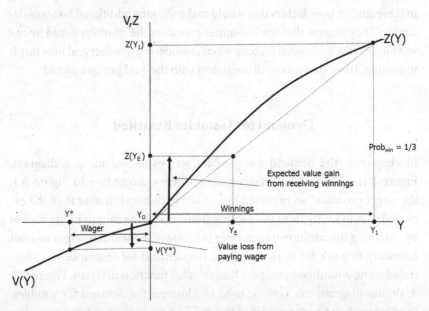

Figure 7.2 Demand for Gambling with Modified Prospect Theory Value Function

for those consumers who gamble, the wager is not viewed as an aversive loss. Moreover, the utility of labor gained from having a job would also decrease the utility loss from paying the wager with earned income, compared to viewing the wager as representing a pure consumption loss. As a result, the wager is evaluated on $V(Y)$ below the origin, showing the loss of value from spending earned income. The winnings, $(Y_1 - Y_0)$, would be evaluated according to $Z(Y)$, because the winnings—and the disproportional consumption generated by unearned income—represent income obtained without work. Moreover, if the gambler also considers the value of the work saved from obtaining the income transfer through gambling, this would alter the reference point of the gain so that $Z(Y)$ is steeper still, increasing the gain from the income transfer (not shown in Figure 7.2) and increasing the demand for gambles. Thus, for gamblers, the loss in value from paying the wager is $V(Y^*)$ and the expected gain in value is $Z(Y_E)$. Because the expected gain in value from the income transfer exceeds the expected loss in value from making this fair wager, this consumer would gamble.[5]

The introduction of prospect theory and other considerations changes some of the expectations regarding who would gamble and how much, compared to the discussion in chapter 3. On the wager cost side of the gambling decision, those who are aversive to losses and regard the wager as an unplanned loss (as shown in Figure 7.1) would be unlikely to gamble (Shang, Duan, and Lu 2021). However, as was initially discussed, those who derive more utility from having a job and consider initial hours at work welfare-increasing would be more likely to part with the income earned and make a wager. On the additional income gain side, those who attach a greater utility to the additional unearned income would be more likely to gamble, as would those whose job characteristics and associated disutility of labor orient them to considering also the disutility saved from not working.

Preference Reversals

What makes this theory of the demand for gambling interesting is that it focuses on a characteristic of gambling that seems obvious and important—the fact that the winnings are obtained without work—but one that appears

---

[5] In addition, if $V(Y)$ represented the perceived gain in utility from unearned income compared to the loss of utility from working for the income transfer, $V(Y)$ might be even steeper.

to have been overlooked by existing research in the explanation of gambling behavior. This may be more generally important because one of the fundamental assumptions of experimental preference research is that the subjects' preferences are independent of the tasks presented to the subject. This assumption has been termed the postulate of "context-free preferences" (Cubitt, Munro, and Starmer 2004). However, the quid pro quo theory suggests that the context of an amount of money, say, US$1,000, may be different if viewed as a wager or as winnings, and in ways related to working and jobs that are understood by subjects but not by researchers. As was suggested in chapter 3, this is especially likely because of the presence of mental accounting, where different amounts of money are implicitly (and unobservedly to researchers) placed into different accounting categories in the mind depending on their origins or intended uses (Thaler 1985).

Some of the experimental studies described in chapter 3 that investigated the preferences of subjects by presenting them with a standard gamble choice between a sure amount of money and an uncertain gamble with the same expected value may be influenced by this accounting. For example, an experiment might give subjects a choice between (a) US$100 with certainty, and (b) a gamble where there is a 0.1 chance of winning US$1,000 and a 0.9 chance of winning US$0. The gamble is fair, so the only difference appears to be between the certainty of the US$100 and the uncertainty of the actuarially equivalent expected US$100. However, the theory of mental accounting (Thaler 1985) suggests that subjects might vary in their interpretation of the amounts of this choice because of their origins. Thus, because the "choice" frame means that the subjects could simply walk away with US$100 as their own, it is as if the US$100 were already owned by the subjects and accounted for mentally as part of their existing income. As a result, the "choice" could instead be viewed by some subjects as a "transaction," and so the question then becomes, would the subject be willing to wager US$100 for a gamble where the winnings are US$1,000 with a 0.1 probability or US$0 with a 0.9 probability? Furthermore, the US$100 of income that the subject interprets as if they already own it may be regarded as part of their *earned* income, and the US$1,000 winnings could represent a transfer of *unearned* income that the subject does not have to work for. Thus, there could be an implicit contextual difference between the choice A and B that is unrelated to the intended certainty/uncertainty preference difference of the research question, but related to the utility of labor as captured in the wager and the absence of the disutility of labor as captured by the winnings. If such a contextual difference existed, it would violate the idea of context-free preferences and may bias the researchers' findings regarding preferences for uncertainty.

Although such a bias would probably be difficult to detect in most cases, some experimental problems may be sufficiently refined that such a bias could be detected. Take, for example, the issue of preference reversals (Lindman 1971; Lichtenstein and Slovic 1971; Slovic and Lichtenstein 1983). With preference reversals, subjects are presented with two standard gambles. One, called the p-bet, is a gamble where the probability of winning is high but the winnings are low, and the other, called the $-bet, is a gamble where the probability of winning is low but the winnings are high. If asked which they prefer, subjects tend to prefer the p-bet to the $-bet. However, if asked how much they would be willing to pay (or accept) for the two bets, many subjects place a higher value on the $-bet than the p-bet, thus reversing their preferences.

Some researchers think this reversal occurs because the higher winnings in the $-bet "anchors" the respondent's evaluation of the gamble at a higher amount than the winnings of the p-bet, so some respondents tend to place a higher value on the $-bet (Grether and Plott 1979; Tversky and Kahneman 1990; Tversky, Slovic, and Kahenman 1990; Seidl 2002). Alternatively, if viewed from the perspective of the quid pro quo model, the higher winnings in the $-bet and the request to the respondent to tell what they would pay for the two bets with dollars could trigger in the respondent a recognition that (1) the payment would be paid with their existing earned income, but (2) the greater winnings in the $-bet would represent an income transfer gained without the need to work. Thus, because the implications regarding the utility and disutility of labor may become more pronounced in the $-bet when it is evaluated by the amount that the respondent would pay with dollars, the dollar evaluation might be greater for the $-bet than the p-bet, even though simple preferences favor the p-bet.

This is pure speculation because the mental accounting difference in the choice between an amount with certainty and the expected winnings from the uncertain gamble has not (to my knowledge) been investigated empirically. Nevertheless, researchers are recognizing more and more that the manner in which preference questions are presented to subjects influences the results of such experiments (Loomes and Pogrebna 2017). This potential bias also suggests that the quid pro quo theory presented here may have implications that go beyond simply explaining the demand for gambles.

Empirical Evidence on Gambling Motivations

As indicated above, economists have identified a number of motivations for gambling: (1) risk seeking, (2) entertainment, and (3) now, the desire for additional income without working for it. Risk seeking is a relatively precise in that it stems only from a certain interpretation of the curvature of the utility function for income, but what causes that convex curvature to exist is not clear. Entertainment has not been precisely defined and could encompass a number of psychological motivations, such as the desire for "fun," "excitement," "social interaction," and so on. The motivation to obtain additional unearned income, however, is relatively precise.

The conventional approach taken by economists in determining the motivation of gamblers is to deduce it from a theoretical model. Psychologists have also worked to identify the motivations that underlie the demand for gambles. Most of their studies focus on the motivations of pathological gamblers, but an increasing number collect and analyze information on the motives of nonpathological or recreational gamblers. In contrast to the deductive approach favored by economists, the approach used by psychologists has been more inductive and empirical: they simply ask respondents what their motivation is. The following paragraphs relate the findings of a series of nine surveys that all request responses from gamblers on their motivation to gamble. In every survey, the motivation that is endorsed most prominently is the desire for additional income.

Neighbors et al. (2002) asked 184 American college students to list their top five reasons to gamble in rank order. Of the 766 different responses that were listed, the analysts distilled 16 distinct motives and then tallied the responses according to these motivational categories. Of the motivations deemed to be most important, "Gambling to make or obtain money" was endorsed by the largest percentage of respondents with 42.7 percent. "Gambling for enjoyment or just to have fun" was the second most endorsed with 23.0 percent, "Gambling as a means of interacting with friends or family, or to meet new people" was third at 11.2 percent, and "Gambling for arousal, thrill, or excitement" was fourth with 7.3 percent. "Gambling in order to take risks or experience uncertainty" was the 9th most cited with only 2.2 percent of respondents indicating it was the most important reason. Thus, in this study, winning money, being entertained, and having a social experience were most important, in that order, with risk seeking appearing not to matter much, at least to these college students.

Lee et al. (2006) reviewed the extant literature and identified 30 potential motivations for gambling. The researchers developed questions with 5 Likert scale responses (for example, 1 = strongly disagree, 3 = neutral, and 5 = strongly agree) and posed questions regarding these motivations to 399 gamblers at a Korean casino, face to face. The motivation that received the largest support was "To win money" with an average Likert score of 4.01. "Because gambling offers excitement" and "Because gambling is enjoyable" received average scores of 3.33 and 3.21, respectively. "To take risks" scored in the disagree range at 2.91, again indicating that monetary motives are the most important and that risk taking is much less important.

Clark et al. (2007) studied the responses of gamblers to 18 motives for beginning to gamble and 13 reasons for continuing to gamble, as suggested by a panel of experts. Among 106 nonpathological gamblers from New Zeeland, the authors found that "I hoped to win some big money" was the most endorsed reason for starting gambling and "I want big wins" was most endorsed for continuing gambling. Responses pertaining to entertainment motives received lower scores. Preference for risk as a motive was not considered.

Barry et al. (2007) used the 1998 Gambling Impact and Behavior Study to determine the motivations of American recreational gamblers with low incomes (less than US$24,000 per year), on the one hand, and those with middle and higher incomes (greater than US$24,000 per year), on the other. From their sample of 727 low-income gamblers, the most prevalent of the five motives listed on the survey was "Gambling to win money" with 59.4 percent endorsing this motive. For the 1,519 middle- and higher-income respondents, 64.0 percent endorsed that same motive. "Gambling for social activity" was endorsed by 36.9 and 37.9 percent for lower- and middle/higher-income respondents, respectively, and "Gambling for excitement" was endorsed by 32.0 and 40.3 percent for the same two income categories. Risk motives were not an option in the survey instrument. Similar results were obtained comparing old and young recreational gamblers, and male and female recreational gamblers by researchers using the same data set (Desai et al. 2004; Potenza, Maciejewski, and Mazure 2006).

Wardle et al. (2011) developed the Reasons for Gambling Questionnaire, a list of 15 possible motives for gambling, and asked a sample of 5,704 British gamblers how often they gambled for each of the reasons specified. The most endorsed motive was "For the chance of winning big money" with 42 percent of respondents indicating they always gambled for that reason. The second most endorsed motive was "Because it's fun" with 30 percent and the third most endorsed was "To make money" with 28 percent always gambling for that reason. A desire for risk did not surface in the motive development process.

One of the instruments that has been used by psychologists to determine gambling motives was derived from an instrument originally intended to determine the motivations for drinking alcoholic beverages. The Gambling Motives Questionnaire (GMQ) identified three core motivations from the 15 questions capturing (1) "enhancement," meaning excitement, fun, and other good feelings, (2) "coping," meaning coping with negative feelings, and (3) social motives (Stewart and Zack 2008). In part because gambling could have a financial motive that drinking did not, Dechant (2014) expanded the GMQ to include four items on financial motivations. To do this, she conducted a telephone survey of 1,014 gamblers in Manitoba, Canada, where she asked the respondents when they gambled how often they did do so for each of 24 reasons: 1 = never or almost never, 2 = sometimes, 3 = often, and 4 = almost always or always. She found that "to win money" was the answer to the motivation question that had the highest endorsement, with 26.4 percent indicating a 4 for "almost always or always"; "because it's fun" was second highest with 22.1 percent indicating a 4; and "because you enjoy thinking about what you would do if you won a jackpot" was third with 11.1 percent indicating a 4. A separate motive regarding the desire for risk was not included in the analysis. The exploratory factor analysis confirmed that the resulting 4 factor Gambling Motives Questionnaire-Financial (GMQ-F) had better psychometric properties than the three-factor GMQ.

Among the more recent gambling motivation studies, Francis et al. (2015) studied the motives of 2,796 Tasmanian gamblers. Using a modification of the British Gambling Prevalence Survey, they found that gambling "For the chance of winning big money" was the reason with the most "almost always" endorsements, with "Because it's fun" and "To make money" receiving the second and third most "almost always" endorsements. Hagfors et al. (2022) found that winning money received endorsements as their primary motive from 52.2 percent of their sample of 5,684 Finnish respondents in 2017 who gambled, and another 24.0 percent as an additional motive. Palleson et al. (2020) found that, of 13 motives listed in a questionnaire sent to about 6,000 Norwegians in 2019, "to win" was the most endorsed, with 60 percent of respondents who gambled endorsing that motive. Second most was "for fun," with 54 percent.

Entertainment and the Desire for Income

Desire for risk rarely shows up in these surveys of gambling motives, and when it does surface in the motive development stage of the study, the motive receives few endorsements as a motivation. It is clear, however, that both obtaining additional income and the factors related to the fun or excitement of gambling—its entertainment function, including the social aspect—are both important motivators of gambling. It has been argued here that the entertainment from gambling is secondary to the desire for income that one obtains without working. It is, of course, possible that the entertainment is the primary motive for gambling and that wagering with money for winnings that do not require work is incidental to the fun of participation and secondary. Some studies have looked into this issue directly.

Wulfert et al. (2008) conducted a randomized experiment where 443 college students were presented with a videotaped horse race. Some subjects simply watched the race, and others were asked to draw a number from a bag and were told that "the number you draw will be the horse you picked to win; let's see if you're lucky and pick a winner," but did not wager. The rest of the subjects bet US$1 on the horse they drew and could win US$2, US$7, or US$15, depending again on the draw. For all those with a horse, some had selected a horse destined (by experimental manipulation) to win and some to be the runner-up, but subjects did not know its fate at the time the horse was selected.

The question being addressed by the study is whether those who gambled for money were more entertained than those who did not gamble for money. Entertainment was captured in part by the subjects' heart rate measured at various times before, during, and after the horse race. Heart rate has been shown in other studies to indicate "arousal," the psychologist's term for excitement (Mackay 1980; Obrist 1981). Subjects were also asked to complete a subjective excitement measure (on a scale of 1 to 10) before, during, and after the horse race. The analysis held constant a measure of gambling engagement (the South Oaks Gambling Screen, Lesieur and Blume 1987) and a measure of impulsiveness (the Eysenck Impulsiveness Questionnaire, Eysenck and Eysenck 1978). The researchers found that (1) both those who simply watched the horse race and those who had drawn a horse experienced increased excitement compared to baseline, but there was no significant difference between these groups; (2) those who also bet money were significantly more excited than those who did not bet, compared to each of their baseline excitement levels; (3) those who could win the top prize of US$15 were significantly more excited than those with lesser prizes; and (4) those who had a winning horse were more excited than those with a runner-up horse at the end of the race. An earlier study from the same laboratory found similar results, except that it did not vary the winning monetary amounts (Wulfert et al. 2005).

Watching horse races can be exciting even without gambling, as the many and varied sports programs aired on television attest. The relative importance of (1) entertainment and (2) the wagering and winning of money in gambling was also tested using video lotteries, a game with minimal intrinsic interest, in contrast to a horse race. Ladouceur et al. (2003) assigned half of their 34 subjects to video lotteries where the subjects could win credits that had no monetary value and the other half to 100 video lotteries where for the first 50 games the subjects were told that winnings averaged 92 percent of wagers, and for the second 50 games that winnings averaged 200 percent of wagers. The subjects' heart rates were used to indicate excitement. For the first 50 games, there was no difference between the excitement of the gamblers and the nongamblers, but for the second 50 games, the gamblers were significantly more excited than the nongamblers. After the experiment, all respondents were asked what was exciting about gambling, and 30 of 34 said it was the potential to win money. They were also asked if they would play even if there was not possibility of winning money, and 28 of 34 said they would play less. These studies suggest that the excitement and entertainment of gambling is derived from the wagering and the possibility of winning money, rather than the other way around.[6]

Mao, Zhang, and Connaughton (2015) use data from the sales of the *Shengfu* lottery of China to estimate the effect of entertainment on the demand for these lottery tickets. The Shengfu is a nationally recognized sports lottery based on the results of 13 or 14 soccer (football) matches selected each

---

[6] This issue was further investigated by Lee et al. (2007) who wanted to determine whether entertainment and the desire for money acted as parallel motivations to gamble, or whether the desire for money was the dominant motivation for gambling, with entertainment being secondary. This study, however, evaluated the statistical fit of their model based on the responses of 234 predominantly pathological gamblers from Korea. The authors found that for pathological gamblers, the desire for money seemed to be dominant and to "mediate" all the motivations related to entertainment (excitement, social engagement, fun) and the more psychological motivation of avoidance of negative feelings. Alternatively, Flack and Morris (2015) addressed the issue of whether financial or emotional motives dominate in again predicting problem gambling. They found that the financial motive appears to work in parallel with the emotional motives considered, and so does not dominate. To my knowledge, there are no similar studies investigating the motives of recreational gamblers.

week from among the prominent European football leagues. The authors' approach was to estimate nationwide *Shengfu* ticket sales using time series data and two ordinary least squares equations: (1) one equation predicted sales with only the effective price of the ticket and four lagged sales variables, and (2) another predicted sales with these variables plus six variables related to the "attractiveness of the football matches" included in the 13 or 14 matches for that week's *Shengfu* lottery. Comparison of the R^2 statistic between these two equations was used to show the importance of the entertainment motive for gambling. Although some of attractiveness variables either acted to increase or decrease sales significantly, overall including these additional variables only represented an increase in the percentage of the variance explained from 71 to 79 percent. Thus, compared to the results based solely on effective price and the lagged sales, representing the expected monetary gain from the purchase of the lottery ticket, the entertainment portion explained only a small share, 8 percent, of the overall variation in sales.

In addition to the empirical work, a few other papers have argued for the dominance of a financial motive for other reasons. For example, Walker, Schelling, and Anjoul (2008) consider the historical context for the development of gambling. Because of the various monetary and financial changes in society that appeared to be prerequisites for the development of widespread gambling, these authors suggest that

> the evidence available suggests that the desire to win money (or item of value) is the core motivation of the gambler. . . . Thus, while people may gamble for amusement, for excitement, for escape, for company, or for induced states of altered consciousness, the common denominator is the desire and hope of winning money. (Walker, Schellink, and Anjoul 2008, 30)

Thus, based on their analysis of the historical origins of gambling, these authors conclude that all other motives to gamble are secondary to the motive to win additional income.

When asked to come up with a list of the most important reasons for gambling or when asked to endorse reasons from a list on the survey they think are most important, survey respondents are probably not considering how the various motives would interact. Specifically, they probably do not consider how the other motives would work in the absence of the possibility of winning money for which they did not need to work. This is because the income winnings and the fact that they come free of work are so familiar to respondents that these factors are either assumed, overlooked, or ignored. For example, respondents may not consider whether repeatedly playing a slot machine would generate the same level of excitement without the lure of a monetary win, or whether, without such a lure, repeatedly playing the same machine for meaningless tokens would become more tedious than exciting. They would certainly not consider how much entertainment would be derived from playing for additional income for which they were required to work. They also may not consider whether sufficient numbers of customers would flock to a casino, racetrack, or bingo parlor, and create the same attractive social environment, if only stage money were to be won or if working were required for the winnings. Thus, respondents may say that the most important motivation for gambling is excitement, entertainment, or socializing, not recognizing the important role played by the desire to win additional unearned income in generating that entertainment or creating the environment where these other motives matter. On the other hand, every one of these surveys found that the most endorsed motivation was a desire to win money, and so gamblers apparently recognize the prime importance of the income transfer, even after considering all the trappings of the gambling venue that might contribute to its excitement, social, or entertainment value.

Welfare Effects of Gambling

Because of the many associations between excessive gambling and negative health or social consequences—depression, suicide, excessive monetary losses, addiction, and so on—it might be surprising to recognize that until recently, most economists viewed gambling through a theoretical lens that implied that fair gambling generated a welfare gain. Just as the welfare gain from insurance derived from the curvature of the utility function, the welfare gain from gambling derived from a similar curvature, only one that is convex.[7] Although a number of studies have used the curvature of the utility function to estimate the welfare gain from insurance (e.g., Feldstein 1973; Friedman

---

[7] Arrow concluded famously that if consumers (1) exhibit a risk-averse utility function, (2) maximize expected utility and (3) are charged actuarially fair premiums, "the welfare case of insurance policies of all sorts is overwhelming" (Arrow 1963b, 961). The same could be said for gambling if the utility function is risk-seeking.

and Feldstein 1977; Feldman and Dowd 1991; Manning and Marquis 1996), to my knowledge, no studies have used the curvature of the utility function of gamblers to estimate the welfare gain from gambling.

A number of recent empirical studies have used alternative approaches to estimate whether gambling generates changes in welfare. Most of these studies, however, have focused on the effect of pathological or disordered gambling on the gambler's health as a measure of welfare. Many of these studies assume that, because the observations represent gamblers on the pathological end of the continuum, the causality of the associations they find runs from excessive gambling to health. Nevertheless, this relationship is most likely endogenous because, as some studies have argued (Nyman et al. 2008; Nyman et al. 2013), those in poor health are more likely to gamble because they find working for additional income from any job difficult. If so, the observed relationship might represent reverse causality to an extent, or might be generated by a third unobserved variable that is correlated with both variables. Therefore, studies that do not account for endogeneity could be biased.

Farrell (2018) is one of the few studies that investigated the welfare implications of recreational gambling. This author uses 6,624 observations from the British Gambling Prevalence Survey 2010 to estimate the effect of gambling on welfare as measured by happiness. The happiness question from the survey is worded: "Taking all things together, on a scale of 1–10, how happy would you say you are these days?" Gambling engagement is measured by the number of endorsed items from the 10-item DSM-IV criteria, then recoded into four categories: (1) never, for those who did not gamble in the last 12 months; (2) social, for those who endorse 0, 1, or 2 items; (3) at risk, for those who endorse 3 or 4 items; and (4) pathological, for those who endorse 5 or more items. In an alternative analysis, gambling engagement was measured by the responses to the Population Gambling Severity Index (PGSI), where respondents could score anywhere from 0 to 27, with the number of endorsed items again assumed to increase the level of gambling engagement. The PGSI scores were again recoded into four categories: (1) nonproblem, with a PGSI score of 0; (2) low-risk problem, with a score of 1 or 2; (3) high-risk, a PGSI score of 3–7; and (4) problem gambler, with a score of 8 or higher. The analysis also used the raw DMS-IV or PGSI scores without categorization in alternative analyses, with those variables treated as continuous. The data indicated that 75.0 percent of respondents gambled, 0.5 percent of respondents were pathological gamblers according to the

DSM-IV, and 0.7 percent of respondents were problem gamblers according to the PGSI.

Ordered probit analyses were used for the categorical dependent variables and ordinary least squares for the continuous dependent variables, with other demographic, income, and health variables from the survey included as control variables in the equations. The categorical analysis indicated that there was no significant difference in happiness between those in the "never" gambled and those who were "social" gamblers, but all the other categorical levels for both the DSM-IV and PGSI showed a significant decline in happiness compared to the excluded "never" or "nonproblem" categories, respectively. In the separate OLS analysis, both of the continuous measures of gambling engagement had negative coefficients that were significant. These relationships, however, were interpreted causally. While the direction of the causality may flow from degree of gambling engagement to the level of unhappiness, it is possible that the direction of causality may flow from the level of unhappiness to degree of gambling engagement. Thus, because the endogeneity is not accounted for, it is difficult to know what conclusions to draw from this study.

Humphreys, Nyman, and Ruseki (2021) investigated the impact of recreational gambling on the health and welfare of Canadians using data from the 2002–2009 Canadian Community Health Surveys. The analysis distinguished between those who did not gamble and four levels of gambling engagement for those who gambled, based on the nine items in the Canadian Problem Gambling Index (CPGI) and the three response levels for each of those items. Respondents were classified as (1) nonproblem, if they had 0 CPGI items endorsed; (2) low-risk, with 1 or 2 CPGI item/levels endorsed; (3) moderate risk, 3–7 item/levels endorsed; and (4) problem, with 8 or more item/levels endorsed. Two comparisons were made: (a) between those who did not gamble and "recreational" gamblers (those who represented the "nonproblem" gamblers according to the CPGI), and (b) between those who did not gamble and "at risk" gamblers (those who fell into the other 3 CPGI categories of gamblers). Although the focus of the study was on comparing nongamblers to recreational gamblers, the second comparison was included in order give a context for the first comparison.

A number of welfare and health measures were used as dependent variables. These variables were all dichotomized from the raw data and, with the exception of the change in health status, defined negatively, meaning that positive coefficients would indicate that gambling reduced welfare

Table 7.1 Humphreys, Nyman, and Ruseki (2021) Dependent Variables

Dependent variable
Life stress: quite a bit or extreme stress = 1, else 0
Life satisfaction: dissatisfied or very dissatisfied =1, else 0
Self-assessed health status: fair or poor = 1, else 0
Change in health status: much or somewhat better = 1, else 0
Migraines = 1, else 0
Stomach ulcers = 1, else 0
High blood pressure = 1, else 0
Stroke = 1, else 0
Heart disease = 1, else 0
Diabetes = 1, else 0

or health. The dependent variables and their coding are listed in Table 7.1. Of the 135,495 Canadians who comprised the observations, 69,727 were nongamblers, 60,867 were nonproblem gamblers according to the CGPI, and 4,901 were problem gamblers.

The theory that was being investigated by Humphreys, Nyman, and Ruseki (2021) was the same theory as is presented in this book: gambling benefits those most for whom the disutility of labor for additional income is the greatest. This theory, however, may represent a more intuitively accessible understanding of the potential welfare gain from gambling than the welfare gain from either uncertainty or entertainment. This is because the gain in welfare is caused by a factor that seems more concrete: the value of additional unearned income and the savings of the disutility of labor from not having to work for the additional income. Regarding the latter, it is easy to imagine working conditions that are so disagreeable or onerous, or personal or health characteristics that make working so difficult, that gambling for additional income that avoids such sources of disutility would increase welfare. More specifically, by avoiding the disutility of labor, the impact of recreational gambling is hypothesized to reduce stress, improve life satisfaction, and perhaps even generate an improvement in self-assessed health status or lead to an improved general health. Moreover, because many of the chronic diseases that workers acquire on the job are caused by unrelenting stress, gambling might act as an outlet to relieve this stress and so reduce the likelihood of some specific illnesses.

The authors were concerned with endogeneity and so estimated the 10 welfare and health equations two ways: (1) a probit model, using an instrumental variable (IV) in the first stage, and (2) a recursive bivariate probit model for endogenous regressors. The instrument used to determine predicted gambling status was the number of gambling facilities per 100,000 population in the province in which the respondent resides. This variable differed across observations both according to the Canadian province and year, was plausibly independent of the welfare and health variables, and yet was predictive of gambling. This variable was also used as an exclusion restriction in the recursive bivariate probit model. The equations included a number of additional demographic, employment, and educational variables.

The results from the IV and bivariate recursive probit are consistent with each other and indicate that, compared to not gambling, recreational gambling significantly (1) reduces stress, (2) increases satisfaction with life, and (3) increases the likelihood of an improvement in general health, but (4) worsens self-assessed health status. The negative effect of gambling on health status and the inconsistency across the results was difficult for the authors to explain. Recreational gambling also (5) reduces the likelihood of a strokes and (6) reduces the likelihood of a stomach ulcer, but the latter appeared significant in only the instrumental variable equation approach and not the bivariate recursive probit equation. In the comparison of not gambling to *at risk* gambling, these authors found that at risk gambling significantly (1) decreases satisfaction with life, (2) reduces the likelihood of an improvement in general health, (3) increases the likelihood of a stroke, and (4) increases the likelihood of a stomach ulcer.

The Humphreys, Nyman, and Ruseki (2021) results suggest that engaging in recreational gambling may have a generally positive effect on welfare and health, compared to never gambling. This may be especially true for those who find themselves in jobs they do not like or in work they have trouble performing. However, the results also suggest that excessive (at risk) gambling engagement has a negative effect on health and welfare, compared to never gambling. The study also shows that it is important to account for the endogeneity of the gambling variable when predicting health and welfare. To my knowledge, these results represent the only extant analysis of the relationship between recreational gambling, on the one hand, and health and welfare variables, on the other, which takes into account this endogeneity. Although this is a very early study—and perhaps the only one to account for endogeneity—it is suggestive of a potentially important health and welfare effect derived from recreational gambling.

Summary

The empirical evidence supporting the quid pro quo theory of the demand for gambling was presented in this chapter. A number of studies show that the preferences for risk either do not generate demand for gambling or do not even register risk as a contributor to demand in the studies that seek to identify the main motives for gambling. The motive "to win money" is invariably the most important and/or the most popular choice when gamblers are simply asked. Although a number of studies also find that entertainment—comprising the fun, excitement, and social aspects of gambling—is an important motive in the demand for gambling, whether it is a primary or stand-alone motive, independent of winning money, is questioned by other studies.

The demand for gambling in order to win additional income for which work is not required is supported by studies showing that the amount of gambling increases with increases in the arduousness of the job or the difficulty of working. Recreational gambling also appears to increase welfare as measured by stress relief and health improvements, both of which are consistent with the connection between gambling, on the one hand, and working in an undesirable, stressful, or otherwise negative work environment, on the other.

The prospect theory value function diagram can, therefore, be modified as in Figure 7.2 to show a value gain from an expected income transfer from gambling that is similar to the utility gain from gambling described in chapter 3. This chapter also speculates that the wager and winnings of a gamble might have an implied context through mental accounting that has implications for understanding the results of unrelated experimental studies. This context provides an alternative explanation for preference reversals. Finally, this chapter mentions that there are a number of alternative motives for gambling and continuing gambling that appear to be unrelated to the desire for additional income. An appendix now discusses one of these, the so-called gambler's fallacy, and shows that, from an alternative rational perspective, no fallacy exists.

Appendix: Gambler's Fallacy

An interesting alternative motive for continued gambling is the gambler's fallacy. The gambler's fallacy refers to the idea that gamblers, after observing a certain outcome occurring time after time, might place a wager on the opposite outcome because it is "due." This behavior is interpreted by gambling researchers as implying that the gambler views the probability of the opposite outcome occurring as having increased. However, because the gambling outcomes are independently and identically distributed (iid), the probabilities of both the original and alternative outcomes occurring remain constant, and so this behavior is viewed as a fallacy.

Nyman (2007b), however, has suggested that the gambler's fallacy might instead represent the likelihood of a streak of similar events occurring, rather than a change in probability. Because most gambling games constrain the gambler to wager on the marginal event (the next spin of the roulette wheel or throw of the dice), it appears that the gambler is fallaciously betting more money on the opposite outcome because they think that the probability of that outcome has increased. For example, in a fair coin toss game, the probability (Pr) of heads (H) is 0.5 [i.e., Pr(H) = 0.5] and the outcome of each toss is iid. If a gambler observes a series of tails (T) and then bets on heads (or raises his bet on heads), it is assumed that they are thinking that the conditional probabilities are increasing:

$$Pr(H) < Pr(H|T) < Pr(H|TT) < \text{etc} \tag{7.3}$$

However, because each toss is iid, increasing conditional probabilities are impossible.

Alternatively, the betting strategy might be established *ex ante* and based the probability of the series of outcomes. Because the probabilities of successively longer series of Ts are in fact diminishing, that is,

$$Pr(T) > Pr(TT) > Pr(TTT) > \text{etc.} \tag{7.4}$$

and at the same time, the probabilities of at least 1 H occurring in a series are increasing as the series increases,

$$Pr(H) < [1 - Pr(TT)] < [1 - Pr(TTT)] < \text{etc.} \tag{7.5}$$

betting on heads or raising the bet on heads after a series of successive tails would be rational if based on the high probability of getting at least one H in a given series of coin tosses.

The following betting strategy based on this conception is then adopted to show that gambler's fallacy behavior is actually rational.

The gambler bets on H with every toss, and wins an amount equal to his wager if H appears, but loses his wager if T appears. The gambler wagers $1 on H on the first toss and on any toss that is subsequent to a win (that is, subsequent to an H appearing). In the event of a loss, (that is, a T has appeared), the gambler wagers double his last wager plus $1 on the next toss of the coin. (Nyman 2007c, 167)

If a gambler were observed to be following this strategy, it would appear as if the gambler were behaving according to the gambler's fallacy. However, the betting strategy is in fact established *ex ante* and based on the probability associated with a series of outcomes.

The rationality of this betting behavior is demonstrated using a computer simulation. In the simulation, the gambler adopts this betting strategy in each game, a game consists of a series of 100,000 random coin tosses, and the game was repeated 100,000 times. Focusing on the fact that each coin toss is iid, each coin toss has a theoretical value of US$0 and so the game has a theoretical expected value of US$0 per game of 100,000 tosses. The simulation results, however, show that this betting strategy resulted in average winnings of US$99,958 per game, and average winnings per coin toss of just under US$1. If the game is stopped on the coin toss with the first H to appear after the 99,999th toss, then the average winnings are US$100,001 and the winnings per coin toss are US$1.

For this betting strategy to be truly rational, however, the gambler must have an initial bankroll sufficient to cover the largest series of bets required. In the coin toss simulation, five of the 100,000 games each experienced a series of 29 consecutive Ts in a row somewhere in the series of tosses, requiring over US$1 billion to cover the bets. The game requiring the median bankroll spent over US$200,000 to cover the 17 Ts in a row.[8] Therefore, if a fallacy exists, it is that the gambler assumes that they will have sufficient resources to cover all bets with this strategy. Other practical issues include whether the house would agree in advance to accept every one of these bets, and whether the game is fair, or more accurately, whether the degree to which the game is unfair prohibits this betting strategy from working. There are also the time cost and tedium of playing a game that requires making 100,000 wagers in a row. In any case, gambling decisions that are based on this practical understanding of the likelihood of streaks are clearly rational, even though these other considerations might, and often should, overrule them.

---

[8] Note that it is possible for such an unusually long streak to occur and affect the average winnings of the St. Petersburg Paradox game. For such a streak to have an effect, it would not only need to occur, but also occur at the start of the sequence of coin tosses representing the St. Petersburg game, rather than anywhere in a sequence of 100,000 coin tosses. The former is a much rarer occurrence than the latter.

8

Price and Income Effects in Insurance

Introduction

The conventional theory of the demand for insurance was presented in
chapter 2. According to the Friedman–Savage (1948) model, insurance is
demanded in order to avoid the risk of an uninsured loss. This motivation is
derived from the risk-averse shape of the utility function and suggests that
the risk of an uninsured loss creates the demand for insurance. In chapter 5,
this theory was updated to take into account the empirical foundations of
prospect theory, perhaps most importantly, the finding that consumers generally prefer risk when losses are at stake (Kahneman and Tversky 1979). It
was further updated in that chapter to account for the realization that the
curvature of the utility function could not possibly account for the demand
for insurance for modest stake losses because of what such a curvature would
then imply for the demand for large stake gambles—gambles that theoretically would not be accepted even though they offered wildly favorable payoffs
and odds (Rabin and Thaler 2000).

Elements of prospect theory were blended with conventional theory
to produce Kőszegi and Rabin's (2006) model. These authors suggest that
consumers demand insurance coverage for modest losses because of the relative impact of gains and losses, as derived from prospect theory, but that
consumers demand insurance coverage for large losses because of a concave shape of the value function, as is consistent with the conventional risk
aversion motivation. They further suggest that consumers may regard the
parameters of a given insurance contract differently because of the alternative reference points from which consumers can view insurance premiums
and payoffs. This model, and its variants, probably represents the current
state of conventional theory of the demand for insurance.

Chapter 5 noted that while the Kőszegi and Rabin (2006) model might
represent a viable model for economists, it is likely to be far too sophisticated to characterize the thought processes of most consumers who are considering the purchase of insurance. The contortions of thinking required to

A Theory of Insurance and Gambling. John A. Nyman, Oxford University Press. © Oxford University Press 2024.
DOI: 10.1093/oso/9780197687925.003.0008

adopt the various perspectives and reference points suggested in their model are not natural and, given what we know about the average consumer's limited understanding of insurance, seem far beyond the capabilities of most insurance buyers. Moreover, in models like theirs, there is a fundament change in the motivation to purchase insurance when going from insurance coverage of modest scale losses and to coverage of large scale losses, but there is no theory explaining why that change in motivation occurs. The change is convenient theoretically, but the intuition for why consumers would change their basic motivation to purchase insurance is not addressed.

Alternatively, chapter 2 suggested instead that consumers regard the purchase of insurance in the same way that they regard the purchase of virtually all of the other goods and services they buy: a quid pro quo exchange. The demand for insurance is, therefore, a desire by consumers to obtain additional income in the *ex post* state of the world where it is more valuable, and for which consumers are willing to pay a premium to obtain it. Moreover, uncertainty is beneficial because it allows consumers to pay a small premium, but gain a much larger income payout if the uncertain event occurs. The additional income is made more valuable because of the additional demands on the consumer's budget generated by the triggering event. It may also be made more valuable because it is evaluated on a portion of a curved utility function where the marginal utility of income is greater because of a loss of income. In chapter 6, the quid pro quo theory of insurance was expanded to acknowledge the potential effect of the aversion to losses in reinforcing this shift in utility when potential losses are at stake and when the benefits of the insurance contract are well understood by the consumer.

The key contribution of the quid pro quo theory to understanding the demand for insurance, however, is the focus on the consumer's desire for additional income in the payoff state. Such a transfer of income from the insurer occurs even when the insurer pays off the insurance contract by reducing the price of the covered commodity. In chapter 2, and as illustrated with Figure 2.3, it was shown that, when insurance pays off by reducing the price, within that price reduction there is an income effect that generates an increase in spending on the covered commodity. This, in turn, results in a welfare gain through increases in the consumer surplus.

Economists have been slow to recognize this income effect. As was discussed in chapter 2 and illustrated with Figure 2.2, many years of health policy have been based on the presumption that health insurance created an incentive to provide too much healthcare because it paid off by reducing the price of healthcare (Pauly 1968). It was widely held that the expansion of health insurance created large increases in healthcare expenditures, increases that were widely regarded by economists as inefficient. The RAND Health Insurance Experiment was intended to determine how much additional inefficient healthcare was being produced by isolating the effect of the price reduction on quantity demanded from selection effects (Newhouse et al. 1993). Because all the additional health expenditures were assumed to represent inefficient moral hazard, economists recommended increased cost sharing—sometimes at absurdly high coinsurance rates and deductibles, and with no stop-loss to provide a limit on total consumer spending—in order to rein in moral hazard spending (e.g., Feldstein 1973; Manning and Marquis 1996). As was also noted in chapter 2, although income effects were identified early on in health insurance (Nyman 1999b; 1999c), some influential economists continue to summarize what we know about moral hazard without acknowledging income effects or their impact on healthcare spending and welfare (Finkelstein 2014; Einav and Finkelstein 2018). This lack of recognition among economists, so long after it was identified and written about, is puzzling.

At the same time, why economists were so quick to label as inefficient all the additional spending associated with insurance coverage is also difficult to understand. For example, it must have been apparent to almost any thoughtful observer that some consumers purchase health insurance in order to gain access to expensive healthcare that they otherwise would not be able to afford, and that this additional care received when ill (and insured) is often very valuable and sometimes even life-saving. This access motive, however, appears to have been lost on the many economists who characterized all the additional healthcare spending when insured as inefficient (e.g., Pauly 1968). While such attitudes are perhaps most notorious among those economists who have written about health insurance, they surface among economists who have written about other forms of insurance as well. For example, with regard to the explaining the longer periods of unemployment of those with unemployment insurance, Gruber writes in his public economics text that unemployment insurance "has a significant moral hazard cost in terms of subsidizing unproductive leisure" (Gruber 2007, 395). Similar sentiments are observed by Bound and Waidmann (1992) with regard to explaining the lower labor force participation of those with disability insurance. The presumption that additional spending with insurance is inefficient and welfare-decreasing appears to have been the default attitude of many economists.

This situation, however, is in the process of changing. Some economists are now beginning to recognize that insurance causes additional spending that can sometimes represent an efficient income effect.[1] Furthermore, some of the new studies have focused on determining the welfare gain from the access value of insurance. These new empirical and theoretical studies are reviewed in this chapter. But before reviewing these studies, the results of a number of surveys that investigate the reasons for purchasing insurance are reviewed. Most of these surveys point to access as an important motivation for the demand for insurance.

Surveys

Ideally, there would be a number of surveys requesting respondents to describe their motives for purchasing insurance, similar to those done to determine the motives for gambling. For whatever reason, such surveys—with an open-ended questions up front and with researchers categorizing the responses into broader categories—do not appear to exist. Only a few surveys list motives and ask respondents to endorse the one that characterizes why they purchased insurance, or would purchase it, if they do not have the insurance already.

One such survey was discussed in chapter 6 with regard to loss aversion. Suter et al. (2017) found that the most popular response to the question of why insured Europeans purchased six different types of insurance was because it provides "peace of mind." Unfortunately, the list of potential responses in the survey was limited, and did not reflect the alternative theoretical motives as broadly or precisely as would have been desirable. The "peace of mind" response was interpreted by the authors as reflecting a loss aversion motive, but one also finds "peace of mind" from insurance if it allowed consumers to gain access to otherwise unaffordable car repairs, jobless days, or healthcare.

---

[1] This book uses the terms "price effect" and "income effect" to refer the decomposition of the additional spending caused by insurance as discussed in the last section of chapter 2. The price effect is inefficient and corresponds to the Hicksian "substitution effect," while the income effect is efficient. When dealing with unemployment insurance, Chetty (2008) uses the term "liquidity effect" instead of income effect. This is because, for those who are unemployed, the additional consumption is financed by assets and other forms of wealth that are liquidated. The unemployed are assumed to have little or no income and so must rely largely on this liquidation of wealth to finance consumption when unemployed and uninsured.

Perhaps the most directly relevant survey is a 2010 Kaiser survey of 1,038 Americans who had purchased health insurance privately (Kaiser Family Foundation, 2010). Although this group is not representative of the US population, their responses are revealing because these respondents had all made the decision to purchase insurance in the market directly themselves. That is, the decision was not made for them by their employer or by their eligibility for a government program, so their motivations to purchase insurance were perhaps more authentic. This survey found that 55 percent of respondents bought health insurance privately because they were either very worried or somewhat worried that "You won't be able to afford the health care services you need" (Kaiser Family Foundation. 2010). Thus, access was the motivation for the demand for health insurance.

A separate survey of 1,326 respondents who had considered purchasing long-term care insurance in 2015 were asked whether they agreed with the statement, "I worry about how I would pay for care if needed" (America's Health Insurance Plans, 2017). In that year, 73 percent of respondents who purchased long-term care insurance said they either "strongly agree" or "agree" with that statement. Interestingly, a slightly larger percentage of the 225 nonbuyers, 76 percent, strongly agreed or agreed with the statement. These findings are not consistent with the conventional aversion to risk explanation because, if one cannot afford a certain commodity, there would be no risk of financial loss associated with it, by definition. They are, however, consistent with and illustrative of an access motive.

Kluender et al. (2021) surveyed consumer credit reports to estimate the amount of medical debt in the US. In June 2020, about 17.8 percent of individuals had debt averaging US$429. Between 2013 and 2020, for those living in states that adopted the Medicaid expansion under the Affordable Care Act, the average debt declined by 34 percentage points compared to the average debt in the nonadopting states. This study does not survey consumer demand motives, but it does illustrate how health insurance provides additional income that would otherwise require going into debt in order to gain access to the needed healthcare. Thus, if consumers desired access to otherwise unaffordable care, insurance could provide it.

Nyman and Trenz (2016) used the Medical Expenditure Panel Survey (MEPS) for the years 1996 to 2008 to estimate the proportion of insured healthcare spending that would be unaffordable without insurance. These authors first found the amount of income that would be required to achieve a minimal subsistence level of consumption—the poverty thresholds from the US Census Bureau—by year and family size. That amount was subtracted from the annual incomes of respondents in the MEPS to find the maximum amount of each household's income that would be available to spend on medical care. This remainder was then compared to the that household's medical spending by insurance in the same year in order to determine the amount of insurance spending that would have been unaffordable given income. These authors estimated that about one-third of all American health insurance expenditures would have been unaffordable to the insured consumers if they had been forced to rely only on their privately available incomes. The percentage was higher for those with government-provided health insurance and lower for those with private health insurance. Thus, a large portion of health insurance expenditures appear devoted to providing access to care.

Many of these studies document the importance of access as the motivation to purchase insurance, and especially access to care as a motive to purchase health insurance. Access, however, is likely important in motivating the purchase of many other types of insurance as well. The inability of consumers to cover any losses with current resources, and the need for insurance coverage as an alternative financing mechanism, is apparent from the surveys of the fragility of household finances.

Lusardi, Schneider, and Tufano (2011) surveyed 9,147 respondents from 13 countries, including 2,148 from the United States, and asked them "How confident are you that you could come up with US$2,000 if an unexpected need arose within the next month?" For Americans, 50 percent of respondents said they would "definitely not" or "probably not" be able to do so. Other countries surveyed had substantial but slightly smaller proportions of respondents with these responses, with the exceptions of the United Kingdom and Germany, which had slightly larger proportions. In a similar study, Ericson and Sydnor (2018) asked 205 adults how they would pay of an unexpected US$1,000 hospital bill. Only 31 percent said they would do so fully from money they already have.

These studies illustrate the level of financial fragility with which households in the US and other developed economies face the possibility of covering the shock of a relatively small expenditure or loss. Such households would likely regard the access that insurance provides to coverage of such expenditures or losses as a motivation for the purchase of a number of different types of insurance.

Empirical Studies

A number of studies have now attempted to evaluate empirically the additional spending generated by insurance that pays off by reducing the price of the covered commodity. Unlike previous studies based on conventional theory, these studies either take account of income transfers explicitly, or the access value of insurance, or both.

Nyman (2001c; 2003) provided an early back-of-the-envelope estimate of the value of health insurance due to moral hazard, based on available data. The approach was to estimate the number of life years gained from having insurance for a year, compared to not having insurance, for an arbitrary group of 40 million Americans aged 25 to 65 and distributed evenly across these 40 age groups. The gained life years are evaluated at US$100,000 per year, the standard used for evaluating a quality-adjusted life year at the time, and then compared to the total additional spending if insured, over and above spending if uninsured. Using an existing estimate of the effectiveness of insurance in generating mortality gains (Franks, Clancy, and Gold 1993), this study found that about 1,225,380 life years would be saved, or an increase of about 0.0009 (0.09 percent) of the total life expectancy for this group of 40 million Americans. At US$100,000 per life year, the estimated value of the additional years of life is US$123 billion. According to the 1996 Medical Expenditure Panel Survey, the average annual medical spending of those under 65 with insurance was US$1,918 and without insurance was US$942, so additional medical spending if insured is US$976. Additional medical spending for a year for these 40 million would therefore be estimated at US$39 billion. Compared to the value of this spending, US$123 billion, the cost is about one-third as great as the additional value. While not a decomposition of the additional spending from insurance into an income effect and a price effect, the welfare gain from this back-of-the-envelope analysis is suggestive that the income effect of insurance would dominate any price effect.

Robertson et al. (2020) conducted two experiments to estimate the relative effects of the income payoff and price reduction in explaining the additional healthcare consumed when insured with health insurance. To do so, these researchers developed a series of realistic vignettes to describe eight different illness and healthcare intervention combinations. In the first experiment, a single vignette was presented to all 613 respondents from a paid online panel, along with additional information on the level of the effectiveness of this intervention—suggesting either that the care was either of low- or high-value—randomly assigned. In the second experiment, one of eight different vignettes (including the vignette from experiment 1) and one of the same two effectiveness levels were randomly assigned to 2,356 respondents from a different online panel of paid respondents. The respondents were told the price of each intervention (ranging from US\$15,000 to US\$125,000). They were also told that they were to assume that a doctor had told each of them that they had contracted the illness and needed the care. They were then asked, given the information provided on each of the vignettes, whether they would take the treatment if they were alternatively (1) uninsured, (2) insured with a traditional policy that paid for all their healthcare, or (3) insured with an indemnity policy that paid them a check for the cost of their care. For the uninsured case, they were told that they should consider their actual income and wealth, but also any sources of formal or informal credit actually available to them, and to be realistic. For the indemnity insurance case, they were assured that they could do anything of their choosing with the insurance money.

Robertson et al. (2020) found similar results for the two experiments. In the second experiment, for the low- and high-value cases, (1) 7 and 9 percent of respondents, respectively, would take the intervention if uninsured; (2) 49 and 65 percent, respectively, would take it if traditionally insured; and (3) 43 and 62 percent, respectively, would take the intervention if insured with an indemnity payment equal to the cost of the intervention (Robertson 2020). The statistical analysis of these differences (using national weighting of the observations for income, gender, and age, plus including a series of demographic control variables) showed a significant difference between the uninsured and insured responses, but no significant difference between traditional and indemnity insurance. That is, although there was some evidence of a small inefficient moral hazard effect, it was too small to be significant statistically. Robertson and his colleagues concluded that the increase in spending with insurance was almost all due to an efficient income effect.

Sometimes studies can be linked so that a study of the effect of insurance on demand can be better understood by pairing its results with the results of a second study that evaluates the effect of income on demand. Autor and Duggan (2007) used such an approach to understand the welfare effect of disability insurance on labor force participation (LFP). They noted that there is a "near consensus" that the Social Security Disability Insurance system has created a substantial disincentive to work. They further noted that virtually all of the policies used by the Social Security Administration to encourage labor supply have focused on removing the price effect disincentives to work, that is, removing the "taxes" whereby disability insurance benefits are eliminated when a disabled worker takes a job. These policies have generally not worked to increase employment among the disabled. The authors, however, suggested that these policies may not have worked because they were directed at removing a seemingly inefficient price effect. The authors further suggested that there is a hitherto "neglected explanation" for these programs not working: LFP for the disabled is determined instead by an efficient income effect.

Autor and Duggan (2007) tested whether income effects might explain the ineffectiveness of disincentive-oriented policies by looking at the effect of a change in the benefits paid under the US Department of Veterans' Affairs Disability Compensation (VDC) program. In 2001, the VDC made cash payments available to a previously ineligible cohort of disabled male veterans, regardless of whether they were working or not. The authors recognized that any change in LFP resulting from these payments would represent an income effect, because whether the disabled veterans received these benefits did not depend on their being unemployed and because the additional income could be spent on anything of their choosing. To address endogeneity, they used a difference-in-difference approach that compared LFP by male *disabled* veterans versus LFP of a nonveteran male control group, before and after this policy change. They found that the income payments resulted in a significant decline in LFP of the disabled veterans relative to controls. Thus, they concluded that the inability of the disincentive-removing programs to increase LFP among those with disability insurance was likely due to the income effect of the program, and so might not be affected by policies directed at a price effect. That is, if the disabled had been given a lump sum income payment of the same amount (as the benefits they received from disability insurance because they were not working), they would have "spent" that payment on not working. Thus, the reduction in labor force participation by disability insurance recipients is efficient because it is caused by disability insurance providing the disabled with income they needed to retire from what the recipients likely regarded as painful or otherwise difficult jobs.

A similar two-part analysis was conducted by Konetzka et al. (2019) and Dong et al. (2021). Konetzka et al. (2019) used the Health and Retirement Survey to estimate the effect of long-term care insurance on the demand for home healthcare and nursing home care. To deal with possible endogeneity, they used as an instrumental variable whether the respondent itemized deductions on their last tax return. Respondents who live in states with tax incentives to purchase long-term care insurance would be more likely to itemize their deductions, so itemization would be predictive of having long-term care insurance. These authors found that long-term care insurance causes demand for home healthcare to increase significantly but not nursing home care.

In the companion study by this same team of researchers, Dong et al. (2021) then used the same Health and Retirement Survey to determine the effect of income on demand for home healthcare and nursing home care by uninsured respondents. To deal with endogeneity here, the researchers used an income shock—whether the respondent "received money or property in the form of an inheritance, a trust fund, or an insurance settlement . . . [or] any other large lump sum payments?" since the last wave of the survey—as the income variable (Dong et al. 2021, 353–354). Controlling for other variables, the authors found that those who received an income shock of US$50,000 or more were more likely to purchase home healthcare, but not nursing home care. The researchers concluded that these findings indicate that the results of the earlier Konetzka et al. (2019) study are likely the reflection of an efficient income effect of insurance in generating the demand for home healthcare, rather than an inefficient price effect.

Chetty (2008) used a similar approach to show the existence of income effects in unemployment insurance, but also to estimate the share of total additional insurance spending that is due to income effects rather than price effects. Chetty observed that unemployment insurance increases the durations of unemployment of those with such insurance, and that this increase is due, at least in part, to a "liquidity" effect. Liquidity refers to the ability of households to liquidate wealth (assets) to use for consumption purposes, and so a liquidity effect would be the equivalent to an income effect in an insurance that makes marginal payments to the insured for every day of unemployment. Moreover, a liquidity (wealth) effect of unemployment insurance that covers the loss of income is analogous to an income effect for insurance that covers the loss of an asset (wealth) like a house or car.

Chetty conducted a two-part empirical analysis. He noted that about half of households with job losers in America have no liquid wealth at the time of the job loss and that consumption in those households would likely be constrained if a job were lost, making an extended period of unemployment to search for a job difficult. He used 4,560 unemployment spells in data

from the Survey of Income and Program Participation (SIPP) over the period 1985–2000 to compare the unemployment durations of those who lose
jobs from wealth-constrained households to the unemployment durations in
households unconstrained by wealth. He found that increases in unemployment insurance benefits appear to increase the unemployment durations of
the constrained group but have no effect on the unemployment durations
of those from the unconstrained group. Chetty concluded from this finding
that price-related inefficient moral hazard is likely to be small, although it
is still possible that the difference he found could be due to a difference in
preferences across the two groups.

In the second part of his analysis, Chetty (2008) used data from a
Pennsylvania survey of job losers in 1991 and data from a survey of unemployment durations in 25 states in 1998 (that oversamples those with unemployment insurance who exhaust their benefits) to investigate the effect of
severance payments on unemployment durations. These data contain the
unemployment durations of 2,441 individuals, of whom 471 received a severance payment. The response to a severance payment would represent an
income effect because it is a lump-sum payment that does not increase with
the duration of the unemployment stint. He found that those with severance
payments have significantly longer unemployment durations than those
without. Unfortunately, in this study, the author was not able to rule out
endogeneity. Nevertheless, he pointed to a different study by Card, Chetty,
and Weber (2007) that found similar results using data from Austria where
the likelihood of an endogeneity effect was diminished by the use of a quasi-
experimental design.

Chetty then estimated the portion of the additional unemployment
durations that is due to liquidity effects in unemployment insurance and the
portion due to inefficient moral hazard. He calculated·that about 60 percent
of the additional unemployment durations with unemployment insurance
are due to income-like liquidity effects and are therefore welfare-increasing,
leaving only about 40 percent due to price-related inefficient moral hazard.

Nyman et al. (2018) used the Medical Expenditure Panel Survey (MEPS)
for the years 1996 to 2010 to demonstrate how the additional healthcare
spending of those with health insurance (compared to those without it) can
be decomposed into price and income effects for various diseases. These
researchers separated MEPS respondents by health conditions: cancer, diabetes, mental illness, heart disease, stroke, chronic obstructive pulmo-
nary disease (COPD) or asthma, arthritis, and hypertension. Employing an

instrumental variable analysis to counter endogeneity, the authors calculated spending with and without insurance for those in each of the eight disease categories. Income elasticities of healthcare spending were then calculated using corresponding data from the Health and Retirement Survey (HRS) for each of the diseases, employing an income shock as the income variable to deal with possible endogeneity. Returning to the MEPS, the amount of spending by the insurer was determined and this was then assumed to be the amount of income that would be transferred to the ill (insured) person if they had been insured with an equivalent indemnity insurance policy. The additional counterfactual medical spending that was generated by that indemnity income transfer was calculated based the application of the income elasticities from the HRS to these indemnity payments. This additional counterfactual spending was deemed to be efficient. The additional medical spending with traditional insurance was then compared to the additional counterfactual spending with the indemnity insurance. These researchers found that the efficient portion of additional insurance spending represented by indemnity insurance ranged from 6 percent for mental health problems to 61 percent for cancer and 71 percent for diabetes. Thus, for at least the latter two diseases, income-transfer effects represented a majority of the additional medical spending when insured. Although the study successfully showed how the quid pro quo welfare effects could be estimated using existing data to simulate the decomposition moral hazard into its efficient and inefficient portions, the researchers noted a number of limitations with the empirical aspects of this study that could be improved upon if reliable trial data were available instead.

These six studies represent the current extent of the empirical work done to estimate the income effects of insurance when a price reduction is used to transfer income from the insurer to the insured. These studies uniformly find that income effects are substantial and are likely in many cases to represent a majority of moral hazard. The findings of these empirical studies are now also reinforced by the following four theoretical studies.

Theoretical Studies

Perhaps the most fundamental questions are: To what extent does insurance increase or decrease welfare, and especially to what extent does insurance result in a welfare gain from the income transfer of insurance net of the welfare loss from the using the price reduction to transfer income? A number of studies address questions that bear on these issues.

In an early analysis, Nyman and Maude-Griffin (2001) and Nyman (2003) presented a theoretical model to estimate the welfare loss from the price effect alone. The plan of the analysis was to estimate the welfare loss from the conventional analysis (Pauly 1968), and then to determine what percentage of that welfare loss would be represented by the welfare loss from the price effect alone in the quid pro quo model. In Figure 2.3, this difference would be represented by area def as a percentage of area abc.

Because of the assumption of linear demands, it is simply necessary to estimate the differences in quantity demanded (inefficient moral hazard) in order to estimate the differences in the magnitude of areas under the demand curves, representing the welfare losses. Three differences in quantity were specified:

$$(M^* - M^u) \approx \eta M^u(c-1) \tag{8.1}$$

$$(M^H - M^u) \approx [\eta M^u + \Theta \varepsilon M^u] (c-1), \text{ and} \tag{8.2}$$

$$(M^N - M^u) \approx [\eta M^u + \Theta \varepsilon M^u](c-1)/[1+(1-c)\Theta \varepsilon] \tag{8.3}$$

representing the welfare loss from the conventional theory, the welfare loss from the Hicksian substitution effect, and the welfare loss from the price effect of the quid pro quo analysis, respectively. M^u is the uninsured quantity demanded, M^* is the quantity demanded after an exogenous reduction in price measured by a movement along the Marshallian demand curve, M^H is the quantity demanded representing the Hicksian substitution effect, and M^N is the quantity demanded representing the new quid pro quo price effect. (These quantity differences were depicted in Figure 2.5 as $[Q_I - Q_O]$, $[Q_H - Q_O]$, and $[Q_N - Q_O]$, respectively.) These equations can be simplified as follows without loss of their ability to capture the relative sizes of the welfare losses:

$$(M^* - M^u)/M^u \approx \eta(c-1) \tag{8.4}$$

$$(M^H - M^u)/M^u \approx [\eta + \Theta \varepsilon](c-1), \text{ and} \tag{8.5}$$

$$(M^N - M^u)/M^u \approx [\eta + \Theta \varepsilon](c-1)/[1+(1-c)\Theta \varepsilon] \tag{8.6}$$

Thus the relative welfare losses depend on four parameters: η, c, Θ, and ε, representing the price elasticity of demand, the coinsurance rate, the share of spending devoted to medical care, and the income elasticity of demand, respectively.

To calculate the relative welfare effects, these parameters must be specified. The price elasticity of demand, η, was chosen to be −0.32, based on the RAND Health Insurance Experiment estimate of the arc elasticity between the 0.25 and the 0.95 coinsurance rates. This was likely an understatement of the responsiveness because the RAND experiment did not account for the added insurance responsiveness to making otherwise unaffordable expenditures affordable.

The coinsurance rate, c, was chosen to be the average rate from the RAND experiment, 0.31. This coinsurance rate seemed to be a reasonable approximation of the percentage of all medical expenditures paid by the insured.

The share of an ill consumer's budget that is devoted to medical care spending, Θ, was problematic. In Nyman (2003), it was pointed out that this value differs across individuals and should be weighted "because the distribution of the expenditures is so skewed" (Nyman 2003, 95). Thus, "an approximation that is perhaps more representative of the ill person's spending share would be to use the medical expenditures share for the 10% of households accounting for 72% of medical spending" (Nyman 2003, 95–96). This number was adjusted to reflect the fact that the insured ill would have less income to spend with insurance because of the premium payment. The analysis, therefore, used 0.54 as a "conservative estimate of the representative ill consumer's spending share" (Nyman 2003, 97).

The income elasticity of demand, ε, was also problematic. Because the estimates of this parameter in the RAND experiment did not account for income transfers, nor did the RAND experiment focus on estimating this parameter for the ill, a parameter was taken from the estimate in Feenberg and Skinner (1994) based on tax returns. These authors estimate this elasticity for the ill to be about 0.38, but this also was likely to be too low because it did not capture income transfers from insurance when ill, which would augment

Table 8.1 Estimate of the Relative Welfare Loss from the Price Effect

	Price effect welfare loss as a percent of original consumption	Price effect welfare loss evaluated with parameters	Price effect welfare loss as a percent of the Marshallian loss
Marshallian demand	$\eta(c-1)$	$(-0.32)(-0.69) = 0.221$	100 %
Hicksian demand	$\eta(c-1) + \Theta\varepsilon(c-1)$	$0.221 + (0.54)(0.38)(-0.69) = 0.079$	36 %
New demand	$[\eta(c-1) + \Theta\varepsilon(c-1)] /[1+ (1-c)\Theta\varepsilon]$	$0.079/ [1 + (0.69)(0.54)(0.38)] = 0.069$	31 %

spending and income equally, and thus increase the spending elasticity of income.

Given these parameters, the various estimates of the welfare loss and the percentage welfare loss relative to the conventional theory are listed in Table 8.1.[2] These calculations indicate that the welfare loss after adjusting for a Hicksian income effect is about 36 percent of the conventional one, and that the quid pro quo welfare loss is about 31 percent of the conventional one. Thus, about 31 percent of the increase in consumption from insurance is inefficient. Note that this difference focuses only on the price-related welfare loss from using a price reduction to transfer income. This change, however, is not the total net change in welfare because it does not account for welfare gains from the increase in consumer surplus associated with either the additional healthcare consumption generated by the income transfer on the healthcare that would have been consumed without insurance.

Boone (2018) conducted a theoretical analysis to estimate the added welfare gain from the access to otherwise unaffordable care by health insurance. Specifically, this author compared (1) the welfare gain from a state provided ("basic") health insurance plus the availability of a supplemental private insurance under the conventional theory (analyzed primarily in a companion piece, Boone 2015), to (2) the welfare gain from the same health insurance regimen when the welfare gain from access to otherwise unaffordable care

---

[2] In Nyman (2003), there were typographical errors in the corresponding table, but the final calculations were correct. The typos have been corrected here.

is also included as a goal of basic insurance. In the conventional theory, the welfare gain from basic insurance is derived from coverage of those relatively healthy consumers who would have been driven out of the private health insurance market by adverse selection. Boone (2018) pointed to an analysis by Pauly (2008) who concluded that, because these excluded consumers are relatively healthy, substituting a state-provided system that covered them (for a private one that did not) would generate a relatively small welfare gain. This is because under a private system, many of those who become uninsured because of adverse selection could purchase the healthcare privately. On the other hand, Boone recognized that many of these consumers represented those who would not be able to gain access to care if uninsured. So in his analysis, he assumed access to be a goal of the basic insurance program and modeled some of the relatively healthy as being constrained by their incomes from gaining access to healthcare if they became ill and were uninsured. Boone found that the gain from instituting a state-provided basic system generates "welfare effects . . . [that] are magnitudes higher in the access to care model" (Boone 2018, 54).[3]

The analysis of insurance in chapter 2 assumes that insurance pays off by resetting the price of the covered commodity at a coinsurance rate instead of the full price (Nyman 1999b; 2003). This analysis further assumes that the price of the covered commodity is fixed exogenously. If so, the purchase of insurance would generate an income-transfer effect that increases welfare through an increase in the consumer surplus, as illustrated in Figure 2.3. However, when the price of the covered commodity is endogenous and determined by sellers with monopoly power, the welfare gains are not as clear.

Besanko, Dranove, and Garthwaite (2020) considered the case of private insurance coverage of a commodity where the firm is a monopolist that can

---

[3] Boone's (2018) study, in addition, showed that introducing access as a goal of basic insurance also changes the policy implications for the cost-effectiveness analysis. Under the conventional use of cost-effectiveness analysis, treatments are ranked according to the quality-adjusted life years (QALYs) gained per dollar spent (Gold et al. 1996; Neumann et al. 2019). A government budget spent according to this ranking until exhausted maximizes the total QALYs gained from the budget. In the standard cost-effectiveness analysis, if distributional issues are considered, they are considered separately. Boone found instead that, once access is specified as a goal of basic insurance, distributional considerations become an endogenous part of the cost-effectiveness analysis. His model concluded that diseases then would not simply be ranked according to their marginal QALY to cost ratios, but also according to the prevalence of a disease/intervention combinations among those who receive the greatest benefit from the intervention. This would likely be the high-risk and low-income types in the population. Thus, "prevalence" would enter into the ranking of illness/treatment coverage decisions as well.

set the price. The authors have in mind the case of pharmaceutical insurance coverage of patented drugs. Using a theoretical model, they showed that the introduction of insurance into a market with a competitively supplied commodity would indeed increase the consumer surplus, but insurance would likely shrink the consumer surplus (compared to the uninsured case) if the firm supplying the commodity had monopoly market power and could set prices. Thus, the monopolist would be able to capture a portion of the increase in consumer surplus from insurance coverage and convert it into firm profits.

The model that these authors developed also showed how cost sharing can have a perverse effect on the distribution of the people who purchase insurance. As discussed above and in chapter 2, insurance has conventionally been seen as a source of inefficient moral hazard and cost-sharing has been the solution that economists have recommended to reduce moral hazard. Higher coinsurance rates and deductibles act to increase the effective prices of covered services to consumers, and thus to choke off additional care, all of which was deemed inefficient under the conventional model. However, cost-sharing provisions may also reduce the ability of insurance to cover otherwise unaffordable healthcare costs to the consumer, thus reducing the demand for health insurance, especially among the low-income consumers. Thus, increased cost sharing may induce some low-income consumers not to purchase health insurance. Because the remaining health insurance purchasers have higher incomes, it may encourage monopolist firms to set prices even higher.

Finally, these authors considered the case of insurance that covers both monopoly-provided drugs and also other forms of healthcare, such as hospital care and physician services, which are assumed to be competitively supplied. They show that such comprehensive insurance could result in the monopolist charging such high drug prices that they exceed the drug's value to the consumer. This is possible because if insurers are compelled to cover both competitive and monopolized commodities, the monopolist could use the high prices for the monopolized commodities to capture not only the consumer surplus from those monopolized commodities (the drugs) but some of the consumer surplus of the competitively supplied commodities as well.

The access value of insurance is therefore not assured and is dependent on market conditions, specifically, the presence of monopoly power held by the providers. These authors summarize their findings this way:

Previous work—most notably Nyman (1998, 1999, 2003)—has shown that when prices are exogenous, this increase in access benefits consumers. However, our analysis—which endogenizes the prices charged by manufacturers of high-value products—demonstrates that while the Nyman access benefit does indeed operate, the welfare gains can be wiped out if the producers of the high-value products have sufficient monopoly pricing power. (Besanko, Dranove, and Garthwaite 2020, 17–18)

These authors then consider policy solutions where monopoly drug prices are either controlled (1) directly by government or (2) indirectly by reforming the market so that the monopolized drugs are supplied (more) competitively. The authors note, however, that the use of these solutions is made difficult because pharmaceutical firms require some level of profits in order to finance continued product innovation. Thus, the solutions to this issue are complex.

Phelps (2022) constructed a theoretical model to derive the conditions for optimal coinsurance and deductibles in health insurance. Phelps's interest in and work on optimal insurance dates back to the early foundational work for the RAND Health Insurance Experiment (Phelps 1973). To my knowledge, Phelps's present model (Phelps 2022) represents the first time that his work has acknowledged the effects of income on welfare.

Unlike the last two papers reviewed in this section where utility was assumed to be risk-neutral with regard to income in order to concentrate on the access value of insurance, Phelps's (2020) model generates a gain from insurance through the curvature of an assumed lognormal utility function. This assumption is used, despite the calculations by Chetty (2006), Gourinchas and Parker (2002), and Rabin (2005) who find that the utility function is, or must be, virtually linear. His calculations of optimal coinsurance rates and deductibles are based on the inclusion of income effects and measures of skewness and kurtosis of the risk distribution. He does not, however, give an intuitive explanation for the consumer behavior that the skewness and kurtosis represents, nor does he explain their connection to the demand for insurance.

Phelps (2022) leveled two criticisms at the calculation in Nyman (2003) that the true welfare loss is only 31 percent of the moral hazard welfare loss as calculated according to the conventional theory. First, he suggested that, because Nyman's welfare loss estimate is based on the difference in the quantities of medical care, instead of the differences in (price*quantity =) expenditures (as represented by areas in a demand curve diagram like Figure 2.3), the estimate is not accurate and overstates the difference. Nyman, however, expressly assumed that the demand curves that describe these welfare losses are linear (Nyman 2003, 91). If so, the areas representing the welfare losses are exactly commensurate with the quantities alone, and so Phelps's criticism is not correct. This is apparent from inspection of Figure 2.3 and a comparison of the areas abc and def.

Second, Phelps suggested that, by choosing a single value for the share of income that an ill person would spend on healthcare, Nyman (2003) has also biased upward the difference between the conventional welfare loss and the welfare loss from a quid pro quo model, making the latter welfare loss too small as a percentage of the conventional welfare loss. Phelps suggested that these shares vary with illness and, if the probability of becoming ill is also accounted for, a probability-weighted estimate of the difference would be smaller. Nyman (2003), too, recognized that there is a distribution of spending, but sought to focus on the spending of those who are ill as being more representative of the type of individual who would generate this welfare loss. While Phelps's analysis may account for the range of spending shares of those on a spending continuum because of health, the spending shares at the low end are unlikely to represent those who are actually ill. Therefore, his estimate likely understates the difference.

Phelps, nevertheless, now acknowledges and accepts the importance of income effects. Despite his issues with the previous quid pro quo calculations, Phelps writes,

> Applying the logic of Nyman's income-effect analysis shows that "countable" welfare losses fall rapidly as event-specific budget shares of income transfers . . . rise, so that the economic value of imposing coinsurance-like payments diminishes and finally vanishes at larger [budget shares]. This result leads directly to the conclusion that stop-loss insurance provides higher value to risk-averse consumers than any plan that has unending coinsurance requirements. (Phelps 2022, 25–26)

In addition to acknowledging the necessity of stop-losses, Phelps's reevaluation of the risk distribution, plus the recognition of income effects, led him to conclude that deductibles should not be fixed amounts, but should vary with the income of the consumer. Most importantly, however, his optimal coinsurance rates are far smaller than those that have been recommended in the literature and that have been used as the justification for much of health insurance policy in the US. Instead of coinsurance rate recommendations of 45 percent with no stop loss provision (Manning and Marquis 1996) or 66 percent (or higher) for all healthcare across the board (Feldstein 1973), Phelps found that "optimal coinsurance rates are quite small, nearing 0 for plausible distributions of medical spending risk" (Phelps 2022, 27).

Price Effects and Policy

When a price reduction is used to transfer income in insurance, the pure price effect represents a welfare loss. As mentioned, this loss was a preoccupation of health economists for much of period following the publication in 1968 of Pauly's influential original study (Pauly 1968). As suggested by Nyman (2003), however, the welfare loss is not nearly as great when income effects from insurance are acknowledged and accounted for. Nevertheless, the latter study estimated the price effect loss at 31 percent of the conventional moral hazard welfare loss, a substantial portion. Is this still a welfare loss that should preoccupy policy analysts, as it has for the last 50 years with regard to health insurance? Should such a welfare loss generate increased cost-sharing, in the form of higher coinsurance rates and deductibles? The quid pro quo theory has at least two insights that bear on this question.

First, the policy question raised by the moral hazard welfare loss has conventionally been presented as a trade-off between "risk spreading and the appropriate incentives" (Zeckhauser 1970) or equivalently "risk pooling and moral hazard" (Manning and Marquis 1996). The welfare gain was conventionally captured with utility function diagrams like Figure 2.1 and the welfare loss with market diagrams like Figure 2.2. An increase in the coinsurance rate would reduce the moral hazard welfare loss, but also reduce the welfare gain from avoiding risk. With the quid pro quo theory, the tradeoff facing policymakers is different. The application of cost sharing might well diminish the welfare loss from the price effect, but it would also simultaneously diminish the consumer surplus welfare gain of the income-transfer effect that causes both (1) an increase in the consumer surplus of those covered commodities already purchased without insurance, and (2) an increase in the consumer surplus of the additional covered commodities consumed (see Figure 2.3). Importantly, the value assigned to the additional commodities in the latter case would also reflect the probability that they might not otherwise be affordable to the consumer, were it not for insurance reducing their cost. Thus, the access value lost to the consumer from the imposition of greater cost-sharing could be substantial because of either not being able to afford to cover the coinsurance payment or deductible during a specific *ex post* triggering episode, or recognizing this possibility *ex ante* and not purchasing insurance at all.

Fels (2016) brings home the effect of cost-sharing policy on access when he considered the value of private long-term care (LTC) insurance compared with the value of government-provided LTC insurance, such as the Medicaid program in the United States. He first points to the number of studies that have lamented the relatively small number of private LTC insurance policies sold in the United States. Most of these studies attribute this lack of demand to the crowding out private LTC insurance by Medicaid (Pauly 1989; 1990; Brown, Coe, and Finkelstein 2007; Brown and Finkelstein 2008). Next, he points to studies that claim that the insurance value of Medicaid is low anyway, when Medicaid is evaluated by the risk reduction gains of conventional theory (Brown and Finkelstein 2008; 2001). Fels points out, however, that the motivation for Medicaid is not risk reduction, but instead the provision of access to LTC services for the poor. Thus, crowding out is only a reasonable criticism if private LTC insurance were able to provide the same level of access that Medicaid does.

Fels (2016) then showed how premiums for private LTC insurance could be made more affordable if deductibles are increased. Deductibles, however, make access to LTC services contingent on being able to pay the deductible when ill. So high deductibles might mean that, even though lower insurance premiums have made LTC insurance more affordable *ex ante* when healthy, insurance is no longer valuable because access to LTC services would be denied due to unaffordably high deductibles *ex post* when ill. As a result, the crowding out of private LTC insurance by Medicaid is not a legitimate issue because private LTC insurance simply cannot provide the same access for poor consumers that Medicaid does.

This analysis and the quid pro quo theory suggest that existing studies of the effect of increasing cost-sharing on the price effect of insurance sometimes overlook the importance of access, and access has important welfare implications. Raising coinsurance rates or deductibles reduces these price effects, but such a policy would also affect access to the covered commodity and may greatly reduce the *ex ante* value of insurance as a result. Such an access effect is also likely to effect the poor disproportionately.

Second, to avoid the welfare loss from using a price reduction to transfer income, an alternative policy would be to use indemnity insurance contracts that pay off with a lump sum and so transfer income directly. For example, with an indemnity health insurance contract, any additional spending on healthcare would occur only (at least, in theory) after all the other goods and services that the consumer could purchase with the indemnity payment had been considered. As a result, any additional consumption of the covered commodity would be efficient. As was suggested in chapter 2, however, such indemnity payments in health insurance would generate other costs. The insurer would incur additional research costs for developing a tariff of payments that differ not only with each disease, but also with each of the various treatments for the disease, with each of the disease's complications, with the patient's comorbidities, with the levels of responsiveness to treatment, and so on. Moreover, the insurer would need to establish a mechanism—probably involving the hiring of expensive medical personnel—for confirming illnesses before a payment is made, in order to eliminate fraud. As a result, adopting an indemnity payment system for health insurance might have costs that exceed the costs of the original market failure, making the original price-payoff insurance the efficient vehicle for transferring income. Similar cost advantages may exist for other types of insurance that use a price reduction to transfer income.

The adoption of a quid pro quo theory would emphasize that an income transfer from insurance is the raison d'être for insurance. If so, the vehicle for making that income transfer would need to be identified in order to determine policy prescriptions. For any insurance that pays off by reducing the price of the covered commodity, this would lead to the recognition that the additional spending can be decomposed into income and price effects, but that the latter could be regarded as a transaction cost of using a price reduction to transfer income. This would then raise the issue of whether any other vehicle was available for transferring income that would have a lower transaction cost. If all the other ways of transferring this income have greater transactions costs, then incurring the price effect in price-payoff insurance would become efficient under the theory of the second best.[4]

[4] The theory of the second best holds that correcting one market failure might cause another market failure that has an even greater welfare cost. So rather than trying to eliminate all such failures when there are such tradeoffs, it is preferred to find the failure that generates the smallest efficiency

Income Transfers and the Consumer Surplus

The quid pro quo model of the welfare gain from insurance that pays off by reducing the price of a covered commodity shows that an income-transfer effect increases welfare through an increase in the consumer surplus of the covered commodity (Nyman 1999b). An important antecedent of the quid pro quo theory is the paper by de Meza (1983) that showed that insurance that pays off directly with an income payment could also generate an increase in demand for the covered commodity. In a recent paper, de Meza and Reyniers (2023) focused on how to evaluate an insurance payoff that is either (1) a direct increase in income or (2) the replacement of a commodity that has an equivalent income value.

De Meza and Reyniers (2023) argue that, when commodities are insured, the value of the insurance is captured in part by the area under a demand curve for the commodities that are insured, that is, by their consumer surplus. As a result, insurance that replaces an actual US$1,000 possession that is lost, stolen, broken, or otherwise fails, has a value that exceeds the value of insurance that pays off with a US$1,000 indemnity payment, even though the US$1,000 cost to the insurer is the same. This is true for consumer durables like washing machines and refrigerators, but it may also be true for more costly consumer possessions such as cars, houses, and services such as LTC and medical care. In the authors' words, "the more surplus a good delivers, the greater the loss if it fails, so the higher will be the [willingness to pay] to insure it" (de Meza and Reyniers 2023, 271–272). This may help to explain why insurance in the form of warranties on consumer items are purchased, despite their high premiums compared to their expected return.

De Meza and Reyniers (2023) support their model with a survey of 300 nonstudent subjects who were asked to choose between insuring one of two commodities that cost the same to purchase, but where the stated willingness to pay value of one was greater than the WTP value of the other. They find that 64 percent of respondents would choose to insure the commodity with the greater consumer surplus, with the rest either choosing the one with the lower consumer surplus or not favoring one or the other. Thus, differences in the consumer surpluses of the commodities that are being replaced by

---

cost and tolerate that level of inefficiency as a second-best solution. Thus, some amount of inefficiency is optimal under the theory of the second best (Lipsey and Lancaster 1956).

insurance seem to explain some of the variation in the demand for insurance for those items.

In chapter 5, the quid pro quo theory considered the findings of prospect theory and how such findings may alter the demand for insurance. In chapter 6, it was concluded that the most likely impact of prospect theory on the demand for insurance was through loss aversion. One possible effect of loss aversion was to reinforce the shifting of up of (1) the utility function or (2) the positive portion of the value function, increasing the demand for insurance as described in Figure 5.3. Similarly, the de Meza and Reyniers (2023) analysis suggests that the consumer surplus gain from the income-transfer effect in insurance that pays off by reducing price may actually be greater than the effect of a direct income payment. This is because the income-transfer effect in price-payoff insurance would more directly capture the consumer surplus associated with that coverage. That is, the value of the income-transfer effect in price-payoff insurance is derived in part from the additional commodities purchased, but the value of an income transfer in indemnity insurance is derived only from the income transfer. This difference would represent a reason why price-payoff insurance may be valued by consumers more than indemnity insurance, even if the cost to the insurer for the two types of payoffs, and the premiums charged to the consumer, were exactly the same. This effect would reinforce the shift of the utility or value functions derived from a change in state.

Summary

This chapter reviewed the important surveys and the existing empirical and theoretical work in support of the quid pro quo theory of the demand for insurance. These studies show that the income effects in insurance and the access to the additional covered consumption that they produce have important implications for welfare and policy, implications not recognized by conventional theory. For health insurance, much of past welfare and policy analysis has been based on the RAND Health Insurance Experiment, the so-called gold standard study that many economists have relied upon for data or for summary statistics to use in their theoretical models. Although the RAND experiment was based on conventional theory and therefore suffered because it did not recognize the importance of income transfers, perhaps an even more important shortcoming was the bias created by the fact that 16 times the percentage of participants dropped out of the cost-sharing arms of the experiment as out of the free fee-for-service arm. The effect of this bias is now reviewed in an appendix.

Appendix: Attrition Bias in the RAND Health Insurance Experiment

The most expensive social experiment ever conducted in the United States was the RAND Health Insurance Experiment (HIE) (Newhouse et al. 1993). It was well known at the time that those with insurance purchased more healthcare, but what was not known was the extent to which this was due to the insured responding to a lower price—the coinsurance rate—or to insurance being disproportionately purchased and used by those who were ill—adverse selection. Isolating the effect of the coinsurance rate on the quantity of healthcare demanded was, therefore, the main reason for conducting the study because it would seem to confirm the welfare loss impact of expansions of health insurance under conventional theory.

The study compared healthcare utilization and spending by participant families randomly assigned to either insurance that provided free care for all medical services or insurance that provided care with various coinsurance payments: 25 percent, 50 percent, and 95 percent. The coinsurance arms had a maximum amount of expenditures of US$1,000 over 12 months, after which any additional care would be provided free. Enrollment in the HIE began in 1974, so the US$1,000 stop-loss provision would be equivalent after accounting for medical care inflation to over US$12,500 in 2022. The experiment also included an analysis of participant families randomly assigned to two deductible plans and a health maintenance organization.

The experiment found that healthcare spending in the free-care arm was greater than in the coinsurance arms. For example, spending was about 45 percent greater in the free-care arm than in the arm with the 95 percent coinsurance rate and the US$1,000 stop-loss (Newhouse et al. 1993, 40). This was expected, but what made this experiment especially influential was the finding that, "the 40 percent increase in services on the free-care plan had little or no measurable effect on health status for the average adult" (Newhouse et al. 1993, 243). The exception was the impact of cost-sharing on the sick poor, whose health was adversely affected by being assigned to a cost-sharing plan (Newhouse et al. 1993, 339). Nevertheless, for many economists, the RAND findings confirmed the conventional theory, as summarized by Pauly's (1968) diagram (Figure 2.2): the additional healthcare consumed when insured had costs that exceed the value of the additional healthcare to consumers. This finding led to the policy conclusion that coinsurance rates could be raised to choke off additional inefficient healthcare with little, if any, adverse consequences to health. Over the years, the RAND HEI came to be regarded as the gold standard study, and so this finding became especially influential in determining health insurance policy. It provided empirical support for the many economists who were already inclined to argue for greater cost-sharing.

The problem with this finding was that the RAND experiment did not explain or account for the large number of participants who dropped out of the coinsurance and deductible arms. Over the course of the experiment, 6.7 percent of those in the cost-sharing arms voluntarily dropped out of the experiment early, compared to only 0.4 percent who dropped out of the free care arm. This represented a 16-fold increase in the attrition rate in the cost-sharing arms compared to the attrition rate in the free arm. This attrition differential represented the most dramatic change in behavior caused by cost-sharing in the entire experiment. Despite its salience and potential for biasing the results, the RAND researchers had never explained why this attrition rate differential existed.

In 2007, however, an article focusing on the potential effect of this attrition differential was published (Nyman 2007a). The article suggested that those who dropped out of the experiment in the cost-sharing arms did so because they had become ill and wanted to avoid paying the coinsurance and deductibles required when obtaining care within the experiment. Those ill who dropped out could revert to the insurance policy in effect prior to their participation in the HEI and could thereby receive care while avoiding the added RAND cost-sharing expenditures, expenditures that could be as much as US$1,000 at the time (or the equivalent of over US$12,000 in 2022). RAND researchers had recognized this potential problem and put in place provisions designed to reduce the incentives for those in the cost-sharing arms to drop out of the experiment: (1) a participation incentive paid to participants every four weeks over the course of the experiment, with a total payment amount equal to the potential financial risk the participant took on to be in the experiment, compared to their risk under their prior insurance policy; and (2) a completion bonus, paid to those participants who stayed in the experiment for the entire three or five years of the participant's study period. These payments, however, were independent of the participant's actual incurred costs, and so the incentive for a newly diagnosed participant to avoid the cost-sharing by dropping out was never totally eliminated. Moreover, as the attrition rate differential demonstrates, these incentives clearly did not work.

The incentive to drop out was likely greatest for those who had become ill with a diagnosis that required hospitalization, because a hospitalization would generally require the largest cost-sharing payment. The results of the experiment are consistent with this attrition-based interpretation. For example, compared to 10.3 percent in the free arm, only 7.9 percent of those in the 95 percent coinsurance rate arm were hospitalized. This represented about a 23 percent decline in hospitalizations. It is, however, difficult to believe that, if such a decline in hospitalizations were entirely due to participants who needed inpatient care opting not to be hospitalized and not to receive a hospital-based procedure because of its costs, this would not have had noticeable effects on the health of these participants. Nevertheless, the RAND experiment found no overall health effects from this decline in healthcare utilization. Moreover, with regard to attrition, the RAND researchers wrote that "there was no statistically significant difference in the rate of use between those who did and those who did not complete the Experiment" so the difference in the rate of attrition did not cause "any appreciable bias" (Newhouse et al. 1993, 25–26).

The RAND researchers defended the experiment against the critical paper on attrition (Nyman 2007a) by presenting a rebuttal piece where they claimed that "we could find no evidence that those who withdrew were importantly different from those who did not" (Newhouse et al. 2008, 302). But in addition to their rebuttal, they also made available on Newhouse's Harvard University website a 1993 paper by RAND researchers (Manning, Duan, and Keeler 1993) that had been referenced in their 1993 book (Newhouse et al. 1993), but with an earlier date, 1988. This paper investigated the effect of attrition on the consumption of healthcare and concluded that,

> The data from the Health Insurance Experiment indicate that individuals who dropped out behaved differently (in ways that measured characteristics and time on the study could not explain) than those who stayed to the end of the study. Thus past

inferences based largely on stayers are biased. For outpatient care, the bias is quite small. But for inpatient care, there was a moderate bias. (Manning, Duan, and Keeler 1993, 15–16)

To my knowledge, these results had never been acknowledged publicly by RAND researchers prior to 2007 when this controversy arose. These findings by Manning, Duan, and Keeler (1993) contradict the oft-repeated RAND statements—and resulting widely held belief among those in the health economics research community—that there was "no appreciable bias" caused by attrition.

The nut of the issue is that RAND researchers did not collect information on either the healthcare utilization or health status of those who left the experiment after they left. Thus, without these additional data it would be difficult to determine the effect of attrition on healthcare spending or health. To my knowledge, no study estimating the attrition bias in the spending differential due to coinsurance in the experiment has ever been conducted. Nevertheless, it is clear that those who remained in the experiment and in the cost-sharing arms were likely to have experienced fewer health issues generally because of the attrition from the experiment by cost-sharing participants with illnesses or other health issues. As a result, even though there was a reduction in healthcare consumed in the cost-sharing arms compared to the healthcare consumed in the free care arm, participants in both arms were essentially receiving the care they needed, and so there was little observable difference in health status.[5] Because of this attrition differential, and the lack of follow-up data and analysis, it is clear that the RAND Health Insurance Experiment is far from a gold standard study and cannot be trusted to show the true effects of increased cost sharing on health.

---

[5] Interestingly, when the responsiveness to being placed in the coinsurance arm vs. the free care arm was disaggregated by high, medium, and low-income ranges, those in the high- and medium-income categories were more responsive to coinsurance than those in the low-income range. We would have expected just the opposite because, if those with high and medium incomes became ill, they would have had more income to cover the coinsurance costs and so would have been less responsive to coinsurance rates. Instead, the high and medium incomes were more responsive. The most likely explanation for this unexpected finding is that high- and medium-income participants had more complete private insurance coverage to fall back on, and so were more likely to drop out when faced with a potential coinsurance payment. If they dropped out, the care they received would not have registered in the RAND accounts, and so the high- and medium-income participants in the cost-sharing arms appeared to consume much less healthcare than their counterparts did in the free care arm. Low-income participants did not have such comprehensive coverage to fall back on and so were more likely to stay in the experiment. They were less responsive to coinsurance rates, compared to the apparent responsiveness of the high- and medium-income participants.

9

The Insurance-Purchasing Gambler

Introduction

A book that juxtaposes a theory of insurance with a theory of gambling might appear an odd combination of topics to those unfamiliar with this literature. To most economists, however, the connection is obvious: it is derived from the famous model by Milton Friedman and L. J. Savage that proposes to explain the purchase of insurance by a preference to avoid the risk of an uninsured loss (Friedman and Savage 1948). This same paper goes on to explain the purchase of a gambling wager based on risk preferences as well, but here it is a desire to obtain the risk of gamble instead of retaining a sure amount, the wager. It would probably be fair to say that this model has represented the basis for understanding the demand for insurance and for gambling held by most economists since the paper was written in 1948.

The Friedman–Savage paper also established one of the classic puzzles in economics: the existence of the insurance-purchasing gambler. To explain this phenomenon, these authors proposed that utility as a function of income could be generally increasing with income at a decreasing rate, but exhibit a portion where utility is increasing with income at an increasing rate, as illustrated by Figure 3.3.[1] Such local convexities were interpreted to mean that the same consumer could find it rational to purchase insurance, because of risk aversion, and to gamble at the same time, because of the convex risk-seeking portion of the function. This diagram has obvious mathematical appeal, but it begs the question of why marginal utility would be decreasing

---

[1] As discussed in chapter 3, Bailey et al. (1980) have argued that nonconcavity actually could not in principle explain gambling because the option of saving and borrowing would dominate when the consumer's rate of time preference differs from the interest rate and there are two periods. Hartley and Farrell (2002) dispute this argument, and there is also the issue of whether consumers (given de Meza's [1983] analysis of insurance) actually regard saving and borrowing as substitutes for gambling, or more generally, if they do, what proportion of gambling behavior can be explained with the model in Bailey et al. (1980).

A Theory of Insurance and Gambling. John A. Nyman, Oxford University Press. © Oxford University Press 2024. DOI: 10.1093/oso/9780197687925.003.0009

over some portions of income and increasing over others. That is, it solved the mathematical problem, but failed to provide the intuition for why people would also gamble.

Because of the widespread prevalence of insurance-buying gamblers and the broad acceptance of risk aversion as the conventional motivation for the demand for insurance, a number of authors have sought to provide a behavioral explanation that preserves the assumption of functional concavity. Some of these models are based on the identification of specific consumer characteristics which create overlapping discontinuities in utility functions and which then make portions of the combined functions convex. Other models postulate indivisibilities in commodities that prompt consumers on occasion to override a basic aversion to risk and gamble in order to gain access to these "lumpy" commodities. Still other models focus on how a subjective reweighting of probabilities would make gambling seem to be a bargain and thus act to override the consumer's basic desire for certainty. And finally, some models explain (as already discussed in chapter 3) that gamblers derive additional utility from its entertainment value and that this additional consumption value of gambling, along with the assumption about the lack of appreciable concavity of the utility function when modest gambles are at stake, enables consumers to override basic risk aversion and gamble. A number of other explanations have been offered as well. These explanations all make it possible for the consumer to purchase insurance for risk aversion reasons, and to gamble at the same time for risk seeking reasons, per the conventional theory.

Overlapping Utility Functions

Friedman and Savage's (1948) theory of the demand for insurance and gambling begins by explaining separately the behaviors of those who purchase insurance and those who gamble. Those who purchase insurance have utility functions that are concave (from below), and those who gamble have convex ones.[2] Then, these authors note the existence of the insurance-purchasing

---

[2] Friedman and Savage (1948) refer to the shapes of these utility functions in just the opposite terms: an insurance-purchasing consumer has a utility function that is "convex" from above, and a gambling consumer has one that is "concave" from above. The present analysis uses the more common perspective of "concave" from below to characterize the utility function of an insurance purchasers and "convex" from below to characterize the utility function of the gambler.

gambler and explain such a consumer's behavior with the famous "wiggly utility curve" (Friedman and Savage 1948, 297) described by Figure 3.3. The authors recognize, however, the potential difficulty with this explanation and seek to head off criticisms by providing additional theory regarding this wiggle. They suggest that consumers have concave utility functions overall, but that these utility functions vary according to "class." Low-income consumers—one class—have a concave function at the low end of the income distribution, and high-income consumers—another class—have a concave function at the higher end of the distribution. Although Friedman and Savage do not further define the term, class might represent a certain set of cultural and economic assumptions held in common and so define its members and that includes, apparently, commonly held notions of how utility varies with income.

In Figure 9.1, curves a and b represent utility functions of the low-income class consumers and the high-income class consumers, respectively. Because income was already captured in the diagram, the notion of income class represents the critical shift variable. Consumers with incomes that fall in the range where these two utility functions overlap (for example, income Y_1 in Figure 9.1) do not, however, represent a separate middle class. Such an income level would belong to a consumer in either the low- or high-income class, but not an intermediate class. Friedman and Savage go on to suggest

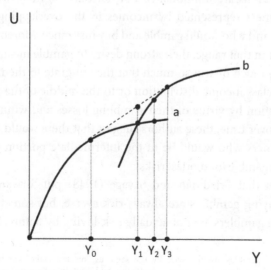

Figure 9.1 Overlapping concave utility functions

instead that there might be a number of classes, each having their own concave utility function and regions of overlap.

This theory leads to specific predictions about the types of gambling and insurance that consumers who find themselves in different income classes would do. For example, this model predicts that some low-income consumers would buy insurance for modest risk losses,[3] but at the same time buy a lottery tickets for the rare chance of large winnings that would place them among the high-income class consumers. These predictions, however, sometimes clash with casual empiricism. For example, the theory also predicts that high-income consumers would buy insurance to protect from modest losses, but not to protect from large losses. (The latter would require premium payments for fair insurance that reduced utility more than the expected utility gain from the insurance payoff that covered a large loss and that would have had placed a consumer in the low-income class.) Nor would high-income consumers ever buy fair lottery tickets for even greater wealth. Both of these predictions are contradicted by observed behavior. Indeed, these authors admit that such cases exist and are problematic, but do not offer a reasonable explanation for their existence (Friedman and Savage 1948, 301).

Friedman and Savage also include refinements in their model that often seem ad hoc. For example, they suggest that the functions of income for upper and lower classes also reflect their frequency distributions, and that these distributions are unimodal (if not normal). So there would be only a few consumers represented by incomes in the overlapping tails of the distributions and who would gamble and buy insurance. Moreover, for those who start out in that range, their strong desire to gamble means they would either lose so much or win so much that they migrate to the middle of the low-income class income distribution or to the middle of the high-income class distribution by virtue of their gambling losses and winnings, respectively. Thus, over time, these authors suggest that there would be fewer and fewer consumers who would be in the intermediate portion of the utility function and gamble for modest risks.

The model that Friedman and Savage (1948) put forward holds that insurance-buying gamblers are always risk-averse, but sometimes seek to gamble. Such gamblers are not actually risk-loving by nature, but may find

---

[3] "Modest risk" gambles are conceptually the same as "modest stake" gambles discussed in chapter 5. These are wagers and income transfers that would result in income positions that are moderately close to the *ex ante* income level.

themselves in situations where they purchase insurance and gamble at the same time because of sociological (class) factors. Such cases, however, are dynamic and are expected to become rarer because of the endogeneity of income levels in their model. Their apparent dismissal of this issue, however, is inconsistent with the many consumers who purchase insurance and engage in repeated gambling for modest risks, the type done at most racetrack, video, and casino venues. Thus, Friedman and Savage (1948) present arguments that gambling and the insurance-purchasing gambling are both rarities, when they are clearly not.

Overlapping utilities have been used by others to explain the insurance-purchasing gambler, but for other reasons. For example, Dobbs (1988) presents a model similar in concept to Friedman and Savage's (1948) model, but suggests that the difference across overlapping utility functions is not between classes, but between those whose incomes are derived from both labor and wealth, and those whose incomes are derived from wealth alone. This model appears to be similar to the quid pro quo model of gambling because it separates utility functions into one that is earned and one that is unearned. One difference is that Dobbs's model is intended to explain the occurrence of both gambling and the purchase of insurance, whereas corresponding the portion of the quid pro quo model is intended to explain only gambling.

Dobbs's model holds that there is a certain amount of wealth that would be sufficient for a person to stop working altogether and rely totally on income derived from wealth to finance his or her consumption, and that one way to achieve that level of wealth is by gambling.[4] Thus, this model is appropriate for explaining gambling for very large income transfers, such as the purchase of lotteries. As Dobbs observes, "this provides an explanation of individuals enthusiasm for purchasing small stake/large prize lottery tickets . . . The point is that lotteries offer the possibility of an alternative life style—the life of leisure" (Dobbs 1988, 173–174). It does not explain the purchase of modest gambles, the explanatory target of the quid pro quo theory and where the motivation is an ongoing desire to gain additional income without working for it. Still, Dobbs's model can explain the simultaneous purchase of insurance to

---

[4] In addition, the motivation in this model is also similar to the consumption indivisibilities discussed next because it suggests that there is a level of wealth that would allow the consumer to stop working altogether and live a life of leisure. This wealth level, however, is not achievable through working, but can only be achieved through winning the large income transfer that a small stake/large prize gambles such as a lottery could provide.

cover modest losses and lotteries for the very large winnings that would place workers in a range of income where they no longer need to work.

Consumption Indivisibilities

Another explanation for gambling that preserves diminishing marginal utility of income is the presence of consumption indivisibilities. Consumption indivisibilities have already been encountered in chapter 2 with regard to the access value of insurance. For example, some medical procedures are so expensive that the consumer cannot afford to purchase them. Moreover, they are indivisible because purchasing a portion of such a procedure would be either worthless or have adverse health consequences, as per the example of stopping a coronary artery bypass graft procedure midcourse. In the case of indivisible medical procedures, insurance exploits the uncertainty of illnesses to multiply an affordable premium into a much larger income transfer that allows for the purchase of the otherwise unaffordable medical care.

In the case of gambling, similar reasoning suggests that there are commodities that are desirable, in the sense that the marginal utility they would render to the consumer is greater than the marginal utility of the last (assumed continuous) commodity actually purchased with existing income. However, these commodities are not purchased because they are indivisible and the consumer's income is not sufficient to cover their price. Again the uncertainty of the gamble would allow for a small wager to be converted into winnings large enough so as to gain access to an otherwise unaffordable "lumpy" commodity. Thus, even with diminishing marginal utility, the indivisibility of some desirable consumption goods provides a reason to gamble.

This explanation of the insurance-purchasing gambler was first suggested by Ng (1965), and was modified by Jones (2008) and Vasquez (2017) to showcase useful implications. Fels (2017) develops the following simple mathematical description of this case. Let V represent consumption utility from consumption good I, the price of which is $p < V$. $I = 1$ if the good is consumed, and I = 0 if not. Good x is divisible and the consumer derives utility, u, from both goods: $u(I, x) = I^*V + x$. Suppose the consumer's budget is B < p. The consumer's utility then relies only on the amount of x that can be purchased, $u_0 = B$. However, if the consumer can purchase a gamble with a probability π of winning p for an actuarially fair price of πp, the gamble would allow for the purchase of I. The consumer's expected utility is

$$u_g = \pi(V + B - \pi p) + (1 - \pi)(B - \pi p) \tag{9.1}$$

$$= u_0 + \pi(V - p) \tag{9.2}$$

That is, the gamble allows the consumer to gain expected utility to the extent that the value of the indivisible commodity exceeds its price. Thus, Fels's model shows that gambling creates the possibility that an unaffordable lumpy commodity is accessible.

Ng (1965) argues that the presence of such an indivisible commodity would create a situation that is again similar to Figure 9.1. In that diagram, a consumer with, say, income of Y_2 cannot purchase a commodity that, if it were continuous and purchased, would add utility b onto utility a, and so shift the combined utility upward. But since the commodity is indivisible, the gain in utility would be lumpy and thus not accessible with the present income. Nevertheless, gambling could allow for access to this indivisible commodity and this potential access to an indivisible commodity would then generate an incentive to gamble. In a similar vein, Hakansson (1970) suggests that borrowing constraints would lead to the same difficulties with indivisible commodities and generate a similar demand for gambles.

Notice that this solution to unaffordability of indivisible commodities might be considered a substitute for insurance by some, but it would surely be an inferior solution. This is because the event that triggers the payoff with gambling has nothing to do with a change in state that makes the indivisible commodity valuable. With insurance, the event that triggers the demand for an indivisible commodity also triggers the income transfer. Therefore, gambling is an inferior substitute compared to insurance in gaining access to some indivisible commodities.

Probability Weighting

This book has not devoted much space to the reweighting of probabilities as an explanation of the demand for insurance or gambling, yet the empirical studies that originally gave support to prospect theory pointed to this factor as being an important determinant of the demand for both. The original prospect theory studies found that consumers generally overstate low probabilities and understate high ones (Kahneman and Tversky 1979; Tversky and Kahneman 1992). By 1992, a diagram like Figure 9.2 was commonly used to translate the actual probabilities into the corresponding decision weights and was strongly supported by empirical studies in the literature (Lattimore, Baker, and Witte 1992; Prelic 1998; Gonzalez and Wu 1999; Abdellaoui 2000; Bruhin, Fehr-Duda, and Epper 2010). Such a diagram would imply that, if a consumer learns that an outcome occurs with a probability of 0.01, because it is at the low end of the conversion function, the consumer's operational understanding of this probability might be consistent with the outcome occurring with a higher probability, say, 0.02 instead. For high probability events, the opposite would be the case. If an outcome occurred with a probability of 0.8, the consumer might reweight it to a lower probability, say, 0.7 operationally. In general, low probabilities have higher subjective probabilities and high probabilities have lower ones. Kahneman and Tversky (1992) emphasized that this reweighting is not an

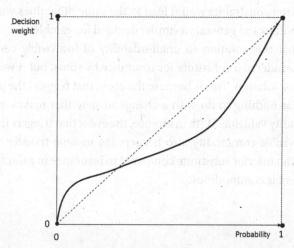

Figure 9.2 Translating probabilities into subjective decision weights

error. Instead, the consumer might know exactly what a 0.1 probability means mathematically, but still reweight it upward for use in economic decision making (Barbaris 2013).

Because most insurance contracts cover outcomes that occur with a low probability, weighting probabilities subjectively acts to increase the demand for insurance. This is because the subjective probabilities would operate to make fair insurance seem favorably unfair to the reweighting consumer. For example, a fair insurance policy that pays US$10,000 with a 0.01 probability might cost US$100 annually, the actuarially fair premium. However, if the consumer instead understands this to mean that the probability of the US$10,000 payment occurring in a year is 0.02 operationally, the actuarially fair premium would instead appear to be US$200 to this consumer. Therefore, paying the true actuarially fair premium of US$100 looks like a bargain and results in a demand for the insurance.

Reweighting no doubt exists and appears to contribute to the demand for insurance (e.g., Collier et al. 2020; Jaspersen, Ragin, and Sydnor 2022), but its effect would be virtually nonexistent if the more fundamental gain (from receiving the income transfer after an event made it more valuable) did not exist. In the above example, if it were not for the increased value of the US$9,900 in income that is transferred because of the event of an illness, or because of a lawsuit due to negligence, or a death, or an increase in longevity, the insurance contract would have little additional value beyond its value as a gamble.

Returning to the issue at hand, the subjective reweighting of probabilities is cited as yet another reason for the existence of the insurance-purchasing gambler (Yaari 1965; Karmarkar 1978; Quiggin 1991). If a consumer is offered a gamble paying US$10,000 with a 0.01 actual probability for a wager of $100, a reweighting of the subjective probability of winning to 0.02 would again mean an increase in the expected payout and fair wager to US$200. As a result, it would again make the actual US$100 cost of the wager seem to be a bargain. For some risk-averse insurance-purchasing consumers, this reweighting of the actual probabilities might be sufficient to motivate the consumer to gamble as well.[5] For gambles with high

---

[5] Quiggin (1982) noticed that applying the probability weighting function to each probability would sometimes lead to violations of dominance. A violation of dominance occurs when an individual decision-maker chooses an inferior alternative when there is a better or dominant one available (see Kourouxous and Bauer 2019). Quiggin's rank dependent expected utility approach applies the probability weighting function to the cumulative probability of each outcome. This preserves the predictions of the reweighting function for the case when one probability is associated with two

probabilities of winning, such as might occur for some favored horses in racetrack gambling, the opposite prediction would apply. That is, the probability weighting would reduce the demand for these high-probability gambles.

Consideration of probability weighting appears to be increasing in gambling studies, but it is still not a common explanation of the demand for gambling (O'Donaghue and Somerville 2018). This is because of problems that exist with understanding the process of reweighting the probabilities. One problem is that the psychological principles that underlie the transformation of probability to decision weights are not clear. Moreover, although probability weighting is refined in that it predicts both increases and decreases the demand for gambles compared to using the actual probabilities, the inflection point is not well defined. This means that erroneous predictions are likely for probabilities around the middle of the reweighting function. O'Donaghue and Somerville (2018) also suggest that to use probability weighting often requires simplifications of the various states considered, but these simplifications might have an important and biasing impact on the conclusions of the analysis.

Entertainment from Gambling

As discussed in chapter 3, an alternative theory of the demand for gambling is that it provides entertainment, and this entertainment is sufficient to overcome, given the modest stakes of most gambling opportunities, what is thought to be a range of income for the consumer's utility function that is linear for all practical purposes (Conlisk 1993). As mentioned in chapter 3, it would probably be fair to say that this theory is so well established among economists that it represents the main alternative to the theory of gambling proposed by Friedman and Savage (1948). Or more accurately, it is a broadly accepted version of the conventional theory, because it accepts that consumers are risk-averse purchasers of insurance and must have a different reason (than their risk preferences) to take on risk and gamble.

As was discussed in chapter 7, however, it is unlikely that the same entertainment value would be derived from the typical casino game—slot

outcomes, but recalculates the subjective probabilities for the cases when more than two outcomes and more than one probability exist (O'Donoghue and Somerville 2018).

machines, roulette, craps, blackjack—if there were no difference between the wager and the winnings in terms of the labor required. And, as Markowitz (1952) observed, playing a slot machine or roulette game for "stage money" would have a limited entertainment value. The social aspect of gambling would also be diminished if the prospect of free money were not drawing others to the gambling venue and thus increasing the social value of gambling.

The difference between the entertainment derived from gambling and the entertainment derived from social card games like bridge or games like checkers or Monopoly® is due to, what might be called, the "edginess" of gambling. This edginess is generated by the willingness of the consumer to wager earned income in exchange for the possibility of a larger income transfer that requires no work. Thus, there is real "skin in the game" with gambling and that feature makes it far more interesting, exciting, and entertaining than these other forms of entertainment, as a number of the empirical studies reviewed in chapter 7 illustrate. And, as a few of these empirical studies also illustrate, consumers recognize that this feature distinguishes the entertainment derived in gambling from other types of gaming entertainment. Without this feature, gambling games, like slot machines and roulette at casinos, would surely exhibit a much-diminished demand.

Quid Pro Quo Approach

A number of other explanations have been offered to explain the existence of the insurance-purchasing gambler over the years. For example, Eden (1980) proposed that the simultaneous demand for insurance and gambling is due to differences in the timing of when these contracts are resolved. Chetty and Szeidl (2007) suggested that the existence of the insurance-purchasing gambler is related to the presence of commodities in the consumer's budget whose consumption is not easily reduced if there were to be a reduction in the consumer's income or wealth. Other models have been proposed (see Flemming 1969; Kim 1973; Dowell 1985), but none has captured the field in the same way that risk aversion has for explaining the purchase of insurance (although the entertainment explanation appears to be the most favored extension of the conventional theory). That the broad acceptance of the risk aversion theory of insurance has survived such a glaring inconsistency as is represented by the insurance-purchasing gambler is perhaps a tribute to the creativity of economists.

Nevertheless, the existence of the insurance-purchasing gambler is only a puzzle if one accepts the premise that insurance and gambling are motivated by utility functions with opposing second derivative signs. If the motivations are not diametrically opposed, the puzzle goes away. The demands for insurance and gambling opportunities proposed under a quid pro quo approach are both derived from a desire for additional income, but these income gains have unrelated motivational origins and so are not mutually exclusive. If so, it should not be regarded as a sign of irrationality, or even of abnormality requiring a special economic model, when one observes the same consumer purchasing a health insurance contract in order to obtain an income transfer in the event of illness and making a bet at a casino in order to obtain a transfer of additional work-free income in the event of a lucky spin of roulette wheel, on the same day.

10

Conclusions

Quid Pro Quo Theory

Any concept is communicated more easily by comparing it to another concept. One way, therefore, to summarize meaningfully the quid pro quo theory is to list the main ways that it differs from conventional theory. Accordingly, for insurance, the quid pro quo theory differs from conventional theory in three important ways:

1. Instead of demanding insurance because of *risk aversion*, that is, because consumers prefer certain losses to uncertain ones of the same expected magnitude, (a) consumers demand insurance to obtain *additional income* (or consumption). (b) Some insurance is also demanded because the additional income allows consumers to gain *access* to commodities that they would not otherwise be able to afford. (c) The uncertainty of the payoff-triggering event is the vehicle by which insurance is able to convert a small *ex ante* premium into a larger income payoff the *ex post* state.

2. Instead of evaluating welfare with a *single utility function* of income, (a) the income payoff is evaluated by a *shifted utility function* of income that reflects the *state dependency of utility*. The shift captures the increase in the value of additional income and is caused by the payoff-triggering event. The increase in value is due primarily to the additional commodities demanded in the consumer's budget as a result of the triggering event. (b) Instead of the utility defined as a function of *other income*, utility is a function of *all income*, including income to purchase the covered commodity.

3. Instead of limiting insurance coverage to the loss that would have occurred if uninsured, and generating a *moral hazard welfare loss* when any additional insured commodities are purchased, (a) the welfare analysis recognizes efficient *income effects*, that is, any commodities purchased because the income transferred from the insurer to the

A Theory of Insurance and Gambling. John A. Nyman, Oxford University Press. © Oxford University Press 2024.
DOI: 10.1093/oso/9780197687925.003.0010

consumer would have increased the consumer's willingness to pay above the price. (b) Any additional inefficient commodities purchased because a price reduction is used to transfer income may represent an irreducible transaction cost of transferring income, if all other mechanisms are more costly.

The quid pro quo theory of gambling differs from conventional theories in the three ways:

4. Instead of demanding gambling because consumers *seek risk*, that is, because they prefer uncertain gains to certain ones of the same expected magnitude, (a) consumers demand gambling because they seek *additional income*. (b) The uncertainty of the payoff-triggering event is the vehicle by which gambling is able to convert a small *ex ante* wager into a larger winnings the *ex post* state.

5. Instead of evaluating the welfare by a *single utility function*, welfare from the additional income is evaluated by a *shifted function*, to reflect the *change in state* caused by the triggering event. The triggering event is a lucky gambling outcome that causes the gambling winnings to be evaluated without the *disutility of labor*. As a result, the additional income is less costly to obtain than by earning it, the standard mechanism for obtaining additional income in a market economy.

6. Instead of assuming all income is *fungible*, the additional income from gambling winnings may represent a reason to *splurge on consumption* for some consumers, and thus represent an additional reason to gamble.

These six points represent the core differences between the conventional and the quid pro quo theories, and are the basis of the welfare analyses. As was noted in the introduction, this book also recognizes that the consumer might have a subtly different and perhaps less sophisticated understanding of the demands for insurance or for gambling than would an analyst interested in determining welfare. Specifically, with insurance that pays off by reducing the price of the covered commodity, the consumer might focus on the commodity that represents the *quo* in the quid pro quo exchange, whereas the analyst would focus on the income that is the provenance for obtaining that commodity. Or, with gambling, the consumer might focus on the *quo* as the additional income obtained from the gambling process, not recognizing that the advantage of winning additional income by gambling is that the income is labor free. Nevertheless, the theory laid out here is the one appropriate for analyzing welfare, even though the consumers' perceptions may not match the theory precisely.

Despite the obvious attractiveness of gaining additional income, not everyone buys insurance, nor does everyone gamble. The theory of insurance presented here suggests that those consumers who view the premium as a potential loss are less likely to purchase insurance because of loss aversion. Studies have shown that the demand for various types of insurance can be manipulated by re-educating consumers into the viewing the premium as a transactional payment for an uncertain income transfer if a specific event occurs. The theory of gambling suggests that those who view the wager primarily in terms of the goods and services foregone are less likely to gamble than those who view the wager in terms of replaceable wages foregone. On the other hand, those who view the additional income gained through gambling as a reason for a splurge in consumption may be more likely to gamble because they value the additional *gambling* income more than just income. Thus, the theory presented here also suggests some of the main sources of variation in the demand for these two commodities.

It is, of course, too early to know to what extent the quid pro quo theory presented in this book will be accepted by economists. As Kuhn (1962) recognized, even if correct, new scientific approaches are often difficult to accept and so it will take time to determine whether a change in thinking has occurred among the profession, if it occurs at all. The reaction of other economists is especially important with regard to theoretical questions because it is often only the acceptance of a theory by other economists that proves its validity. As Heyne notes, "Statements, propositions or judgements are made and held by subjects and are therefore always subjective . . . There is consequently no way to establish the validity of a proposition in economic science except by persuading other economists. . . . Science is a social activity" (Heyne 2008, 18). Nevertheless, even though all theories rely on their acceptance by the economics profession for their legitimacy, some theories are demonstrably more worthy of acceptance and legitimacy than others because they fit the data better, are more predictive, or are more complete. Over time, the acceptance of such theories by a rational and unbiased profession seems inevitable.

Because some of the differences between the conventional and the alternative theories listed above have already been identified and have been known for a number of years, the reaction of economists to these differences is known. These alternative theories are also part of the quid pro quo approach, so this experience might provide a basis for predicting the degree of acceptance of the quid pro quo theory more generally. An appendix to this chapter presents some of the speculation regarding why two of the components of conventional theory—the *risk aversion* assumption and the lack of recognition of *income effects*, points 1 and 3 on the above list—have been so durable.

Empirical Challenges

There are a number of empirical challenges for economists in applying the quid pro quo theory. First, it is difficult to decompose moral hazard into an income and a price effect, but such a decomposition would be necessary in any randomized controlled trial that seeks to understand the welfare implications of insurance that pays off by reducing price. For example, with health insurance, to determine the income transferred from insurance and so incorporate a third indemnity payment arm into the trial, it would be necessary to observe a consumer with standard health insurance and determine how much the insurer spent on that consumer's healthcare. To determine the income effect, it would then be necessary to find a matching consumer in the indemnity arm and pay them, upon becoming ill, a lump-sum amount equal to what the insurer would have spent, and then determine how much that consumer spends on care. Because of the idiosyncrasy of diseases, complications, comorbidities, effectiveness of treatments, and so on, finding two ill consumers that match exactly would be difficult in any randomized controlled trial. Finding a third consumer with exactly the same illness for the no insurance arm (if such an arm would even be permitted) would be equally difficult for the same reasons.

Second, estimating the true welfare loss from using a price reduction to transfer income requires estimating the effect (on *ex post* spending) of having to pay increasingly larger *ex ante* premiums for increasingly smaller coinsurance rates. The theoretical effect has been approximated using static estimates for the various health-sector-wide parameters (Nyman and Maude-Griffen 2001; Nyman 2003), but a dynamic approach would be required in order to calculate insurance demand precisely. This would be a challenge in any study that sought to determine the welfare consequences of insurance that paid off by reducing price.

Third, estimating the welfare effects from insurance would require a different approach than has been used previously. As shown in Figure 2.7, the expected welfare loss from paying the insurance premium would be determined by the loss of utility (or value) from a movement along the no event utility function of all income. The expected welfare gain from the insurance *when no loss occurs* would be determined by the expected increase from (1) the utility of income in the event state after the premium had been paid to (2) the utility of income after the income payoff has been received in the event state. As shown in Figure 2.8, the expected welfare gain from insurance *when a loss of income (or assets) occurs* would be determined by the expected increase from (1) the utility of income after the income loss and premium payment are accounted for in the event state to (2) the utility of income after the income payoff in the event state. This welfare gain would capture the effect of both the income loss in increasing the marginal utility of income and the factors that make the income dearer in the event state.

For health insurance, a number of existing studies have attempted to determine the difference between utility of income when healthy and when ill (Sloan et al. 1988; Viscusi and Evans 1990; Evans and Viscusi 1991; Lillard and Weiss 1997; Edwards 2008; Finkelstein, Luttmer, and Notowidigdo 2009). Finkelstein, Luttmer, and Notowidigdo (2009) review these studies and suggest alternative empirical approaches for estimating these differences. The approaches used by these authors, however, seek to estimate the "effect of health on the marginal utility of a constant amount of non-medical consumption" (Finkelstein, Luttmer, and Notowidigdo 2009, 116). In contrast, a quid pro quo approach would seek to estimate the effect of health (or illness) on the marginal utility of income spent on *all* consumption, including the healthcare covered by this insurance. Moreover, it would be necessary to obtain an estimate of the utility function when ill so that the impact on utility from an income gain could be estimated. To my knowledge, studies containing both these modifications do not exist in the current literature. Thus, new ground would need to be broken to obtain empirical estimates of the welfare effects.

Fourth, estimating the welfare effect of gambling would also require a new approach. As shown in Figure 3.1, the expected loss from the wager on utility could be estimated along a no event utility function that captured both the utility from income used in consumption and the utility of having a job and earning the income during a standard workday. The expected gain from the additional income would be determined (assuming a utility gain as described in equation 3.1) by the additional income evaluated along the event utility function, which captured the gain in utility based solely on its consumption value. Such an empirical study would also break new ground.

These four represent only a portion of the empirical challenges that adopting the quid pro quo approach would generate. A complete inventory of these challenges and their solutions is beyond the scope of this theoretical analysis.

Contributions of the Quid Pro Quo Model

The quid pro quo model represents important progress in understanding why insurance is demanded. For those types of insurance where the triggering mechanism does not mean a loss of either income or an asset, but simply a change in state (such as health insurance, annuities, long-term care insurance, and pharmaceutical insurance), the gains in understanding derive from the recognition that the demands for additional commodities (that must be included in the household budget after the triggering event occurs) make additional income more valuable. This increase in value of income is the main reason for the demand for such insurance.

For those types of insurance that pay off with a reduction in price, the advance in understanding derives from the recognition that the price reduction contains an income effect. Moreover, for those types of insurance that pay off with a price reduction and where the trigger is a loss of income or an asset, the quid pro quo approach does not limit insurance coverage to replacing the consumption that was the uninsured loss. Instead, insurance generates welfare gains from *any* additional consumption that increases the consumer surplus. This is true for both increases in the consumer surplus of those covered commodities that would be purchased without insurance and for a portion of those covered commodities purchased anew because of insurance. That is, they derive in part from the moral hazard purchases. These purchases might be especially welfare-increasing if they represent access to otherwise unaffordable purchases.

For those types of insurance where the triggering event is a loss of income or assets, the gains in welfare may also derive from the conventional assumption that utility is increasing at a decreasing rate. Because the loss of a large amount of income or a very valuable asset would cause the gain from the income payoff to be evaluated along a portion of the event utility function where marginal utility of income is greater, the additional income represented by the payoff is also more valuable. This change in the reference point is a component of the conventional theory and, with diminishing marginal utility of income, may generate an important portion of the demand for insurance.

Perhaps the most important advance in understanding from the quid pro quo approach is derived from the recognition that the gain in welfare for the consumer has little if anything to do with a preference for certainty. This advance is derived primarily from the recognition of the implications of the experimental work supporting prospect theory, but also of the other empirical work that has shown a lack of a consistent relationship between the purchase of insurance and measures of risk aversion. The removal of risk preferences from the theory of the demand for both insurance and gambling, and their replacement with the quid pro quo model, further means that the insurance-purchasing gambler is no longer a puzzle.

With regard to gambling, the most important contribution of the quid pro quo model to its understanding is derived from the recognition that there is a difference between the utility of the additional income represented by the gambling winnings and the utility of the same winnings if earned. If both were to require labor, the demand for gambling would decrease dramatically. For example, it is difficult to imagine that consumers would derive the same level of pleasure from playing a slot machine where instead the tokens won represented obligations to perform additional work in order to receive the winnings. Similarly, if neither required labor, the demand for gambling would also decrease dramatically. For example, it is difficult to imagine gambling for money that could be exchanged for real commodities, but where consumers had access to any amount of that money they wanted without working. That is, if income could always be obtained free of work, work-free gambling winnings would be meaningless as well. This difference is the core contribution of the quid pro quo theory to the understanding of gambling behavior.

Finally, although the acquisition of additional income represents the focus of the demand motivation for both insurance and gambling, the theory suggests that whether either is actually purchased depends on how the consumer perceives the insurance premium or the gambling wager. If consumers view the payment of an insurance premium as a potential unplanned loss without a sure corresponding gain, they will be reluctant to purchase insurance. However, if they are taught to view the insurance premium as a routine payment in exchange for a valuable income that occurs coincidentally with an increase in its value, then consumers will be more likely to purchase insurance. Similarly, with gambling, whether the consumer views the wager as a loss that reduces present consumption, or as spending out of the replaceable income from an ongoing employment source, also determines demand for gambles. Thus, another contribution is the recognition that, even though the demand incentive rests mainly with the desire for additional income (the *quo*), how the premium or wager cost (the *quid*) is perceived by the consumer is largely responsible for the variation in that demand.

Importance

One way to grasp the importance of the quid pro quo approach is to imagine it as the basis of an alternate reality. Imagine, therefore, that the Friedman–Savage model had concluded, from only a slightly different analytical specification, that the demand for insurance is motivated by a desire for additional income. Imagine that the accepted analysis further held that such an increase in income occurs in a state of the world where additional income is more valuable and one where the intended insurance coverage is not limited to the amount of the uninsured loss. In the case of health insurance, the transfer and augmentation of income from a healthy state to an ill state for the individual consumer would lead to the realization that health insurance exists at the societal level in order to transfer income from those who are healthy to those who become ill, as Evans (1983) had suggested some 40 years ago.[1] If such a model were ascendant in the US, it might also lead to the realization that government could perform this redistribution function more efficiently and equitably than could private firms, as Thomas (2017) has suggested more recently.[2] To the extent that economists can and actually do influence the course of the economy by their policy recommendations, private health

---

[1] It should be noted that the Canadian health economist, Robert Evans, also recognized these same distributional aspects of health insurance and discussed their welfare implications (Evans 1983).

[2] With regard to efficiency, the administrative costs for those Parts of Medicare (A, B and D) that are administered solely by the government has averaged less than 2 percent of healthcare expenditures (Sullivan 2013), whereas the Affordable Care Act limited private health insurance firms in the US to administrative costs and profits of 15 percent of healthcare expenditures (The Patient Protection and Affordable Care Act 2010). With regard to equity, replacing private insurance with a Medicare-type program that would cover all Americans and, including the additional long-term care and dental coverage, would reduce total healthcare expenditures in the US by about 4 percent, according to a critical review and revision of six independent estimates (Nyman 2021).

insurance might have largely been replaced by a comprehensive national health insurance program in the US, as has happened in almost all other developed countries and in some less developed ones as well.

Again tracing out the arc of the counterfactual with health insurance, a correctly modified Pauly diagram (Figure 2.3) of the welfare effects of health insurance would show the effect of this income transfer in shifting demand for medical care, and generating a moral hazard welfare gain. Health economists might therefore no longer be preoccupied by the notion of a moral hazard welfare loss and increased cost-sharing in their policy recommendations. Such an analysis might include an analysis of the welfare loss from using a price reduction to transfer income, but recognize that this loss is limited to only the portion of healthcare services that did not require illness in order to be demanded, that is, limited to only "routine physicians' services, prescriptions, dental care, and the like" (Pauly 1983, 83). For the vast remainder of additional medical procedures consumed by the ill—cataract removals, C-sections, joint replacements, broken bone repairs, angioplasty and atherectomy, stent procedures, hysterectomies, gall bladder removals, heart bypass surgery, and so on—the income effect from insurance would generate a welfare gain.[3] This gain might take the form of an increase in the consumer surplus for procedures that would have been purchased without insurance but are now purchased with an increased willingness to pay (area igah in Figure 2.3). It might take the form of the moral hazard welfare gain (area gda in Figure 2.3) for that medical care that becomes worthwhile to purchase because the income effect has now increased the consumer's willingness to pay enough to cover the price. The important and often expensive care that would otherwise be unaffordable if uninsured would be included as a portion of this latter welfare gain. It would also be shown that the welfare gains from these income-generated healthcare services would far exceed the welfare losses from the overconsumption, if the moral hazard welfare loss were limited to the types of healthcare identified by Pauly (1983).

Such a study might have a number of implications, large and small. As mentioned, it might provide the basis and impetus for the establishment of a comprehensive national health insurance program in the US or for expansions of an existing government insurance program like Medicare. Or, it might simply alter the wording of survey questions used to obtain

---

[3] It is difficult to imagine a consumer with more "skin in the game" than one who has decided to go ahead with a serious procedure like a recommended heart bypass procedure.

economists' opinions of moral hazard by asking about the size of both the welfare gain and welfare loss caused by health insurance, instead of only the welfare loss.

The RAND Health Insurance Experiment would need to be redesigned to estimate the welfare gain from insurance that transferred income by reducing price. The redesigned Experiment would therefore have three arms: (1) free fee-for-service, (2) cost-sharing, and (3) indemnity insurance with payments equal to the expenditures under free fee-for-service. The difference between the spending in arms (1) and (2) would represent moral hazard, and the difference between the spending in arms (3) and (2) would represent the portion of moral hazard that was welfare-increasing. The Experiment would also need to be redesigned in such a way to avoid the attrition from the cost-sharing arms when a participant became ill and was destined to be admitted to the hospital, a difficult redesign. If these issues could be solved, the Experiment would then focus on showing the relative health gains from the participants who represented the efficient and inefficient portions of moral hazard.

While the application of conventional theory to insurance may have had the most egregious impact on policy recommendations and implementations in the healthcare sector, and while replacing its analysis with the quid pro quo analysis may generate the most dramatic welfare gains there, the errors of the conventional analysis of health insurance have clear parallels in other forms of insurance. For example, disability insurance, workers compensation, and long-term care insurance all exhibit moral hazard and economists have long assumed that the additional days of disability, job injury, or home healthcare, respectively, that occur with these types of insurance were inefficient, in the same way that additional medical care was considered inefficient for those with health insurance.[4] As is clear from some of the studies cited in chapter 8, this perception is changing. These studies have recognized that at least some of the additional days of disability, job injury, or home healthcare are efficient and related to income transfers instead of price effects. There may be other

---

[4] The exception here might be unemployment insurance. It has long been recognized that unemployment insurance increases the length of unemployment episodes, but that these episodes do not only increase leisure time. They also increase the time devoted to job search and therefore are beneficial by allowing for the beneficiary to find a better job (Holan 1977). Thus, an efficiency was recognized early on that was associated with the additional unemployed days generated by insurance if used for job search. It was left to Chetty (2008) and his followers (e.g., Krueger and Muller 2010) to separate the additional days of unemployment into the price and "liquidity" effects that are consistent with the welfare analysis of the present book.

forms of insurance, such as pharmaceutical insurance, consumer warranties, or even annuities, where this may also be the case.

Thesis of the Book Summarized

Seventy-five years ago, Friedman and Savage (1948) published a paper that established the lens through which almost all economists who came after them viewed insurance and gambling. Because of that perspective, a great deal of behavior—behavior which was clearly rational and in the interest of consumers—has been overlooked, deemed welfare-decreasing, or even thought to be irrational, in favor of behavior that fit the Friedman–Savage model. This meant that, for example, the purchase of health insurance in order to gain access to otherwise unaffordable care would be ignored as a benefit of insurance. This is because such purchases would mean that consumers used insurance to consume care beyond that which would have been consumed if uninsured, and so would have violated the Friedman–Savage motive of achieving certainty. For the same reason, it meant that welfare-increasing income effects would be ignored in insurance contracts that paid off by reducing the price, even though income effects had long been identified as a welfare-increasing result of a price reduction. It meant that the self-evident motive of gambling to "obtain additional income without working for it" would be ignored in favor of gambling explained by a desire for risk. It meant that unrelated consumer decisions, such as purchasing car insurance and playing blackjack, if done together, would be deemed irrational economic behavior, even though such combined purchases were as commonplace as the cars in the parking lot of a Las Vegas casino. For some, after reading this book, the Friedman–Savage frame of reference will still be difficult to shed, but for others, once all the contradictions and shortcomings of the conventional model have been recognized and the alternative perspective of the quid pro quo model explained, the shedding of the Friedman–Savage perspective will seem, well, obvious. The book now closes with a restatement of the thesis of the book as found in the book's abstract.

This book holds that the demand for insurance is best understood not by focusing on risk preferences, but by focusing on the additional income, the states of the world that trigger the income transfer from the insurer, and the value of income (and consumption) in those states. It is unlikely that demand can be understood if the analyst limits the gain from insurance to coverage of the uninsured loss alone. It is also unlikely that the demand can be understood if the analyst limits the analysis to a movement along a static risk-averse utility or value function, rather than acknowledging that a shift of this function, and thus in the utility or value of additional income, often coincides with the occurrence of the event that triggers the payout.

This book also holds that the demand for recreational gambling is not motivated by a desire for risk, but by a desire for additional income that does not require work. This additional work-free income is obtained because of an uncertain change in the state of the world, such as a lucky roll of the dice or spin of the roulette wheel. Although gambling motives are multifaceted, and include, for example, the desire for entertainment or social interaction, none of these alternative motivations would be able to generate the level of gambling behavior commonly observed if gamblers had to work for their winnings, like they normally would need to in order to obtain the same additional income without gambling.

Appendix: Speculation on the Durability of Risk Aversion and the Ignoring of Income Effects

Durability of Risk Aversion

Difference 1 on the list of differences between the conventional theory of insurance and the quid pro quo theory focuses on risk preferences: under the conventional theory, consumers are averse to the risk of loss and purchase insurance because it allows them to substitute a certain loss for an uncertain one of the same expected magnitude (Friedman Savage 1948). In contradiction to this conventional theory, however, the extensive experimental work by Kahneman and Tversky found that most respondents prefer an uncertain loss to a certain one of the same expected magnitude (Kahneman and Tversky 1979; Tversky and Kahneman 1981; 1986; 1988; 1991). Further evidence from other empirical studies, such as those conducted or reviewed by Eling, Ghavibazoo, and Hanewald (2021), suggested that risk preferences are, at best, an unreliable explanation for the demand for insurance. Thus, if risk preferences were the motivator, only a limited number of consumers would purchase insurance, yet the purchase of insurance is a common behavior.

Even though some of these empirical findings have been known for 40 or more years, they have had only limited success in displacing the conventional explanation. For example, a recent text on health insurance does not cite prospect theory at all or any of the empirical work by Kahneman and Tversky, and explains the demand for health insurance entirely as an aversion to risk (Morrisey 2020). Perhaps more revealing is the relatively recent paper that explained that, if based on the prospect theory diagram and the conventional economic conceptualization of the insurance problem, consumers should not purchase insurance (Sydnor 2010). This paper is revealing because it means that, as late as 2010, the contradiction of conventional insurance theory by the empirical work behind prospect theory was deemed to be worthy of being spelled out in a scientific paper.

Moreover, Fels (2019) points out that many economists are so invested in the conventional theory that they think tautologically about risk aversion and insurance: consumers purchase insurance because they are risk-averse, and consumers are risk-averse because they purchase insurance. This tautology, and the primacy of risk aversion as a motive in the demand for insurance, is implicit in several empirical papers that estimate risk aversion from information on demand for insurance (Halek and Eisenhauer 2001; Cohen and Einav 2007; Sydnor 2010). Sydnor (2010) finds, however, that the constant relative risk aversion (CRRA) coefficient based on the deductibles of home insurance is astronomically large (over 14,000 for one of the cases he calculated), far higher than the CRRA coefficient found when based on labor market (1.25 in Chetty 2006) or other analyses. Such a result should cast even more doubt on the existence of a link between an aversion to the risk of loss and the demand for insurance.

Most economists today would likely acknowledge the importance of prospect theory. However, whether they have made the connection between prospect theory and the empirical evidence supporting it, on the one hand, and its contradiction of the conventional explanation that consumers demand insurance because they are averse to risk of losses, on the other, is not clear. This is pure speculation because to my knowledge, no surveys of economists have asked the relevant questions. Nevertheless, it seems clear that a large portion of the profession would label a utility function that is increasing with income at a decreasing rate as a risk-averse utility function. Moreover, if asked why consumers purchase insurance, most economists would say it is because consumers are risk-averse.

One reason for the durability of the conventional explanation derives from the widespread intuitive appeal and theoretical necessity of the concept of diminishing marginal utility of income as described in Figure 2.1. In addition, diminishing marginal utility of income is connected to risk aversion for many economists by the uncertainty-based process by which von Neumann and Morgenstern (1947) proposed to measure the utility of income. Of course, the concept of a utility function is independent of the process by which it is measured. And, at an even more fundamental level, it is without doubt a leap of faith to base conclusions about the importance of certainty in motivating this behavior solely on the basis of deductive reasoning and the difference between two mathematical equations. This is especially true when there is such extensive empirical evidence pointing to the contrary and when the specification of those equations can so readily be rearranged to show an entirely different motivation.

As has been argued here, uncertainty in insurance (and gambling) is important, but its actual role appears to be largely mechanical rather than motivational. Uncertainty is exploited by firms to multiply a small premium into an augmented payoff, and thus by consumers to multiply a portion of their income and shift it into states of the world where it is more valued, sometimes to multiply the income to a level that would be unobtainable by any other means. This mechanical role of uncertainty is different than the motivational role it plays in conventional theory.

Another reason for its durability is that risk aversion explanation is unquestionably clever. By now, many generations of economics students have had the opportunity to be impressed by the steps of logic with which Friedman and Savage (1948)—and von Neumann and Morgenstern (1946) before them—used to tease out aversion to risk from the utility function represented by Figure 2.1. Economics teaches that one of the ways in which a profession is able to gain monopoly power is through jargon and by making the acquisition of some relevant information unduly difficult. The derivation of risk aversion from diminishing marginal utility of income may be one such story. Yet it also appears to be logically reasonable and therefore acceptable to those who have made the effort to understand it, as long as the empirical evidence is ignored that most consumers prefer the uncertainty of a loss to an actuarially equivalent certain loss. Such a theory serves the profession by contributing to the body of knowledge that is inaccessible to those on the outside.

Thomas (2017) agrees with this critique but sees it as a part of a more general explanation of the ability of questionable assumptions to live on in economic theory. In his book that questions the assumption that all adverse selection in health insurance is undesirable, Thomas suggests that, for wide-spread success, an economic theory needs to be clever, but not too clever. That is, it needs to be clever enough to make people feel smart for understanding it, but not so clever (or distant from extant theories) that the cognitive cost of entry is too high. He calls such arguments "one-way hash arguments," because they remind him of the way that messages are encrypted: the mathematical rule (that is, the complexity of the theory) is known by the person doing the encrypting (that is, the one doing the theorizing), but for the one reading the encrypted message, the encryption rule (that is, understanding the complexity of the theory) is difficult, if not impossible, to understand. Thus, such theories to most nonexpert readers are "flawed or incomplete, but nevertheless intuitive, plausible and appealing" (Thomas 2017, 143).

It would be hazardous to venture a guess as to what proportion of economists are aware of the contradiction of conventional insurance theory represented by the empirical evidence supporting prospect theory. Some might be aware of this evidence, but opt to explain the demand for insurance as risk aversion anyway. It would probably be fair to conclude simply that the impact of the empirical evidence behind prospect theory and of the other contradictory empirical findings on economists' understanding of the demand for insurance is far from complete.

Durability of Absence of Income Effects

Difference 3 on the list of differences is that quid pro quo theory recognizes income effects of insurance but convention theory does not. Income effects were first written about some 40 years ago by de Meza (1983) with regard to insurance that paid off with an income payoff. Some 20 or so years ago, Nyman (1999b; 2003; 1999c) showed that insurance that pays off by reducing the price of the covered commodity can also generate income effects. The conventional view, originating with Pauly (1968), is that all additional healthcare consumed because of insurance (that is, moral hazard consumption) represents an inefficient price effect. Moreover, it is widely held that this additional consumption from expansions of health insurance represents the main reason for the growth in healthcare expenditures in the US over the years and the main cause of the healthcare or medical cost "crisis" (Newhouse et al. 1993).

The alternative theory is that, when insurance pays off with an income payment (as was assumed in the original Friedman–Savage model), such income payments would generate moral hazard if the insured commodity were a normal good (de Meza 1983). Even when insurance paid off by reducing the price of the covered commodity, moral hazard could represent an income effect to the extent that the income used to pay for the insured commodity would have been spent on more of that commodity, if the insurer had paid that amount to the beneficiary in a lump sum indemnity payment (Nyman 1999b; 1999c; 2003). Moreover, this is sometimes healthcare that consumers would not be able to afford without insurance. The portion of the additional purchases generated by an income effect would increase welfare to the extent that the consumer's willingness to pay for this additional income exceeds the cost.

It would probably be fair to say that there has been a level of acceptance of the income effects among health economists. Nevertheless, there is evidence to suggest that the conventional view still dominates the profession. First, surveys have found that, for most economists, moral hazard is associated primarily with welfare losses rather than welfare gains. In 1989, Feldman and Morrisey surveyed 273 US and Canadian health economists (Feldman and Morrisey 1990). The survey asked whether the respondents agreed that, "the level and type of health insurance held by most U. S. families generate substantial welfare loss due to over consumption of medical care services," and found that 63 percent strongly agreed or agreed. In 1995, Fuchs asked 50 leading health economists whether they agreed with the statement that, "Third-party payment results in patients using services whose costs exceed their benefits, and this excess of costs over benefits amounts to at least 5 percent of total health care expenditures" (Fuchs 1996). He found that 84 percent of these economists agreed with the statement. In 2005, shortly after the work pointing out the existence of income effects and the access value of health insurance was published, Morrisey and Cawley asked the same question that Fuchs used of 460 health economists and found that 65 percent agreed (Morrisey and Cawley 2008). Clearly, such questions and responses are not sufficiently refined to determine whether the respondents believe that the welfare loss is greater than the welfare gain, but the fact that only a welfare loss is assumed by the questioners, and that no welfare gain is even acknowledged in the question, is a testament to the continued dominance of moral hazard welfare loss in the thinking of most economists.

Second, how this issue is covered in textbooks is also an indicator of acceptance by the field. On the one hand, some health economics texts devote considerable space to explaining the view that moral hazard derives from both an income effect and a price effect. For example, Santerre and Neun devote eight pages of their text to explaining the income effects theory with regard to health insurance (Santerre and Neun 2010). On the other hand, many texts ignore income effects altogether in explaining moral hazard in health insurance. For example, Phelps's textbook does not reference any of the original work describing the welfare gain from moral hazard, and does not broach the possibility that the change in quantity demanded from becoming insured might have anything to do with income (Phelps 2018). Similarly, Morrisey's text on health insurance also does not allude to the possibility that moral hazard could generate anything other than a welfare loss (Morrisey 2020). In their review the treatment of moral hazard in nine health economics textbooks published since 1990, Grignon et al. (2018) characterize six of these texts as presenting the Pauly analysis as being the only accepted analysis, with the other three presenting Pauly's as the conventional approach but with the income effects approach as an important alternative.

Third, the academic literature has also been uneven in its acceptance of the notion of income effects generating gains in welfare. As indicated in chapter 8, a number of important papers are now based on the theory of a welfare-increasing income-transfer effect and an access value of insurance (Autor and Duggan 2007; Chetty 2008; Fels 2016;

Boone 2018; Besanko, Dranove and Garthwaite 2020; Robertson et al. 2020; Phelps 2022). On the other hand, many papers do not recognize income effects at all. One highly visible example of such a paper is Finkelstein's essay entitled "Moral Hazard in Health Insurance: Developments Since Arrow (1963)" (Finkelstein 2014). This essay, given as the prestigious 5th annual Kenneth J. Arrow Lecture, was purported to capture all that had been learned about moral hazard since the publication in 1963 of Arrow's famous article, which was, perhaps, the first to notice and write on this phenomenon. In her essay, Finkelstein presents the issue as a dispute over whether moral hazard exists at all, and poses as a straw man an article by the popular science writer Malcolm Gladwell, which Finkelstein claims to argue that "medical care is determined not by price but by needs" (Finkelstein 2014, 16). She supports her position that medical care is determined by price with her work on the Oregon Health Insurance Experiment (Finkelstein et al., 2012) and earlier work by others on the RAND Health Insurance Experiment (Newhouse et al. 1993), both of which show that medical care consumption is responsive to price.

The actual argument in the Gladwell article, however, is that, although insurance generates an increase in demand for medical care, this increase in demand is an interaction between a low insurance prices and the presence of a health condition requiring medical care (Gladwell 2005). Moreover, moral hazard is often, and especially in the case of expansions of Medicaid like the one that Finkelstein analyzed in Oregon, due to the presence of a health condition in those who would not otherwise have access to medical care because they cannot afford it. In Finkelstein's essay, there is no recognition that anything other than a price effect exists. Of the commentaries (Gruber 2014; Arrow 2014; Stiglitz 2014; Newhouse 2014), only Gruber's identifies Finkelstein's disregard for income effects as a shortcoming of her analysis. It is clear, however, that Finkelstein's disregard for income effects is not an oversight because in a subsequent article by Einav and Finkelstein that covers the same ground, income effects are again not acknowledged (Einav and Finkelstein 2018).

The ignoring of income-transfer effects has been noticed by a number of other economists. These observers have sometimes offered their own explanations for this phenomenon. One of the most extensive treatments of this issue is found in Kelman and Woodward's (2013) review of Nyman (2003). These authors are puzzled both by the lack of acknowledgment of the income effects issue in the literature and by the lack of appreciation of its importance. As evidence, they cite two highly visible talks on moral hazard—Newhouse's presidential address to the American Society of Health Economists (Newhouse 2006) and Feldstein's presidential address to the American Economic Association (Feldstein 2005)—where neither author mentions income effects. Kelman and Woodward go on to write,

> There has been no review and discussion [of the issue of income effects] in journals or conferences as panel sessions . . . Why has not there been more notice of the work [on income effects] and its implications for health policy? Why have not the health policy and health economics annual meetings, journals, and other publications presented or debated the work [on income effects]? If it is wrong, it should be challenged in the usual arenas of scholarly debate. If the burden of opinion after open debate is that the work is found wanting, then it should be dismissed. Surely, standard scholarly practice is to engage the argument and see where the dust settles.
>
> The response of the leadership of the field perhaps can be best understood within the sociology of knowledge that explains changes in science. Half a century ago Kuhn [1962] introduced a new way of thinking about these changes, which is called

the theory of scientific revolutions. . . . Even in those cases where the new ideas are revealed to be superior to what they are challenging, the process of its adoption is often protracted. . . .

The Friedman–Savage (risk aversion) formulation of the demand for insurance has been settled economic doctrine for more than 50 years, and . . . it is inapplicable to the circumstances of health insurance coverage . . . [thus] the theory is seriously flawed. As a result the insurance payoff has been misinterpreted as a reduction in the price of the covered services rather than as an income transfer from the insurance fund to the sick insured. The welfare implications, as discussed previously, are reversed with major policy implications. (Kelman and Woodward 2013, 5)

To these authors, the reluctance to confront the issue seems unusually strong, but it may actually be no different than the effect of prospect theory on risk aversion in conventional theory, and consistent with the usual temporal delays that accompany the acceptance of a new scientific theory, especially one that would lead to an extensive invalidation of work by leaders of the field.

Thomas (2017) also notes the lack of recognition of the income effects theory in the analysis of health insurance and suggests that the theory has received little attention because it is ideologically unappealing to some economists. This is because, in this theory of the demand for health insurance, insurance represents a redistribution of income from those who are healthy to those who are ill, rather than a way to avoid uncertainty. Although such insurance can still be represented by a purely private transaction, the acknowledgment of a basic redistribution function of insurance leads quickly to the realization that the state could redistribute more effectively, cheaply, and fairly. Thomas thinks that this political implication would grate on some economists and so they have been reluctant to accept the theory.

Thomas (2017) also suggests that, because most economists are accustomed to thinking that any commodity provided free would be overconsumed, they may have tended to dismiss the core welfare argument because it holds that the additional consumption of free healthcare is not overconsumption. He explains this reluctance to accept a moral hazard welfare gain by suggesting that many economists may have failed to recognize that to consume more medical care when insured, it is necessary not only for the price to fall, but also for the consumer's health state to have changed as well. Expensive medical procedures are generally not demanded by healthy consumers, even if free.

Grignon et al. (2018) suggest that the income effects theory was slow to be accepted because it has been misperceived as the standard Hicksian compensated demand, when in fact it is different and new. These authors think that, were the correct analysis of the decomposition of insurance demand into income and price effects more widely understood, its novelty would have perhaps generated a greater acceptance.

Robertson (2019) suggests that income effects have been ignored because they do not lend themselves to empirical testing. This is mainly due to the difficulty in giving the insured consumer who becomes ill an income transfer equal to what the insurer would have paid for their care, and then determining how much healthcare the consumer would purchase. Moreover, Robertson suggests the theory has also made it more difficult to identify succinct policy recommendations. That is, it seems easier to deny the existence of the moral hazard welfare gain or the access value of insurance, than to design cost-sharing policies that targeted only the inefficient portion of moral hazard for elimination.

These explanations are all important, but they seem insufficient in themselves to explain the lack of recognition of income effects. That is, it is simply difficult to understand why so many have been blind to the insurance income effects since most are surely aware of Hicks's and Slutsky–Friedman's decompositions of the change in quantity demand that results from an exogenous price change. This is especially difficult to understand because, to many of these same economists, there appears to be no difference between an exogenous reduction in a market price and paying for the reduction of the price of medical care if ill by buying insurance.

Moreover, the main proponent of the moral-hazard-welfare-loss theory disavowed it not long after it was published. In a 1983 comment, Pauly wrote that his 1968 model was in fact directed not at all moral hazard spending, but should be applied only to that portion of moral hazard spending representing "routine physicians' services, prescriptions, dental care, and the like" (Pauly 1983, 83). It was not directed at the more serious care that represents the majority of healthcare spending. This distinction was not made in his 1968 article and was lost on the many economists who subsequently applied his 1968 conceptualization of the moral hazard welfare loss to *all additional healthcare spending* (e.g., Manning and Marquis 1996). Pauly went on to write in 1983 that "it is nevertheless true that the relevant theory, empirical evidence, and policy analysis for moral hazard in the case of serious illness has not been developed. This is one of the most serious omissions in the current literature" (Pauly 1983, 83). Because of the persistence of the application of the moral hazard welfare loss to all additional healthcare expenditures, even after this comment was published, it seems clear that many economists did not get the memo.

Two other factors are important in explaining the durability of the conventional view of the moral hazard welfare loss and the lack of a recognition of income effects. First, for those economists who teach a health economics course, the famous moral hazard welfare loss diagram (Figure 2.2) that Pauly used in his 1968 comment and the theory behind it are ideal pedagogical tools. The diagram is easy for students to redraw, consists of concepts with which students were already familiar, and is just difficult enough to be a challenging subject for test questions. Plus, it explains why the "medical cost crisis" was a crisis, and would seemingly show how increasing coinsurance rates would represent a solution for it. Thus, the notion that this diagram is wrong (compare Figure 2.3 to Figure 2.2) and that much of the additional healthcare represents a welfare gain is a change in theory that many health economics professors may have been reluctant to make.

Second, the scientific work of many of the leading health economists would have been impacted, and some negated, by the acceptance of the income effects theory. It would be difficult for such acclaimed and often prize-winning economists to have to back-pedal on an analysis so central to their own work. Thus, it was easier to ignore this issue than to take it on and so legitimize it. For example, none of the other authors who gave recommendations for optimal coinsurance have later qualified or disavowed their earlier work in the same way that Phelps (2022) has. Policy prescriptions derived from conventional theory would need to be revised drastically if it were recognized that a large portion of the moral hazard actually generated a welfare gain rather than a welfare loss.

As another example, Newhouse and his colleagues designed the RAND Health Insurance Experiment to determine the welfare implications of health insurance by comparing spending in two arms: (1) participants who faced coinsurance rates, and (2) participants who were provided free care (Newhouse et al. 1993). If the welfare gain from income transfers were acknowledged, the design of the experiment would have needed to include spending in a third arm: (3) participants who, upon becoming ill, were paid a lump-sum amount of income equal to what the insurer would have spent on them under the free care arm. It would only be with this arm that the researchers could tell what portion of the free care spending was due to price alone and therefore inefficient. Thus, basing welfare calculations on RAND estimates of the assumed Marshallian demand elasticities from only two arms could not determine welfare, and would result in biased estimates of the welfare effects. Indeed, because of the difficulty in determining the amount of the income transfer required in the third arm, if the moral hazard welfare gain had been accepted knowledge when the RAND Health Insurance Experiment was being designed and proposed for funding, the study might never have been done at all. Thus, to recognize income effects would again be tantamount to recognizing that the RAND experiment is far from the gold standard it is generally thought to be.[5]

---

[5] In addition, the effect of paying an insurance premium on subsequent demand for medical care would need to be captured by the experiment in order to truly capture the insurance demand. Furthermore, the issue of attrition bias would need to be effectively addressed.

References

Abdellaoui, Mohammed. 2000. "Parameter-Free Elicitation of Utility and Probability Weighting Functions." *Management Science* 46, no. 11: 1497–1512.

Addobbati, Andrea. 2016. "Italy 1500–1800: Cooperation and Competition." In *Marine Insurance: Origins and Institutions, 1300–1850*, edited by A. B. Leonard, 46–77. Houndmills, UK: Palgrave Macmillan.

Alchian, A., and Harold Demsetz. 1972. "Production, Information Costs, and Economic Organization." *American Economic Review* 62, no. 5: 777–795.

America's Health Insurance Plans. 2017. *Who Buys Long-Term Care Insurance? Twenty-Five Years of Study of Buyers and Non-Buyers in 2015-2016.* Waltham, MA: LifePlans, Inc.

Aretino, Pietro. (1537) 1976. *Selected Letters*, edited and translated by George Bull. Harmondsworth, UK: Penguin.

Arkes, Hal R., Cynthia A. Joyner, Mark V. Prezzo, Jane G. Nash, Karen Siegel-Jacobs, and Eric Stone. 1994. "The Psychology of Windfall Gains." *Organizational Behavior and Human Decision Processes* 59, no. 3: 331–347.

Arrow, Kenneth J. 1963a. " 'Comment' on James S. Dusenberry, 'The Portfolio Approach to the Demand for Money and other Assets." *Review of Economics and Statistics* 45, no. 1, February, Part 2, Supplement: 24–27.

Arrow, Kenneth J. 1963b. "Uncertainty and the Welfare Economics of Medical Care." *American Economic Review* 53, no. 5: 941–973.

Arrow, Kenneth J. 1963c. "Utility and Expectation in Economic Behavior." In *Psychology: A Study of a Science. Study II. Empirical Substructure and Relations with Other Sciences. Vol. 6. Investigations of Man as Socius: Their Place in Psychology and the Social sciences*, edited by S. Koch, 724–752. New York: McGraw-Hill.

Arrow, Kenneth J. 1965. *Aspects of the Theory of Risk Bearing.* Helsinki: The Academic Bookstore.

Arrow, Kenneth J. 1974a. *Essays in the Theory of Risk-Bearing.* Amsterdam: North-Holland.

Arrow, Kenneth J. 1974b. "Optimal Insurance and Generalized Deductibles." *Scandinavian Actuarial Journal* 1: 1–42.

Arrow, Kenneth J. 2014. "Commentary." In *Moral Hazard in Health Insurance*, edited by Amy Finkelstein with Kenneth J. Arrow, Jonathan Gruber, Joseph P. Newhouse, and Joseph E. Stiglitz, 55-63. New York: Columbia University Press.

Autor, David, and Mark G. Duggan. 2007. "Distinguishing Income from Substitution Effects in Disability Insurance." *American Economic Review* 97, no. 22: 119–124.

Babcock, Bruce A. 2015. "Using Cumulative Prospect Theory to Explain Anomalous Crop Insurance Coverage Choice." *American Journal of Agricultural Economics* 97, no. 5: 1371–1384.

Bailey, Martin J., Mancur Olson, and Paul Wonnacott. 1980. "The Marginal Utility of Wealth Does Not Increase: Borrowing, Lending, and Friedman–Savage Gambles." *American Economic Review* 70 no. 3: 372–381.

Baker, Thomas. 1996. "On the Genealogy of Moral Hazard." *Texas Law Review* 75, no. 2: 237–292.

Barberis, Nicholas C. 2013. "Thirty Years of Prospect Theory in Economics: A Review and Assessment." *Journal of Economic Perspectives* 27, no. 1: 173–196.

Barberis, Nicholas, and Ming Huang. 2001. "Mental Accounting, Loss Aversion and Individual Stock Returns." *Journal of Finance* 56, no. 4: 1247–1292.

Barberis, Nicholas, Ming Huang, and Tano Santos. 2001. "Prospect Theory and Asset Prices." *Quarterly Journal of Economics* 116, no. 1: 1–53.

Barbour, Violet. 1929. "Marine Risks and Insurance in the Seventeenth Century." *Journal of Economic and Business History* 1, no. 4: 561–596.

Barry, Declan T., Paul K. Maciejewski, Rani A. Desai, and Marc N. Potenza. 2007. "Income Differences and Recreational Gambling." *Journal of Addiction Medicine* 1, no. 3: 145–153.

Barseghyan, Levon, Francesca Molinari, Ted O'Donoghue, and Joshua C. Teitelbaum. 2013. "The Nature of Risk Preferences: Evidence from Insurance Choices" *American Economic Review* 103, no. 6: 2499–2529.

Barseghyan, Levon, Jeffrey Prince, and Joshua Teitelbaum. 2011. "Are Risk Preferences Stable across Contexts? Evidence from Insurance Data." *American Economic Review* 101 (April): 591–631.

Barsky, Robert B., F. Thomas Juster, Miles S. Kimball, and Matthew D. Shapiro. 1997. "Preference Parameters and Behavioral Heterogeneity: An Experimental Approach in the Health and Retirement Study." *Quarterly Journal of Economics* 112, no. 2, May: 537–579.

Basham, A. L. 1954. *The Wonder That Was India: A Survey of the Culture of the Indian Sub-Continent before the Coming of the Muslims*. New York: Grove Press.

Bateman, Ian, Daniel Kahneman, Alistair Munro, Chris Starmer, and Robert Sugden. 2005. "Testing Competing Models of Loss Aversion: An Adversarial Collaboration." *Journal of Public Economics* 89, no. 8: 1561–1580.

Becker, Gary. 1971. *Economic Theory*. New York: Knopf.

Bell, David E. 1982. "Regret in Decision Making under Uncertainty." *Operations Research* 30, no. 5: 961–981.

Bell, David E. 1983. "Risk Premiums for Decision Regret." *Management Science* 29, no. 10: 1156–1166.

Bell, David E. 1985. "Disappointment in Decision Making under Uncertainty." *Operations Research* 33, no. 1: 1–27.

Bellhouse, David. 2005. "Decoding Cardano's *Liber de Ludo Aleae*." *Historia Mathematica* 32, no. 2: 180–202.

Bernoulli, Daniel. (1738) 1954. "Specimen Theoriae Novaede Mensura Sortis (Exposition of a New Theory on the Measurement of Risk)." Translated from Latin by Louise Sommer. *Econometrica* 22, no. 1: 23–36.

Bernoulli, Jakob. (1713) 2005. *On the Law of Large Numbers, Part Four of Ars Conjectandi* Translated from Italian by Oscar Sheynin. Berlin: NG Verlag.

Bernstein, Peter L. 1996. *Against the Gods: The Remarkable Story of Risk*. New York: Wiley.

Besanko, David, David Dranove, and Craig Garthwaite. 2020. "Insurance Access and Demand Response: Pricing and Welfare Implications." *Journal of Health Economics* 73 (September): 102329.

Binde, Per, and Ulla Romild. 2020. "Risk of Problem Gambling among Occupational Groups: A Population and Registry Study." *Nordic Studies on Alcohol and Drugs* 37, no. 3: 262–278.

Boksberger, Philipp E., and Lisa Melsen. 2011. "Perceived Value: A Critical Examination of the Definitions, Concepts and Measures for the Service Industry." *Journal of Services Marketing* 25, no. 3: 229–240.

Boone, Jan. 2015. "Basic versus Supplementary Health Insurance: Moral Hazard and Adverse Selection." *Journal of Public Economics* 128, no. 4: 50–58.

Boone, Jan. 2018. "Basic versus Supplementary Health Insurance: Access to Care and the Role of Cost-Effectiveness." *Journal of Health Economics* 60: 53–74.

Bound, John, and Timothy Waidmann. 1992. "Disability Transfers, Self-Reported Health, and the Labor Force Attachment of Older Men: Evidence from the Historical Record." *Quarterly Journal of Economics* 107, no. 4: 1393–1419.

Bradley, Steve, Colin Green, and Gareth Leeves. 2007. "Worker Absence and Shirking: Evidence from Matched Teacher-school Data." *Labor Economics* 14, no. 3: 319–334.

Brown, Jeffrey R., Norma B. Coe, and Amy Finkelstein. 2006. "Medicaid Crowd-out of Private Long-Term Care Insurance Demand: Evidence from the Health and Retirement Survey." *Tax Policy and the Economy* 21, no. 1: 1–34.

Brown, Jeffrey R., and Amy Finkelstein, 2008. "The Interaction of Public and Private Insurance: Medicaid and the Long-term Care Insurance Market." *American Economic Review* 98, no. 3: 1083–1102.

Brown, Jeffrey R., and Amy Finkelstein. 2011. "Insuring Long-term Care Insurance in the United States." *Journal of Economic Perspectives* 25, no. 1: 119–142.

Brown, Jeffrey R., Jeffrey R. Kling, Sendhil Mullainathan, and Marian V. Wrobel. 2008. "Why Don't People Insure Late-Life Consumption? A Framing Explanation of the Under-Annuitization Puzzle." *American Economic Review: Papers and Proceedings* 98, no. 2: 304–309.

Bruhin, Adrian, Helga Fehr-Duda, and Thomas Epper. 2010. "Risk and Rationality: Uncovering Heterogeneity in Probability Distortion," *Econometrica* 78, no. 4: 1375–1412.

Card, David, Raj Chetty, and Andrea Weber. 2007. "Cash-on-hand and Competing Models of Intertemporal Behavior: New Evidence from the Labor Market." *Quarterly Journal of Economics* 122, no. 4: 1511–1560.

Carvalho, Leandro, Stephan Meier, and Stephanie W. Wang. 2016. "Poverty and Economic Decision-Making: Evidence from Changes in Financial Resources at Payday." *American Economic Review* 106, no. 2: 260–284.

Chetty, Raj. 2006. "A New Method of Estimating Risk Aversion." *American Economic Review* 96, no. 5: 1821–1834.

Chetty, Raj. 2008. "Moral Hazard versus Liquidity and Optimal Unemployment Insurance." *Journal of Political Economy* 116, no. 2: 173–234.

Chetty, Raj, and Adam Szeidl. 2007. "Consumption Commitments and Risk Preferences." *Quarterly Journal of Economics* 122, no. 2: 831–877.

Clark, David, Samson Tse, Max W. Abbott, Sonia Townsend, Pefi Kingi, and Wiremu Manaia. 2007. "Reasons for Starting and Continuing Gambling in a Mixed Ethnic Community Sample of Pathological and Non-problem Gamblers." *International Gambling Studies* 7, no. 3: 299–313.

Clotfelter, Charles T., and Philip J. Cook. 1989. *Selling Hope: State Lotteries in America.* Cambridge, MA: Harvard University Press.

Cohen, Alma, and Liran Einav. 2007. "Estimating Risk Preferences from Deductible Choice." *American Economic Review* 97, no. 3: 745–788.

Collier, Benjamin L., Daniel Schwartz, Howard C. Kunreuther, and Erwann O. Michel-Kerjan. 2022. "Insuring Large Stakes: A Normative and Descriptive Analysis of Households Flood Insurance Coverage." *Journal of Risk and Insurance* 89, no. 3: 273–310.

Conlisk, John. 1993. "The Utility of Gambling." *Journal of Risk and Uncertainty* 6, no. 3: 255–275.

Connor, Robert A. 1996. "More Than Risk Reduction: The Investment Appeal of Insurance." *Journal of Economic Psychology* 17, no. 1: 39–54.

Cook, P. J., and C. T. Clotfelter. 1993. "The Peculiar Scale Economies of Lotto." *American Economic Review* 83, no. 3: 634–643.

Cook, Philip J., and Daniel A. Graham. 1977. "The Demand for Insurance and Protection: The Case of Irreplaceable Commodities." *Quarterly Journal of Economics* 91, no. 1: 143–156.

Courant, P., E. Gramlich, and J. Laitner. 1986. "A Dynamic Micro Estimate of the Life-Cycle Model." In *Retirement and Economic Behavior*, edited by H. G. Aaron and G. Burtless, 832–857. Washington, DC: Brookings Institution.

Cubitt, Robin P., Alistair Munro, and Chris Starmer. 2004. "Testing Explanations of Preference Reversal." *Economic Journal* 114, no. 497: 709–726.

Cummins, J. David. 1974. "Insurer's Risk: A Restatement." *Journal of Risk and Insurance* 41, no. 1: 147–157.

Curry, S. R., D. C. Hodgins, J. Wang, N. el-Guebaly, H. Wynne, and S. Chen. 2006. "Risk of Harm among Gamblers in the General Population as a Function of Level of Participation in Gambling Activities." *Addiction* 101, no. 4: 570–580.

Curry, S. R., D. C. Hodgins, J. Wang, N. el-Guebaly, H. Wynne, and N. V. Miller. 2008. "Replication of Low-Risk Gambling Limits Using Canadian Provincial Gambling Prevalence Data." *Journal of Gambling Studies* 24, no. 3: 321–335.

Cutler, David M., and Richard J. Zeckhauser. 2000. "Chapter 11: The Anatomy of Health Insurance." In *Handbook of Health Economics vol. I, part A*, edited by Anthony J. Culyer and Joseph P. Newhouse, 563–643. Amsterdam: Elsevier.

David, F. N. 1962. *Games, Gods and Gambling: A History of Probability and Statistical Ideas*. Mineola, NY: Dover Publications, Inc.

de Meza, David. 1983. "Health Insurance and the Demand for Medical Care." *Journal of Health Economics* 2, no. 1: 47–54.

de Meza, David, and Diane Reyniers. 2023. "Insuring Replaceable Possessions." *Economica* 90, no. 357: 271–284.

de Roover, Florence Edler. 1945. "Early Examples of Marine Insurance." *Journal of Economic History* 5, no. 2: 172–200.

Dechant, Kristianne. 2014. "Show Me the Money: Incorporating Financial Motives in the Gambling Motives Questionnaire." *Journal of Gambling Studies* 30, no. 4: 949–965.

Dechant, Kristianne, and Michale Ellery. 2011. "The Effect of Including a Monetary Motive Item on the Gambling Motives Questionnaire, in a Sample of Moderate Gamblers." *Journal of Gambling Studies* 27, no. 2: 331–344.

Dembe, Allard E., and Leslie I. Boden. 2000. "Moral Hazard: A Question of Morality?" *New Solutions: A Journal in Environmental and Occupational Health Policy* 10, no. 3: 257–279.

Desai, Rani A., Paul K Maciejewski, David J. Dausey, Barbara J. Caldarone, and Marc N. Potenza. 2004. "Health Correlates of Recreational Gambling in Older Adults." *American Journal of Psychiatry* 161, no. 9: 1672–1679.

Diffie, Bailey W., George D. Winius. 1977. *Foundations of the Portuguese Empire 1415–1580*. Minneapolis: University of Minnesota Press.

Dobbs, Ian M. 1988. "Risk Aversion, Gambling and the Labour-Leisure Choice." *Scottish Journal of Political Economy* 35, no. 2: 171–175.

Dolan, Paul, Tessa Peasgood, and Matthew White. 2008. "Do We Really Know what Makes Us Happy? A Review of the Economic Literature on the Factors Associated with Subjective Well-Being." *Journal of Economic Psychology* 29, no. 1: 94–122.

Dong, Jing, Daifeng He, John A. Nyman, R. Tamara Konetzka. 2021. "Wealth and the Utilization of Long-Term Care Services: Evidence from the United States." *International Journal of Health Economics and Management* 21, no. 3: 345–366.

Dowell, Richard. 1985. "Risk Preferences and the Work-Leisure Trade-Off." *Economic Inquiry* 23, no. 4: 691–701.

Eadington, William R. 1999. "The Economics of Casino Gambling." *Journal of Economic Perspectives* 13, no. 3: 173–192.

Eben, Benjamin. 1980. "The Insurance-Buying Gambler." *Economic Inquiry* 18, no. 3: 504–508.

Edwards, Ryan D. 2008. "Health Risk and Portfolio Choice." *Journal of Business and Economic Statistics* 26, no. 4: 472–485.

Ehrlich, Issac, and Gary S. Becker. 1972. "Market Insurance, Self-Insurance and Self-Protection." *Journal of Political Economy* 80, no. 4: 623–648.

Einav, Liran, and Amy Finkelstein. 2018. "Moral Hazard in Health Insurance: What We Know and How We Know It." *Journal of the European Economic Association* 16, no. 4: 957–982.

Eisner, Robert, and Robert H. Strotz. 1961. "Flight Insurance and the Theory of Choice." *Journal of Political Economy* 69, no. 4: 355–368.

Eling, Martin, Omid Ghavibazoo, and Katja Hanewald. 2021. "Willingness to Take Financial Risks and Insurance Holdings: A European Survey." *Journal of Behavioral and Experimental Economics* 95 (December): 101781.

Ericson, Matthew Marzilli, and Justin R. Sydnor. 2018. "Liquidity Constraints and the Value of Insurance." Working paper 24993. Cambridge, MA: National Bureau of Economic Research.

Evans, Robert G. 1983. "The Welfare Economics of Public Health Insurance: Theory and Canadian Practice." In *Arne Ryde Symposium on Social Insurance*, edited by Lars Söderström, 71–103. Amsterdam: Elsevier.

Evans, William N., and W. Kip Viscusi. 1991. "Estimation of State-Dependent Utility Functions Using Survey Data." *Review of Economics and Statistics* 73, no. 1: 94–104.

Eysenck, S. B. G., and H. J. Eysenck, H. J. 1978. "Impulsiveness and Venturesomeness: Their Position in a Dimensional System of Personality Description." *Psychological Reports* 43, no. 3: 1247-1255.

Farrell, Lisa, Edgar Morgenroth, and Ian Walker. 1999. "A Time-Series Analysis of U.K. Lottery Sales: Long and Short Run Price Elasticities." *Oxford Bulletin of Economics and Statistics* 61, no. 4: 513–526.

Feenberg, Daniel, and Jonathan Skinner. 1994. "The Risk and Duration of Catastrophic Health Care Expenditures." *Review of Economics and Statistics* 76, no. 4: 333–347.

Fehr, Ernst, and Lorenz Goette. 2007. "Do Workers Work More if Wages Are High? Evidence from a Randomized Field Experiment." *American Economic Review* 97, no. 1: 298–317.

Feldman, Roger, and Bryan Dowd. 1991. "A New Estimate of the Welfare Loss from Excess Health Insurance." *American Economic Review* 81, no. 1: 297–301.

Feldman, Roger, and Michael A. Morrisey. 1990. "Health Economics: A Report on the Field." *Journal of Health Politics, Policy and Law* 15, no. 3: 627–646.

Feldstein, Martin S. 1973. "The Welfare Loss of Excess Health Insurance." *Journal of Political Economy* 81, no. 2: 251–280.

Feldstein, Martin. 2005. "Rethinking Social Insurance." *American Economic Review* 95, no. 1: 1–24.

Feldstein, Martin, and Bernard Friedman. 1977. "Tax Subsidies, the Rational Demand for Insurance and the Health Care Crisis." *Journal of Public Economics* 7, no. 2: 155–178.

Fels, Markus. 2016. "When the Affordable Has No Value, and the Valuable Is Unaffordable: The U.S. Market for Long-term Care Insurance and the Role of Medicaid." KIT Working Paper Series in Economics, No. 84. Karlsruhe: Karlsruher Institut für Technologie (KIT), Institute für Volkswirtschaftslehre (ECON).

Fels, Markus. 2017. "A Note on the Equality of Insurance and Gambling Motives." Karlsruhe: Karlsruhe Institute of Technology, Institute of Economics. https://ssrn.com/abstract=2943324 or http://dx.doi.org/10.2139/ssrn.2943324

Fels, Markus. 2019 and 2021. "Why People Buy Insurance: A Modern Answer to an Old Question." Kiel, Hamburg: Beiträge zur Jahrestangung des Vereins für Socialpolitic 2021: Climate Economics, ZBW—Leibniz Information Center for Economics.

Finkelstein, Amy. 2014. "Moral Hazard in Health Insurance: Developments since Arrow (1963)." In *Moral Hazard in Health Insurance*, edited by Amy Finkelstein, with Kenneth J. Arrow, Jonathan Gruber, Joseph P. Newhouse, and Joseph E. Stiglitz, 13-43. New York: Columbia University Press.

Finkelstein, Amy, Erzo F. P. Luttmer, and Matthew J. Notowidigdo. 2008. "What Good Is Wealth without Health? The Effect of Health on the Marginal Utility of Consumption." NBER Working Paper 14089. Cambridge, MA: National Bureau of Economic Research.

Finkelstein, Amy, Erzo F. P. Luttmer, and Matthew J. Notowidigdo. 2009. "Approaches to Estimating the Health State Dependence of the Utility Function." *American Economic Review: Papers and Proceedings* 99, no. 2: 116–121.

Finkelstein, Amy, Sarah Taubman, Bill Wright, Mira Bernstein, Jonathan Gruber, Joseph P. Newhouse, Heidi Allen, and Katherine Baicker. 2012. "The Oregon Health Insurance Experiment: Evidence from the First Year." *Quarterly Journal of Economics* 127, no. 3, 1057–1106.

Fishburn, Peter C., and Gary A. Kochenberger. 1979. "Two-Piece Von Neumann-Morgenstern Utility Functions." *Decision Sciences* 10, no. 4: 503–518.

Fisher, Jonathan D., David S. Johnson, Timothy M. Smeeding, Jeffrey P. Thompson. 2020. "Estimating the Marginal Propensity to Consume Using the Distributions of Income, Consumption, and Wealth." *Journal of Macroeconomics* 65 (September): 103218.

Fisher, Susan. 2000. "Measuring the Prevalence of Sector-Specific Problem Gambling: A Study of Casino Patrons." *Journal of Gambling Studies* 16, no. 1: 25–51.

Flemming, J. S. 1969. "The Utility of Wealth and the Utility of Windfalls." *Review of Economic Studies* 36, no. 1: 55–66.

Folkhälsomyndigheten. 2016. *Tabellsamanställning för Swelogs prevalensstudie 2015.* Östersund & Stockholm, Sweden: Author.

Forrest, D., O. D. Gulley, and R. Simmons. 2000. "Elasticity of Demand for U.K. National Lottery Tickets." *National Tax Journal* 53, no. 4: 853–863.

Forrest, David, Robert Simmons, Neil Chesters. 2002. "Buying a Dream: Alternative Models of Demand for Lotto." *Economic Inquiry* 40, no. 3: 485–496.

Francis, K. L., N. A. Dowling, A. C. Jackson, D. R. Christensen, and H. Wardle. 2015. "Gambling Motives: Application of the Reasons for Gambling Questionnaire in an Australian Population Survey." *Journal of Gambling Studies* 31, no. 3: 807–823.

Franks, Peter, Carolyn M. Clancy, Marthe R. Gold. 1993. "Health Insurance and Mortality: Evidence from a National Cohort." *Journal of the American Medical Association* 270, no. 69: 737–741.

Frederick, Shane, Nathan Novemsky, Jing Wang, Ravi Dhar, and Stephen Nowlis. 2009. "Opportunity Cost Neglect." *Journal of Consumer Research* 36, no. 4: 553–561.

Friedman, Milton. 1962. *Price Theory: A Provisional Text*. Chicago: Aldine Publishing Co.

Friedman, Milton, and L. J. Savage. 1948. "The Utility Analysis of Choices Involving Risk." *Journal of Political Economy* 56, no. 4: 279–304.

Fuchs, Victor R. 1996. "Economists, Values, and Healthcare Reform." *American Economic Review* 86, no. 1: 1–24.

Gächter, Simon, Eric J. Johnson, and Andreas Herrmann. 2022. "Individual-Level Loss Aversion in Riskless and Risky Choices." *Theory and Decision* 92, nos. 3-4: 599–624.

Genesove, David, and Christopher Mayer. 2001. "Loss Aversion and Seller Behavior: Evidence from the Housing Market." *Quarterly Journal of Economics* 116, no. 4: 1233–1260.

Gerstein, D., S. Murphy, M. Toce, et al. 1999. *Gambling Impact and Behavior Study: Report to the National Gambling Impact Study Commission*. Chicago: National Opinion Research Center, University of Chicago.

Gladwell, Malcolm. 2005. "The Moral-Hazard Myth: The Bad Idea behind Our Failed Health-care System." *The New Yorker*, August 29, 2005.

Gold, Marsha R., Joanna E. Siegel, Louise B. Russell, and Milton C. Weinstein, eds. 1996. *Cost-Effectiveness Analysis in Health and Medicine*. New York: Oxford University Press.

Gomes, Francisco J. 2005. "Portfolio Choice and Trading Volume with Loss-Averse Investors." *Journal of Business* 78, no. 2: 675–706.

Gonzales, Richard, and George Wu. 1999. "On the Shape of the Probability Weighting Function." *Cognitive Psychology* 38, no. 1: 129–166.

Gottlieb, Daniel, and Olivia S. Mitchell. 2019. "Narrow Framing and Long-Term Care Insurance." *Journal of Risk and Insurance* 87, no. 4: 861–893.

Gourinchas, Pierre-Oliver, and Jonathan A. Parker. 2002. "Consumption over the Life Cycle." *Econometrica* 70, no. 1: 47–89.

Greene, Mark R. 1963. "Attitudes toward Risk and a Theory of Insurance Consumption." *Journal of Insurance* 30, no. 2: 165–182.

Grether, David M., and Charles R. Plott. 1979. "Economic Theory of Choice and the Preference Reversal Phenomenon." *American Economic Review* 69, no. 4: 623–638.

Grignon, Michel, Jeremiah Hurley, David Feeney, Emmanuel Guindon, and Christina Hackett. 2018. "Moral Hazard in Health Insurance." *Œconomica: History, Methodology, Philosophy* 8, no. 3: 367–405.

Gruber, Jonathan. 2007. *Public Finance and Public Policy*, 2nd ed. New York: Worth.

Gruber, Jonathan. 2014. "Commentary." In *Moral Hazard in Health Insurance*, edited by Amy Finkelstein, with Kenneth J. Arrow, Jonathan Gruber, Joseph P. Newhouse, and Joseph E. Stiglitz, 45-63. New York: Columbia University Press.

Gulley, O. D., and F. A. Scott, Jr. 1993. "The Demand for Wagering on State-Operated Lottery Games." *National Tax Journal* 45, no. 1: 13–22.

Hacking, Ian (2006). *The Emergence of Probability: A Philosophical Study of Early Ideas about Probability and Statistical Inference*, 2nd ed. Cambridge: Cambridge University Press.

Hagfors, Heli, Sari Castrén, Anne H. Salonen. 2022. "How Gambling Motives Are Associated with Socio-demographics and Gambling Behavior—A Finnish Population Study." *Journal of Behavioral Addictions* 11, no. 1:63-74.

Hakannson, Nils H. 1970. "Friedman–Savage Utility Functions Consistent with Risk Aversion." *Quarterly Journal of Economics* 84, no. 3: 472–487.

Halek, Martin, and Joseph G. Eisenhauer (2001). "Demography of Risk Aversion." *Journal of Risk and Insurance* 68, no. 1: 1–24.

Hannum, Robert C. n.d. *A Guide to Casino Mathematics*. Las Vegas: UNLV Gaming Studies Research Center.

Hanson, B. 1988. "Risk Aversion as a Problem of Conjoint Measurement." In *Decision, Probability and Utility*, edited by P. Gardenfors and N.-E. Sahlin, 136-158. Cambridge, MA: Cambridge University Press.

Harrison, Glenn W., and Jia Min Ng. 2016. "Evaluating the Expected Welfare Gain from Insurance." *Journal of Risk and Insurance* 83, no 1: 91–120.

Hartley, Roger, and Lisa Farrell. 2002. "Can Expected Utility Theory Explain Gambling?" *American Economic Review* 92, no. 3: 613–624.

Hartman, Raymond S., Michael J. Doane, and Chi-Keung Woo. 1991. "Consumer Rationality and the Status Quo." *Quarterly Journal of Economics* 106, no. 1: 141–162.

Hershey, John C., Howard C. Kunreuther, and Paul J. H. Schoemaker. 1982. "Sources of Bias in Assessment Procedures for Utility Functions." *Management Science* 28, no. 8: 936–954.

Hershey, John C., and Paul J. H. Schoemaker. 1980a. "Prospect Theory's Reflection Hypothesis: A Critical Examination." *Organizational Behavior and Human Performance* 25 (June): 395–418.

Hershey, John C., and Paul J. H. Schoemaker. 1980b. "Risk Taking and Problem Context in the Domain of Losses: An Expected Utility Analysis." *Journal of Risk and Insurance* 47, no. 1: 111–132.

Hershey, John C., and Paul J. H. Schoemaker. 1985. "Probability versus Certainty Equivalence Methods in Utility Measurement: Are They Equivalent?" *Management Science* 31, no. 10: 1213–1231.

Heyne, Paul. 2008. "Economics and Ethics: The Problem of Dialogue." In *Are Economists Basically Immoral? and Other Essays on Economics, Ethics, and Religion*, edited and with an introduction by Geoffrey Brennan and A. M. C. Waterman, 10-28. Indianapolis: Liberty Fund.

Hicks, John R. 1946. *Value and Capital*, 2nd ed. Oxford: Clarendon Press.

Hilgert, Marianne A., Jeanne M. Hogarth, and Sondra G. Beverly. 2003. "Household Financial Management: The Connection between Knowledge and Behavior." *Federal Reserve Bulletin* 89, no. 7: 309-322.

Hirshleifer, J. 1966. "Investment Decision under Uncertainty: Applications of the State-Preference Approach." *Quarterly Journal of Economics* 80, no. 2: 252–277.

Holen, Arlene. 1977. "Effects of Unemployment Insurance Entitlement on Duration and Job Search Outcome." *Industrial and Labor Relations Review* 30, no. 4: 445–550.

Hsee, Christopher K., and Howard C. Kunreuther. 2000. "The Affection Effect in Insurance Decisions." *Journal of Risk and Uncertainty* 20, no. 2: 141–159.

Hu, Wei-Yin, and Jason S. Scott. 2007. "Behavioral Obstacles in the Annuity Market." *Financial Analysts Journal* 63, no. 6: 71–82.

Humphreys, Brad R., John Nyman, and Jane E. Ruseski. 2021. "The Effect of Recreational Gambling on Health and Well-Being." *Eastern Economic Journal* 47, no. 1: 29–75.

Hwang, In Do. 2021. "Prospect Theory and Insurance Demand: Empirical Evidence on the Role of Loss Aversion." *Journal of Behavioral and Experimental Economics* 95 (December): 1–16.

Jaspersen, Johannes G., Marc A. Ragin, Justin R. Sydnor. 2022. "Predicting Insurance Demand from Risk Attitudes." *Journal of Risk and Insurance* 89, no. 1: 63–96.

Jevons, Stanley (1871) 1970. *The Theory of Political Economy*. With an introduction by Collinson-Black. Harmondsworth: Penguin.

Johnson, Eric J., Gerald Häubl, and Anat Keinan. 2007. "Aspects of Endowment: A Query Theory of Value Construction." *Journal of Experimental Psychology: Learning, Memory and Cognition* 33, no. 3: 461–474.

Johnson, Eric J., John Hershey, Jacqueline Meszaros, and Howard Kunreuther. 1993. "Framing Probability Distortions and Insurance Decisions." *Journal of Risk and Uncertainty* 7 (August): 35–51.

Jones, Larry E. 2008. "A Note on the Joint Occurrence of Insurance and Gambling." *Macroeconomic Dynamics* 12, no. 1: 97–111.

Kahneman, Daniel, Jack Knetsch, and Richard Thaler. 1990. "Experimental Test of the Endowment Effect and the Coase Theorem." *Journal of Political Economy* 98, no. 6: 1325–1348.

Kahneman, Daniel, Jack Knetsch, and Richard Thaler. 1991. "Anomalies: The Endowment Effect, Loss Aversion, and Status Quo Bias." *Journal of Economic Perspectives* 5, no. 1: 193–206.

Kahneman, Daniel, and Amos Tversky. 1979. "Prospect Theory: An Analysis of Decision under Risk." *Econometrica* 47, no. 2: 263–291.

Kahneman, Daniel, and Amos Tversky. 1984. "Choices, Values, and Frames." *American Psychologist* 39, no. 4: 341–350.

Kaiser Family Foundation. 2010. *Survey of People Who Purchase Their Own Insurance.* Publication #8077-R. Menlo Park, CA: Henry J. Kaiser Family Foundation.

Kandel, Shmuel, and Robert F. Stambaugh. 1991. "Asset Returns, Investment Horizons and Intertemporal Preferences." *Journal of Monetary Economics* 27, no. 1: 39–71.

Karmarkar, Uday S. 1978. "Subjectively Weighted Utility: A Descriptive Extension of the Expected Utility Model." *Organizational Behavior and Human Performance* 21 (February): 61–72.

Kelman, Sander, and Albert Woodward. 2013. "John Nyman and the Economics of Health Care Moral Hazard." *ISRN Economics* 2013, no. 3: 1–8.

Kim, Young Chin. 1973. "Choice in the Lottery-Insurance Situation Augmented-Income Approach." *Quarterly Journal of Economics* 87, no. 1: 148–156.

Kingston, Christopher. 2014. "Governance and Institutional Change in Marine Insurance 1350–1850." *European Review of Economic History* 18, no. 1: 1–18.

Kluender, Raymond, Neale Mahoney, Francis Wong, and Wesley Yin. 2021. "Medical Debt in the US, 2009–2020." *Journal of the American Medical Association* 326, no. 3: 250–256.

Kourouxous, Thomas, and Thomas Bauer. 2019. "Violations of Dominance in Decision-Making." *Business Research* 12, no. 1: 209–239.

Knetsch, Jack L. 1989. "The Endowment Effect and Evidence of Nonreversible Indifference Curves." *American Economic Review* 79, no. 5: 1277–1284.

Knetsch, Jack L, and J. A. Sinden. 1984. "Willingness to Pay and Compensation Demanded: Experimental Evidence of an Unexpected Disparity in Measures of Value." *Quarterly Journal of Economics* 99, no. 3: 507–521.

Knetsch, Jack L., and J. A. Sinden. 1987. "The Persistence of Evaluation Disparities." *Quarterly Journal of Economics* 102, no. 3: 691–695.

Knight, Frank H. 1921. *Risk, Uncertainty, and Profit*. Boston: Houghton Mifflin.

Kontezka, R. Tamara, Daifeng He, Jing Dong, and John A. Nyman. 2019. "Moral Hazard and Long-term Care Insurance." *Geneva Papers in Risk and Insurance: Issues and Practice* 44: 231–251.

Kőszegi, Botond, and Matthew Rabin. 2006. "A Model of Reference-Dependent Preferences." *Quarterly Journal of Economics* 121, no. 4: 1133–1165.

Kőszegi. Botund, and Mathew Rabin. 2007. "Reference-Dependent Risk Attitudes." *American Economic Review* 97, no. 4: 1047–1073.

Krueger, Alan B., and Andreas Mueller. 2010. "Job Search and Unemployment Insurance: New Evidence from Time Use Data." *Journal of Public Economics* 94, no. 3–4: 298–307.

Kuhn, Thomas S. 1963. *The Structure of Scientific Revolution*. Chicago: University of Chicago Press.

Kunreuther, H., R. Ginsberg, L. Miller, P. Sagi, and P. Slovic. 1977. *Limited Knowledge and Insurance Protection: Implications for Natural Hazard Policy*. Washington, DC: National Science Foundation.

Kunreuther, H., R. Ginsberg, l, Miller, P. Sagi, P. Slovic, B. Borkam, and N. Katz. 1978. *Disaster Insurance Protection: Public Policy Lessons*. New York: Wiley.

Kunreuther, Howard, and Mark Pauly. 2004. "Neglecting Disaster: Why Don't People Insure against Large Losses?" *Journal of Risk and Uncertainty* 28, no. 1: 5–21.

Kunreuther, Howard, and Mark. Pauly. 2005. "Insurance Decision-Making and Market Behavior." *Foundations and Trends in Microeconomics* 1, no. 2: 63–127.

Kunreuther, Howard, and Mark V. Pauly. 2018. "Dynamic Insurance Decision-Making for Rare Events: The Role of Emotions." *Geneva Papers on Risk and Insurance—Issues and Practice* 43: 335–355.

Kunreuther, Howard, Warren Sanderson, and Rudolf Vetschera. 1985. "A Behavioral Model of the Adoption of Protective Activities," *Journal of Economic Behavior and Organization*, 6, no. 1: 1–15

Kwak, James. 2017. *Economism: Bad Economics and the Rise of Inequality*. New York: Pantheon.

Ladouceur, Robert, Serge Sevigny, Alexander Blaszczynski, Kieron O'Connor, and Marc E. Lavoie. 2003. "Video Lottery: Winning Expectancies and Arousal." *Addiction* 98, no. 6: 733–738.

Lampe, Immanuel, and Daniel Würtenberger. 2020. "Loss Aversion and the Demand for Index Insurance." *Journal of Economic Behavior and Organization* 180, no. C: 678–693.

Lanciani, Rudolfo. 1892. "Gambling and Cheating in Ancient Rome." *North American Review* 155, no. 428: 97–105.

Langer, Ellen J. 1975. "The Illusion of Control," *Journal of Personality and Social Psychology* 32, no. 2: 311–328.

Lattimore, Pamela K., Joanna R. Baker, and Ann D. Witte. 1992. "The Influence of Probability on Risky Choice: A Parametric Examination." *Journal of Economic Behavior and Organization* 17, no 3: 377–400.

Lee, Choong-Ki, Yong-Ki Lee, Bo Jason Bernhard, and TooShik Yoon. 2006. "Segmenting Casino Gamblers by Motivation: A Cluster Analysis of Korean Gamblers." *Tourism Management* 27, no. 5: 856–866.

Lee, Heung-Pyo, Paul Kyuman Chaw, Hong-Seock Lee, and Yong-Ku Kim. 2007. "The Five-Factor Gambling Motivation Model." *Psychiatry Research* 150, no. 1: 21–32.

Lesieur, H. R., and S. B. Blume. 1987. "The South Oaks Gambling Screen (SOGS): A New Instrument for the Identification of Pathological Gamblers." *American Journal of Psychiatry.*144, no. 9:1184-1188.

Lichtenstein, Sarah, and Paul Slovic. 1971. "Reversals of Preference between Bids and Choices in Gambling Decisions." *Journal of Experimental Psychology* 89, no. 1: 46–55.

Lillard, Lee A., and Yoram Weiss. 1997. "Uncertain Health and Survival: Effects on End- of- Life Consumption." *Journal of Business and Economic Statistics* 15, no. 2: 254–268.

Lin, Judy T., Christopher Burncrot, Tippy Ulieny, Annamaria Luscardi, Gary Mottola, Christine Kieffer, and Gerri Walsh. 2016. *Financial Capability in the United States 2016.* Washington, DC: FINRA Investor Education Foundation.

Lindman, Harold R. 1971. "Inconsistent Preferences among Gambles." *Journal of Experimental Psychology* 89: 590–597.

Lipsey, R. G., and Kelvin Lancaster. 1956. "The General Theory of Second Best." *Review of Economic Studies* 24, no. 1: 11–32.

Loewenstein, George, Joelle Y. Friedman, Barbara McGill, Sarah Ahmad, Suzanne Linck, Stacey Sinkula, John Beshears, James J. Choi, Jonathan Kolstad, David Laibson, Brigitte C. Madrian, John A. List, and Kevin G. Volpp. 2013. "Consumer's Understanding of Health Insurance." *Journal of Health Economics* 32, no. 5: 850–862.

Loomes, Graham, and Ganna Pogrebna. 2017. "Do Preference Reversals Disappear When We Allow for Probabilistic Choice?" *Management Science* 63, no. 1: 166–184.

Loomes, Graham, and Robert Sugden. 1982. "Regret Theory: An Alternative Theory of Rational Choice under Uncertainty." *Economic Journal* 92 (December): 805–824.

Loomes, Graham, and Robert Sugden. 1986. "Disappointment and Dynamic Consistency in Choice under Uncertainty." *Review of Economic Studies* 53, no. 2: 271–282.

Lopes, Lola L. 1987. "Between Hope and Fear: The Psychology of Risk." *Advances in Experimental Social Psychology* 20, : 255–295.

Lowenstein, George F., and Drazen Prelec. 1993. "Preferences for Sequences of Outcomes." *Psychological Review* 100, no. 1: 91–108.

Lusardi, Annamaria, Daniel J. Schneider, and Peter Tufano. 2011. "Financially Fragile Households: Evidence and Implications." NBER Working Paper No. 17072. Cambridge, MA: National Bureau of Economic Research.

Mackay, C. J. 1980. "The Measurement of Mood and Psycho-Physiological Activity Using Self-Report Techniques." In *Techniques in Psychophysiology*, edited by I . Martin and P. H. Venables, 501-562. Chichester: John Wiley and Sons.

Manning, Willard G., Naihua Duan, and Emmett B. Keeler. (1988) 1993. "Attrition Bias in a Randomized Trial of Health Insurance." Santa Monica, CA: RAND Corporation.

Manning, Willard G., and M. Susan Marquis. 1996. "Health Insurance: The Tradeoff be- tween Risk Pooling and Moral Hazard." *Journal of Health Economics* 15, no. 5: 609–639.

Mao, Luke Lunhua, James J. Zhang, and Daniel P. Connaughton. 2015. "Sports Gambling as Consumption: Evidence from Demand for Sport Lottery." *Sports Management Review* 18, no. 3: 436–447.

Markowitz, Harry. 1952. "The Utility of Wealth." *Journal of Political Economy* 60, no. 2: 151–158.

Marshall, Alfred. (1890) 1910. *Principles of Economics*, 6th ed. London: Macmillan.

Mayers, David, and Clifford W. Smith, Jr. 1983. "The Interdependence of Individual Portfolio Decisions and the Demand for Insurance." *Journal of Political Economy* 91, no. 2: 304–311.

McConnell, Campbell R., Stanley L. Brue, and Sean M. Flynn. 2012. *Economics*, 19th ed. New York: McGraw-Hill Irwin.

McGrath, Daniel, Tessa Neilson, Kibeom Lee, Christina L. Rash, and Mandana Rad. 2018. "Associations between the HEXACO Model of Personality and Gambling Involvement, motivations to Gamble, and Gambling Severity in Young Adult Gamblers." *Journal of Behavioral Addictions* 7, no. 2: 392–400.

Milkman, Katherine L. and John Beshears. 2009. "Mental Accounting and Small Windfalls: Evidence from an Online Grocer." *Journal of Economic Behavior and Organization* 71, no. 2: 384–394.

Miller, Joshua B., and Adam Sanjurjo. 2018. "Surprised by the Hot hand Fallacy: A Truth in the Law of Small Numbers." *Econometrica* 68, no. 6: 2019–2047.

Morrisey, Michael A. 2020. *Health Insurance*, 3rd ed. Chicago: Health Administration Press.

Morrisey, Michael A., and John Cawley. 2008. "US Health Economists: Who We Are and What We Do." *Health Economics* 17, no. 4: 535–543.

Mossin, Jan. 1968. "Aspects of Rational Insurance Purchasing." *Journal of Political Economy* 76, no. 4: 553–568.

Mrkva, Kellen, Eric J. Johnson, Simon Gächter, and Andreas Herrmann. 2019. "Moderating Loss Aversion: Loss Aversion Has Moderators, But Reports of Its Death Are Greatly Exaggerated." *Journal of Consumer Psychology* 30, no. 3: 407–428.

Muir, Jane. (1961) 1996. *Of Men and Numbers: The Story of the Great Mathematicians*. New York: Dover.

Nagy, Bálint Zsolt, Mónika Anetta Alt, Botond Benedek, and Zsuzsa Săplăcan. 2020. "How Do Loss Aversion and Technology Acceptance Affect Life Insurance Demand?" *Applied Economic Letters* 27, no. 12: 977–981.

National Council on Problem Gambling. 2021. *National Survey on Gambling Attitudes and Gambling Experiences 1.0, National Detailed Report*. Washington, DC: National Council on Problem Gambling.

Neighbors, Clayton, Ty W. Lostutter, Jessica M. Cronce, and Mary E. Larimer. 2002. "Exploring College Student Gambling Motivation." *Journal of Gambling Studies* 18: 361–370.

Nelli, Humbert O. 1972. "The Earliest Insurance Contract—A New Discovery." *Journal of Risk and Insurance* 39, no. 2: 215–220.

Neumann, Peter J., Gillian D. Sanders, Louise B. Russell, Joanna E. Siegel, Theodore G. Ganiats, eds. 2016. *Cost-Effectiveness in Health and Medicine*, 2nd ed. New York: Oxford University Press.

Newhouse, Joseph P. 2006. "Reconsidering the Moral Hazard-Risk Avoidance Tradeoff." *Journal of Health Economics* 25, no. 5: 1005–1014.

Newhouse, Joseph P. 2014. "Introduction." In *Moral Hazard in Health Insurance*, edited by Amy Finkelstein, with Kenneth J. Arrow, Jonathan Gruber, Joseph P. Newhouse, and Joseph E. Stiglitz, 1-12. New York: Columbia University Press.

Newhouse, Joseph P., and the Insurance Experiment Group. 1993. *Free for All? Lessons from the RAND Health Insurance Experiment*. Cambridge, MA: Harvard University Press.

Newhouse, Joseph P., Robert H. Brook, Naihua Duan, Emmett B. Keeler, Arleen Leibowitz, Willard G. Manning, M. Susan Marquis, Carl N. Morris, Charles E. Phelps, and John E. Rolph. 2008. "Attrition in the RAND Health Insurance Experiment: A Response to Nyman." *Journal of Health Politics, Policy and Law* 33, no. 2: 295–308.

Newman, James. 1956. "Commentary on the Law of Large Numbers." In *The World of Mathematics, Volume 3*, edited by J. Newman, 1448-1451. Garden City, NY: Dover Publications, Inc.

Ng, Yew Kwang. 1965. "Why Do People Buy Lottery Tickets? Choices involving Risk and the Indivisibility of Expenditure." *Journal of Political Economy* 73, no. 5: 530–535.

Novemsky, Nathan, and Daniel Kahneman. 2005. "The Boundaries of Loss Aversion." *Journal of Marketing Research* 42: 119–128.

Nyman, John A. 1988a. "Excess Demand, the Percentage of Medicaid Patients and the Quality of Nursing Home Care." *Journal of Human Resources* 23, no. 1: 76–92.

Nyman, John A. 1998b. "Theory of Health Insurance." *Journal of Health Administration Education* 16, no. 1: 41–66.

Nyman, John A. 1999a. "The Economics of Moral Hazard Revisited." *Journal of Health Economics* 18, no. 6: 811–824.

Nyman, John A. 1999b. "The Value of Health Insurance: The Access Motive." *Journal of Health Economics* 18, no. 2: 141–152.

Nyman, John A. 1999c. "The Welfare Economics of Insurance Contracts that Pay Off by Reducing Price." Discussion Paper No. 308. Minneapolis: University of Minnesota, Center for Economics Research.

Nyman, John A. 2001a. "The Demand for Insurance: Expected Utility Theory from a Gain Perspective." Discussion Paper No. 313. Minneapolis: University of Minnesota, Department of Economics.

Nyman, John A. 2001b. "The Income Transfer Effect, the Access Motive and the RAND Health Insurance Experiment." *Journal of Health Economics* 20, no. 2: 295–298.

Nyman, John A. 2001c. "The Theory of the Demand for Health Insurance." Discussion Paper #311. Minneapolis: University of Minnesota, Department of Economics.

Nyman, John A. 2003. *The Theory of Demand for Health Insurance.* Palo Alto, CA: Stanford University Press.

Nyman, John A. 2004. "A Theory of Demand for Gambles." Discussion Paper No. 322. Minneapolis: University of Minnesota, Department of Economics.

Nyman, John A. 2007a. "American Health Policy: Cracks in the Foundation." *Journal of Health Politics, Policy and Law* 32, no. 5: 759–783.

Nyman, John A. 2007b. "Is the Gambler's Fallacy Really a Fallacy?" *Journal of Gambling Business and Economics* 1, no. 3: 165–170.

Nyman, John A. 2008. "Health Plan Switching and Attrition Bias in the RAND Health Insurance Experiment." *Journal of Health Policy, Politics and Law* 33, no. 2: 309–317.

Nyman, John A. 2020/2021. "The Theory of Insurance and Gambling." May 12, 2020, and a revised version, "The Theory of Insurance and Gambling: Replacing Risk Preferences with *Quid pro Quo.*" April 19, 2021l. Cambridge, MA: Social Science Research Network.

Nyman, John A. 2021. "Cost of Medicare for All: Review of the Estimates." *Applied Health Economics and Health Policy* 19 (January): 453–461.

Nyman, John A., Bryan E. Dowd, Jahn K. Hakes, Ken Winters, and Serena King. 2013. "Work and Non-Pathological Gambling." *Journal of Gambling Studies* 29, no. 1: 61–81.

Nyman, John A., Cagatay Koch, Bryan Dowd, Ellen McCreedy, and Helen Markelova Trenz. 2018. "Decomposition of Moral Hazard." *Journal of Health Economics* 57, no. 1: 168–178.

Nyman, John A., and R. Maude-Griffin. 2001. "The Welfare Economics of Moral Hazard." *International Journal of Health Care Finance and Economics* 1, no. 1: 23–42.

Nyman, John A., and Helen M. Trenz. 2016. "Affordability of the Health Expenditures of Insured Americans before the Affordable Care Act." *American Journal of Public Health* 106, no. 2: 264–266.

Nyman, John A., J. W. Welte, and Bryan E. Dowd. 2008. "Something for Nothing: A Model of Gambling Behavior." *Journal of Socio-Economics* 37, no. 6: 2492–2504.

O'Curry, Suzanne Bradley. 1999. "Consumer Budgeting and Mental Accounting." In *The Elgar Companion to Consumer Research and Economic Psychology*, edited by P. E. Earl and S. Kemp, 63-68. Northhamption, MA: Cheltnham.

O'Curry, Suzanne. 1999. "Income Source Effects." Working paper, Depaul University, Chicago.

O'Curry, Suzanne, and Michal Strahilevitz. 2001. "Probability and Mode of Acquisition Effects on Choices Between Hedonic and Utilitarian Options." *Marketing Letters* 12, no. 1: 37–49.

O'Donoghue, Ted, and Jason Somerville. 2018. "Modeling Risk Aversion in Economics." *Journal of Economic Perspectives* 32, no. 2: 91–114.

Obrist, Paul A. 1981. *Cardiovascular Psychophysiology: A Perspective*. New York: Plenum.

Odean, Terrance. 1998. "Are Investors Reluctant to Realize Their Losses?" *Journal of Finance* 53: 1775–1798.

Orford, Jim, Heather Wardle, Mark Griffiths, Kerry Sproston, and Bob Erens. 2010. "The Role of Social Factors in Gambling: Evidence from the 2007 British Gambling Prevalence Survey," *Community, Work and Family* 13, no. 3: 257-271.

Parkin, Michael. 2016. "Opportunity Cost: A Reexamination." *Journal of Economic Education* 47, no. 1: 12–22.

Pashigian, Peter, Lawrence L. Schkade and George H. Menefee. 1966. "The Selection of an Optimal Deductible for a Given Insurance Policy." *Journal of Business* 39, no. 1: 35–44.

Patient Protection and Affordable Care Act. 2010. Pub. L. No. 111-48, 124 Stat. 119.

Pauly, Mark V. 1968. "The Economics of Moral Hazard: Comment." *American Economic Review* 58, no. 3: 531–537.

Pauly, Mark V. 1983. "More on Moral Hazard." *Journal of Health Economics* 2, no. 1: 81–85.

Pauly, Mark V. 1989. "Optimal Public Subsidies of Nursing Home Insurance in the United States." *Geneva Papers on Risk and Insurance* 14, no. 50: 3–10.

Pauly, Mark V. 1990. "The Rational Purchase of Long-term-care Insurance." *Journal of Political Economy* 98, no. 1: 153–168.

Pauly, Mark V. 2008. "Adverse Selection and Moral Hazard: Implications for Health Insurance Markets." In *Incentives and Choice in Health Care*, edited by Frank A. Sloan and Hirschel Kasper, 103-130. Cambridge, MA: MIT Press.

Pallesen, Ståle, Rune Aune Mentzoni, Torbjorn Torsheim, Eilin Erevik, Helge Molde, and Arne Magnu Morken. 2020. *Omfang av Penge og Dataspillproblemer i Norge*. Universitetet i Bergen, Institutt for samfunnspsykologi. Bergen, Finland.

Phelps, Charles E. 1973. *Demand for Health Insurance: A Theoretical and Empirical Investigation*. Rand R-1054-OEO. Santa Monica: Rand Corporation.

Phelps, Charles E. 2018. *Health Economics*, 6th ed. New York: Routledge.

Phelps, Charles E. 2022. "Optimal Health Insurance." *Journal of Risk and Insurance* 90, no. 1:213-241.

Piccinno, Luisa. 2016. "Genoa, 1340–1620: Early Development of Marine Insurance." In *Marine Insurance: Origins and Institutions, 1300–1850*, edited by A. B. Leonard, 25-46. Houndmills, UK: Palgrave Macmillan.

Potenza, Marc N., Paul K. Maciejewski, and Carolyn M. Mazure. 2006. "A Gender-based Examination of Past-year Recreational Gamblers." *Journal of Gambling Studies* 22, no. 1: 41–64.

Pratt, John W. 1964. "Risk Aversion in the Small and in the Large." *Econometrica* 32, no. 1–2: 122–136.

Prelec, Drazen. 1998. "The Probability Weighting Function." *Econometrica* 66, no. 3: 497–527.

Purfield, Catriona, and Patrick Waldron. 1999. "Gambling on Lotto Numbers: Testing for Substitutability or Complementarity Using Semi-Weekly Turnover Data." *Oxford Bulletin of Economics and Statistics* 61, no. 4: 527–544.

Putler, Daniel. 1992. "Incorporating Reference Price Effects into a Theory of Consumer Choice." *Marketing Science* 11, no. 3: 287–309.

Quiggin, John. 1991. "On the Optimal Design of Lotteries." *Economica* 58, no. 229: 1–16.

Rabin, Matthew. 2000. "Diminishing marginal Utility of Wealth Cannot Explain Risk Aversion." In *Choices, Values, and Frames*, edited by Daniel Kahneman and Amos Tversky, 202–208. New York: Cambridge University Press.

Rabin, Matthew, and Richard H. Thaler. 2001. "Anomalies: Risk Aversion." *Journal of Economic Perspectives* 15, no. 1: 219–232.

Rätzel, Steffan. 2012. "Labor Supply, Life Satisfaction, and the (Dis)Utility of Work." *Scandinavian Journal of Economics* 114, no. 4: 1160–1181.

Robbins, Lionel. 1930. "On the Elasticity of Demand for Income in Terms of Effort." *Economica* 10, no. 2: 123–129.

Robertson, Christopher T. 2019. *Exposed: Why Our Health Insurance Is Incomplete and What Can Be Done about It.* Cambridge, MA: Harvard University Press.

Robertson, Christopher T., Andy Yuan, Wendan Zhang, and Keith Joiner. 2020. "Distinguishing Moral Hazard from Access for High-cost Healthcare under Insurance." *PLoS One* 15, no. 4: e0231768.

Rotermann, Michelle, and Health Gilmour. 2022. "Who Gambles and Who Experiences Gambling Problems in Canada." *Insights on Canadian Society*. Ottawa: Statistics Canada.

Samuelson, Paul. 1952. "Probability, Utility, and the Independence Axiom." *Econometrica* 20, no. 4: 670–678.

Samuelson, Paul A. 1963. "Risk and Uncertainty: A Fallacy of Large Numbers." *Scientia* 57, no. 98: 108–113.

Samuelson, William, and Richard Zeckhauser. 1988. "Status Quo Bias in Decision Making." *Journal of Risk and Uncertainty* 1, no. 1: 7–59.

Sanchez-Fernandez, Raquel, and M. Angeles Iniesta-Bonillo. 2007. "The Concept of Perceived Value: A Systematic Review of Research." *Marketing Theory* 7, no. 4: 427–451.

Santerre, Rexford E., and Stephen P. Neun. 2010. *Health Economics: Theory, Insights, and Industry Studies*, 6th ed. Mason, OH: South-Western, Centage Learning.

Schildberg-Hörisch, Hannah. 2018. "Are Risk Preferences Stable?" *Journal of Economic Perspectives* 32, no 2: 135–154.

Schlesinger, Harris, and Neil A. Doherty, 1985. "Incomplete Markets for Insurance: An Overview." *Journal of Risk and Insurance* 52, no. 3: 402–423.

Schmidt, Ulrich. 2016. "Insurance Demand under Prospect Theory: A Graphical Analysis." *Journal of Risk and Insurance* 83, no. 1: 77–89.

Schmidt, Ulrich, Chris Starmer, and Robert Sugden. 2008. "Third-Generation Prospect Theory." *Journal of Risk and Uncertainty* 36: 203–223.

Schoemaker, Paul J. H., Howard C. Kunreuther. 1979. "An Experimental Study of Insurance Decisions." *Journal of Risk and Insurance* 46, no. 4: 603–618.

Schwartz, David G. 2013. *Roll the Bones: The History of Gambling*. Casino Edition. Las Vegas, NV: Winchester Books.

Scott, Frank A., and O. David Gulley. 1995. "Rationality and Efficiency in Lotto Markets." *Economic Inquiry* 33, no. 2: 175–188.

Seidl, Christian. 2002. "Preference Reversal." *Journal of Economic Surveys* 16, no. 5: 621–655.

Shafer, Glenn. 1996. "The Significance of Jacob Bernouilli's *Ars Conjectandi* for the Philosophy of Probability Today." *Econometrica* 75, no. 1: 15–32.

Shang, Xuesong, Hebing Duan, and Jingyi Lu. 2021. "Gambling versus Investment: Lay Theory and Loss Aversion." *Journal of Economic Psychology* 84 (June): 102367.

Shapiro, Carl, and Stiglitz, Joseph. 1984. "Equilibrium Unemployment as a Worker Discipline Device." *American Economic Review* 74, no. 3: 433–444.

Shefrin, Hersh M. and Richard H. Thaler. 1988. "The Behavioral Life-Cycle Hypothesis." *Economic Inquiry* 26, no. 4: 609–643.

Simon, Jonathan. 1998. "Four Essays and a Note on the Demand for Lottery Tickets and How Lotto Players Choose Their Numbers." Ph.D. dissertation. European University Institute, Department of Economics.

Sloan, Frank A., W. Kip Viscusi, Harreil W. Chesson, Christopher J. Conover, and Kathryn Whetten-Goldstein. 1998. "Alternative Approaches to Valuing Intangible Health Losses: The Evidence for Multiple Sclerosis." *Journal of Health Economics* 17, no. 4: 475–497.

Slovic, Paul, Baruch Fischhoff, and Sarah Lichtenstein. 1988. "Response Mode, Framing, and Information-processing Effects in Risk Assessment." In *Decision Making: Descriptive, Normative and Prescriptive Interactions*, edited by E. D. Bell, H. Raiffa, and A. Tversky, 152–166. Cambridge: Cambridge University Press.

Slovic, Paul, Baruch Fischhoff, Sarah Lichtenstein, Bernard Corrigan and Barbara Combs. 1977. "Preference for Insuring against Probable Small Losses: Insurance Implications." *Journal of Risk and Insurance* 44, no. 2: 237–258.

Slovic, Paul, and Sarah Lichtenstein. 1968. "Importance of Variance Preferences in Gambling Decisions." *Journal of Experimental Psychology* 78, no. 4: 646–654.

Slovic, Paul, and Sarah Lichtenstein. 1983. "Preference Reversals: A Broader Perspective." *American Economic Review* 73, no. 4: 596–604.

Slutsky, E. E. (1915) 1952. "On the Theory of the Budget of the Consumer." Translated by Olga Ragusa. Homewood, IL: Irwin.

Smith, Adam. (1776) 2000. *The Wealth of Nations*. New York: The Modern Library.

Smith, Adam. 1759. *Theory of Moral Sentiments*, Part II. Section iii. Chapter 1. London.

Souleles, Nicholas S. 1999. "The Response of Household Consumption to Income Tax Refunds." *American Economic Review* 89, no. 4: 947–958.

Spencer, David A. 2003. "Love's Labor's Lost? The Disutility of Work and Work Avoidance in the Economic Analysis of Labor Supply." *Review of Social Economy* 61, no. 2: 236–250.

Stewart, Sherry H., and Martin M. Zack. 2008. "Development and Psychometric Evaluation of a Three Dimensional Gambling Motives Questionnaire." *Addiction* 103:1110–1117.

Stiglitz, Joseph E. 2014. "Forward." In *Moral Hazard in Health Insurance*, edited by Amy Finkelstein, with Kenneth J. Arrow, Jonathan Gruber, Joseph P. Newhouse, and Joseph E. Stiglitz. New York: Columbia University Press.

Stone, Deborah. 2011. "Behind the Jargon: Moral Hazard." *Journal of Health Politics, Policy and Law* 36, no. 5: 889–896.

Substance Abuse and Mental Health Services Administration. 2016. *Impact of the DSM-IV to DSM-5 Changes on the National Survey on Drug Use and Health*. Rockville (MD): Substance Abuse and Mental Health Services Administration (US). 2016 Jun. Table 3.38, DSM-IV to DSM-5 Gambling Disorder Comparison.

Suits, Daniel B. 1979. "The Elasticity of Demand for Gambling." *Quarterly Journal of Economics* 93, no. 1:155–162.

Sullivan, Kip. 2013. "How to Think Clearly About Medicare Administrative Costs: Data Sources and Measurement." *Journal of Health Politics, Policy and Law* 38, no. 3: 479–504.

Suter, James, Charlotte Duke, Annette Harms, Alexander Joshi, Julia Rzepecka, Luce Lechardoy, Pierre Hausemer, Camille Wilhelm, Femke Dekeulenaer, and Elena Lucica. 2017. *Study on Consumers' Decision Making in Insurance Services: A Behavioral Economics Perspective, Final Report*. Brussels: European Commission.

Sydnor, Justin. 2010. "(Over)insuring Modest Risks." *American Economic Journal: Applied Economics* 2, no. 4: 177–199.

Tanaka, Tomomi, Colin F. Camerer, and Quang Nguyen. 2010. "Risk and Time Preferences: Linking Experimental and Household Survey Data from Vietnam." *American Economic Review* 100, no. 1: 557–571.

Thaler, Richard. 1980. "Toward a Positive Theory of Consumer Choice." *Journal of Economic Behaviour and Organization* 1, no. 1: 39–60.

Thaler, Richard. 1985. "Mental Accounting and Consumer Choice." *Marketing Science* 4, no. 3: 199–214.

Thaler, Richard H. 1994. "Psychology and Savings Policies." *American Economic Review* 84, no. 2: 186–192.

Thaler, Richard. 1999. "Mental Accounting Matters." *Journal of Behavioral Decision Making* 12 (July): 183–206.

Thaler, Richard. 2008. "Mental Accounting and Consumer Choice." *Marketing Science* 27, no. 1: 15–25.

Thaler, Richard H., and Eric J. Johnson. 1990. "Gambling with the House Money and Trying to Break Even: The Effects of Prior Outcomes on Risk Choice." *Management Science* 36, no. 6: 643–660.

Thomas, Guy. 2017. *Loss Coverage: Why Insurance Works Better with Some Adverse Selection*. Cambridge: Cambridge University Press.

Tversky, Amos, and Daniel Kahneman. 1981. "The Framing of Decisions and the Psychology of Choice." *Science* 211 (January): 453–458.

Tversky, Amos, Daniel Kahneman. 1986. "The Framing of Decisions and the Evaluation of Prospects." *Studies in Logic and the Foundations of Mathematics* 114: 503–520.

Tversky, Amos, and Daniel Kahneman. 1988. "Rational Choice and the Framing of Decisions." In *Decision Making: Descriptive, Normative and Prescriptive Interactions*, edited by David E. Bell, Howard Raiffa, and Amos Tversky, 167–191. Cambridge: Cambridge University Press.

Tversky, Amos, and Daniel Kahneman. 1991. "Loss Aversion in Riskless Choice: A Reference Dependent Model." *Quarterly Journal of Economics* 106, no. 4: 1039–1062.

Tversky, Amos, and Daniel Kahneman. 1992. "Advances in Prospect Theory: Cumulative Representation of Uncertainty." *Journal of Risk and Uncertainty* 5, no. 4: 297–323.

Tversky, Amos, Paul Slovic, and Daniel Kahneman. 1990. "The Causes of Preference Reversal." *American Economic Review* 80, no. 1: 204–217.

Tversky, Amos, and Richard H. Thaler. 1990. "Anomalies: Preference Reversals." *Journal of Economic Perspectives* 4, no. 2: 201–211.

Ungarelli, Donald L. 1984. "Insurance and Prevention: Why and How?" *Library Trends* 33, no.1: 57–67.

United States Census Bureau. 2021. *Wealth, Asset Ownership, & Debt of Households Detailed Tables: 2019*. Washington, DC: United States Census Bureau.

United States Department of Housing and Urban Development. 2022. "Estimated Median Family Incomes for Fiscal Year (FY)2021." Memorandum from Todd R. Richardson. Washington, DC: United States Department of Housing and Urban Development.

Van Winssen, K. P. M., R. C. van Kleef, W. P. M. M. van de Ven. 2016. "Potential Determinants of Deductible Uptake in Health Insurance: How to Increase Uptake in the Netherlands?" *European Journal of Health Economics* 17, no. 9: 1059–1072.

Vance, W. R. 1908. "The Early History of Insurance Law." *Columbia Law Review* 8, no. 1: 1–17.

Vasquez, Markus. 2017. "Utility of Wealth with Many Indivisibilities." *Journal of Mathematical Economics* 71, no. C: 20–27.

Viscusi, W. Kip, and William N. Evans. 1990. "Utility Functions That Depend on Health Status: Estimates and Economic Implications." *American Economic Review* 80, no. 3: 353–374.

von Neumann, John and Oskar Morgenstern. 1947. *Theory of Games and Economic Behavior*, 2nd ed. Princeton, NJ: Princeton University Press.

Walker, I. 1998. "The Economic Analysis of Lotteries." *Economic Policy* 13, no. 27: 359–392.

Walker, Jonathan. 1999. "Gambling and Venetian Noblemen: c. 1500–1700," *Past and Present* 162, no. 1: 28–69.

Walker, Michael, Tony Schellink, and Fadi Anjoul. 2008. "Explaining Why People Gamble." In *Pursuit of Winning: Problem Gambling Theory, Research and Treatment*, edited by Masood Zangeneh, Alex Blaszczynski, and Nigel Turner, 11–32. New York: Springer.

Wardle, Heather, Alison Moody, Suzanne Spence, Jim Orford, Rachel Volberg, Dhriti Jotangia, Mark Griffiths, David Hussey, and Fiona Dobbie. 2011. *British Gambling Prevalence Survey*. London: National Center for Social Research.

Welch, Evelyn. 2008. "Lotteries in Early Modern Italy." *Past and Present* 199, no. 1: 71–111.

Welte, John W., Grace M. Barnes, William F. Wieczorek, Marie-Cecile Tidwell, and John Parker. 2002. "Gambling Participation in the U.S.—Results from a National Survey." *Journal of Gambling Studies* 18, no. 4: 313–337.

Welte, John W., Grace M. Barnes, William F. Wieczorek, Marie-Cecile Tidwell, and John Parker. 2004. "Risk Factors for Pathological Gambling." *Addictive Behaviors* 29, no. 2: 323–335.

Williamson, Oliver. 1985. *The Economic Institutions of Capitalism*. New York: Free Press.

Winer, Russel S. 1986. "A Reference Point Model of Brand Choice for Frequently-purchased Products." *Journal of Consumer Research* 13 (September): 250–256.

Wulfert, Edelgard, Christine Franco, Kevin Williams, Brian Roland, and Julie Hartley Maxson. 2008. "The Role of Money in the Excitement of Gambling." *Psychology of Addictive Behaviors* 22, no. 3: 380–390.

Wulfert, Edelgard, Brian Roland, Julie Hartley, N. Wang, and Christine Franco. 2005. "Heart Rate Arousal and Excitement in Gambling: Winners versus Losers." *Psychology of Addictive Behaviors* 19, no. 3: 311–316.

Yaari, Menahem E. 1965. "Convexity in the Theory of Choice under Risk." *Quarterly Journal of Economics* 79, no. 2: 278–290.

Zeckhauser, Richard. 1970. "Medical Insurance: A Case Study of the Tradeoff between Risk Spreading and Appropriate Incentives." *Journal of Economic Theory* 2, no. 1: 10–26.

Zelizer, Viviana A. 1994. *The Social Meaning of Money: Pin Money, Paychecks, Poor Relief, and other Currencies*. New York: Basic Books.

Zeno, Riniero. 1936. *Documenti per la storia del diritto maritime nei secoli XIII e XIV*. Torino: S. Lattes & C.

Zhang, C. Yiwei, and Abigail B. Sussman. 2017. "The Role of Mental Accounting in Household Spending and Investing Decisions." Working Paper No. 19–07. Chicago: University of Chicago, Booth School of Business.

Index